D1766515

HRD in a Complex World

HRD in a Complex World presents a strong challenge to traditional HRD. Over the past ten years notions of complexity have emerged from the hard sciences and are now being applied to the social sciences. This is a highly contested area, but what is clear is that the ideas and language of complexity offer the chance to reinterpret traditional views of theory and practice. This collection addresses HRD from within the notions and language of complexity, presenting multifaceted alternative perspectives to the current practice and theory of HRD.

Divided into four sections, each containing four chapters, this book presents sixteen different perspectives and represents the current state of the art, as portrayed by twenty internationally renowned academics and practitioners. The first section, 'Reviewing the bases of HR: the depth' addresses this issue from a theoretical perspective, exploring the roots of the debate more deeply. Chapters in the second section 'Reflections of HR: the width' build on and widen the debate. In the third section 'Realising HR: applying the theories' the chapters each extend the previous debates to introduce possible tools for practice. The fourth section 'Realities of HR: aspects of practice' looks directly at the implications these debates hold for practice. A range of themes which cut across these sections is highlighted in short introductory passages.

Some authors address aspects of complexity theory directly, others only by implication; some focus on theory, others on practice; some talk globally, others locally; some address issues critically, others present them as they are. But in each case, the main message is that as the world changes and our understandings of the world develop, so the theory and practice of HRD must expand. This collection argues that we can no longer live and work in a non-complex world and if we choose to do so we are in danger of blindfolding ourselves and simplifying our existence to the point of impotence.

Monica Lee is Visiting Professor at Northumbria University, and is based at Lancaster University, UK. She is Editor in Chief of *Human Resource Development International* and Editor of the monograph series *Routledge Studies in Human Resource Development*. She is intrigued by the dynamics around individuals and organisations and most of her work is about trying to make sense of these. This can be seen in recent publications in *Human Relations, Human Resource Development International, Management Learning* and *Personnel Review*.

Routledge Studies in Human Resource Development
Edited by Monica Lee
Lancaster University, UK

HRD theory is changing rapidly. Recent advances in theory and practice, how we conceive of organisations and of the world of knowledge, have led to the need to reinterpret the field. This series aims to reflect and foster the development of HRD as an emergent discipline. Encompassing a range of different international, organisational, methodological and theoretical perspectives, the series promotes controversy and reflective practice.

1 **Policy Matters**
   Flexible learning and organizational change
   Edited by Viktor Jakupec and Robin Usher

2 **Science Fiction and Organization**
   Edited by Warren Smith, Matthew Higgins, Martin Parker and Geoff Lightfoot

3 **HRD and Learning Organisations in Europe**
   Challenges for professionals
   Edited by Saskia Tjepkema, Jim Stewart, Sally Sambrook, Martin Mulder, Hilde ter Horst and Jaap Scheerens

4 **Interpreting the Maternal Organisation**
   Edited by Heather Höpfl and Monika Kostera

5 **Work Process Knowledge**
   Edited by Nick Boreham, Renan Samurçay and Martin Fischer

6 **HRD in a Complex World**
   Edited by Monica Lee

7 **Human Resource Development in Small Organisations**
   Research and practice
   Edited by Jim Stewart and Graham Beaver

8 **New Frontiers in Human Resource Development**
   Edited by Jean Woodall, Monica Lee and Jim Stewart

9 Human Resources, Care Giving, Career Progression and Gender
Beulah S. Coyne, Edward J. Coyne and Monica Lee

Also published as part of the series in paperback:

Action Research in Organisations
Jean McNiff, accompanied by Jack Whitehead

Understanding Human Resource Development
A Research-based approach
Edited by Jim Stewart, Jim McGoldrick and Sandra Watson

HRD in a Complex World

Edited by Monica Lee

Routledge
Taylor & Francis Group

LONDON AND NEW YORK

First published 2003
by Routledge
11 New Fetter Lane, London EC4P 4EE

Simultaneously published in the USA and Canada
by Routledge
29 West 35th Street, New York, NY 10001

Routledge is an imprint of the Taylor & Francis Group

Typeset in Baskerville by GreenGate Publishing Services, Tonbridge, Kent

Printed and bound in Great Britain by MPG Books Ltd, Bodmin

British Library Cataloguing in Publication Data
A catalogue record for this book is available from the British Library

Library of Congress Cataloging in Publication Data
A catalog record for this book has been requested

ISBN 0-415-31013-X

Contents

Illustrations	ix
Notes on contributors	xi
Acknowledgements	xvi

Introduction by Monica Lee — 1

PART I
Reviewing the bases of HR: the depth — 5

1 The complex roots of HRD — 7
MONICA LEE

2 Complexity, HRD and organisation
development: towards a viable systems
approach to learning, development and
change — 25
PAUL ILES AND MAURICE YOLLES

3 Worldviews that enhance and inhibit HRD's
social responsibility — 42
TIMOTHY G. HATCHER

4 Strategic quest and the search for the primal
mother — 57
HEATHER HÖPFL

PART II
Reflections of HR: the width — 67

5 Human resource development in the Arab
Middle East: a 'fourth paradigm' — 69
DAVID WEIR

6 **The ethics of HRD**   83

JIM STEWART

7 **Reconciling autonomy and community:**
 the paradoxical role of HRD   100

CAROLE ELLIOTT AND SHARON TURNBULL

8 **The urge to destroy is a creative urge**   117

KIM JAMES

PART III
Realising HR: applying the theories   129

9 **Clarifying the complexity of emotion in HRD:**
 the use of visualisation technology   131

JAMIE L. CALLAHAN AND DENIS GRAČANIN

10 **Complexifying organisational development and HRD**   147

MAURICE YOLLES AND PAUL ILES

11 **A new perception for a new millennium**   166

CAROLE MCKENZIE

12 **Individual learning from exceptional events**   179

LLOYD DAVIES AND PAUL KRAUS

PART IV
Realities of HR: aspects of practice   193

13 **Leadership principles and reflections for**
 unravelling the stranglehold of organisational
 boundaries: challenges for health services   195

SARAH FRASER

14 **Propositions for incorporating a pedagogy**
 of complexity, emotion and power in HRD
 education   204

KIRAN TREHAN AND CLARE RIGG

15 **The line manager as a facilitator of team**
 learning and change   218

CHRISTINA MARY MACNEIL

16 **A practitioner's reflections on HRD research:**
 a case of internalized complexity?   231

ROSEMARY HILL

Index   243

Illustrations

Figures

A.1	The structure of the book	3
1.1	Four approaches to management (after Lee, 1997a)	9
1.2	Four types of 'development' (after Lee, 1977b)	10
1.3	Mapping of typologies	12
1.4	Movement through typologies (after Lee, 1996)	15
1.5	A typology of typologies	17
2.1	The OD cycle, based on Mabey (1986)	31
2.2	More recent form of OD (Mabey, 1995a)	32
2.3	Diagnosis cycle, linking with traditional OD (Harrison, 1994)	32
2.4	Influence diagram: cognitive purpose of HRD	33
2.5	HRD as methodological inquiry	37
2.6	Evolving model of HRD	39
6.1	An interpretation of Patrick Bateson and Paul Martin (2000) 'Design for a life: How behaviour develops'	88
6.2	A model of HRD	89
6.3	Darwin's contribution. Based on Mary Midgley (1996)	93
6.4	Psychological domains of experience. Based on Stewart (1996)	94
6.5	Circle of being	94
9.1	Key components of the general theory of action	135
9.2	Visualisation framework	138
9.3	Ordinary Petri net example	139
9.4	Parameterised Petri net example	139
9.5	Parameterisation using emotion values	140
9.6	Simple Parameterised Petri net	141
9.7	Outcome based parameterisation	142
10.1	Relationship diagram showing the outline concept of the viable system model	153
10.2	Relationship between the behavioural and cognitive domains in the three domains model	155
12.1	A model of experiential learning	181

13.1   Accelerating the spread of good practice, Fraser (2002),
       Kingsham Press   199
16.1   Summary of *a priori* differences noted between HRD in
       SMEs and UK National HRD (N/HRD)   234
16.2   Summary of HRD approaches in the three cases   237
16.3   A comparison of HRD interaction and intervention   239

Tables

2.1   Steps of the traditional OD methodological cycle   29
2.2   New version of OD (Mabey, 1995a)   29
2.3   The diagnosis phases of Harrison   30
2.4   Definition of the system and metasystem for HRD   33
2.5   Methodological inquiry in a reconceptualised HRD   35
2.6   Steps of a reconceptualised HRD model and action tools   36
2.7   HRD methodology – complex systems model   38
3.1   Bounded and unbounded worldviews   49
9.1   Adaptation example: serving customers (10 incidents)   141
10.1   A focussed view of the organisation through organisational
       development   150
10.2   Actions relating to problems and needs for change, learning
       and development   151
10.3   The three domains, their cognitive properties, and
       organisational patterning   156
10.4   Extending organisational patterning of HRD   162

Boxes

6.1   Definitions of 'intervention' and 'interfere'   95
6.2   Syllogism   98
12.1   Water Main Bursts – 140,000 people affected!   186

Notes on contributors

Jamie L. Callahan is an Assistant Professor in the Educational Human Resource Development Program at Texas A&M University. She is actively involved in the Academy of Human Resource Development and the Academy of Management. Her primary research interests focus on emotion management and its relationship to organisational learning, leadership and culture. Her work has appeared in journals such as *Human Resource Development Quarterly, Human Resource Development International, Management Learning, Organization Studies*; she recently edited a special issue on emotion for the journal *Advances in Developing Human Resources*. A former United States Air Force officer specialising in human resources and organisation development consulting, she continues to consult actively with public, private and nonprofit institutions.

Lloyd Davies had a career in HR in the textiles, steel, engineering and water industries, working on various development aspects at all levels from national to shop floor. His final job before retiring was as HR Director for Yorkshire Water, which, post-privatisation in 1989, entailed a substantial proportion of senior management development and recruitment. Since retiring he has worked as a consultant in the public, private and not-for-profit sectors, and in parallel has researched managerial experiential learning for a PhD at Lancaster University's Department of Management Learning.

Carole Elliott began her academic career at Lancaster University having completed an MSc in HRD. She has taught on a number of postgraduate and undergraduate programmes, and has directed the MA in HRD and Management Learning at Lancaster. She currently directs two undergraduate degree programmes: the BBA in Management and the BBA in European Management. Her research interests include: critical perspectives of HRD; the socio-political context of management education; women managers; and feminist theory.

Sarah Fraser is well known in healthcare for her work on how good practice spreads, how improvements can be made at practitioner level and how organisations and teams can best work together. She is in demand as a speaker and workshop presenter, and has written numerous papers, articles and guides around the topics of spread, complexity, networks, collaboratives and improvements. As an independent consultant Sarah spends much of her time working with large-scale improvement initiatives in the NHS. She is an Executive Board Member of Buckinghamshire Community Action (Council for Voluntary Services and Council for Protection of Rural England). Her formal education comprises various degrees, certificates and diplomas in arts, economics, applied social sciences and technology. Sarah is an Honorary Visiting Professor at Middlesex University.

Denis Gračanin is an Assistant Professor in the Computer Science Department at Virginia Tech. He is a member of several professional organisations including the Association for Computing Machinery (ACM), the Institute of Electrical and Electronics Engineers, Inc. (IEEE) and the Society for Computer Simulation International (SCS). His primary research interests focus on distributed virtual environment, distributed simulation and Internet computing. His work has appeared in journals such as *IEEE Transactions on Systems, Man, and Cybernetics, IEEE Control Systems Magazine, Machine Intelligence and Robotic Control.* He is a Director of the recently established Distributed Virtual Environment research laboratory at the Virginia Tech's Northern Virginia Center.

Tim G. Hatcher is Associate Professor of HRD at the University of Louisville, Louisville, Kentucky, USA. He is a sought after speaker, consultant and author of numerous articles and books on ethics and HRD including *Ethics and HRD: A New Approach to Leading Responsible Organizations,* 2002, Perseus Publishing, Cambridge, MA.

Rosemary Hill is an independent HRD consultant and researcher with both private and public sector experience across a wide range of industry sectors. Her PhD research, which examined HRD approaches in small organisations, has led to the publication of several journal articles and book chapters including a chapter in Routledge's recently published volume *Understanding Human Resource Development: A research-based approach,* edited by McGoldrick, Stewart and Watson (2002). Rosemary is also an Associate Lecturer and Consultant in the Liverpool Business School, Liverpool John Moores University.

Heather Höpfl is Professor of Organisational Psychology at the University of Northumbria, UK. Her research interests focus mainly on new organisational forms and the humanisation of organisation. In 2002 she edited *Casting the Other* with Barbara Czarniawska and *Interpreting the Maternal Organisation* with Monika Kostera. She is Joint Editor of *Culture and Organization* and a Visiting Professor of the University of South Australia, Adelaide and the Academy of Entrepreneurship in Warsaw.

Paul Iles is a Professor of Strategic HRM at Teesside Business School, Teesside University and a Visiting Professor at the University of Mauritius and the University of Baotou, Inner Mongolia, China. He is a Fellow of CIPD, a

Chartered Psychologist and Associate Fellow of the British Psychological Society. He was previously Professor of HRD and Head of the Liverpool Centre of HRD at Liverpool Business School, Liverpool John Moores University and Senior Lecturer in HRM at the Open University Business School. His main research interests are in assessment and development, career development, organisation development, knowledge management, and international HRM and diversity. He has written many articles in scholarly journals and is the author or co-author of several books, including *Changing Patterns of Management Development in the UK*, 2001, Blackwells and *Managing Staff Selection and Assessment in Organisations*, 2000, Sage.

Kim James was born in 1928 and educated at Wellingborough Grammar School between 1939–45. He served in the Royal Armoured Corps (1945–8). Following this, he attended the Borough Polytechnic School of Art (1948–53); London University Education Department (1953–4); the Royal College of Art from where he gained an MA degree (1972–4); Brunel University School of Applied Biology (1974–6) and Brunel University School of Electrical Engineering Division of Cybernetics (1976–83). He has been a practising sculptor since 1954, and his works include a wall relief at St Matthews Church, Bethnal Green; decorated ceilings at St Nicolas, Hayes, Middlesex and St Edmunds, Hillingdon, Middlesex; the Nottingham Trent University Mammoth sculpture and the Middleheim Sculpture Biennale.

Paul Kraus has a law degree and an MBA, qualifications in counselling and NLP, and had a career in HR up to director level. He applies his experience and eclectic approach to change management at the organisational and individual levels through his consultancy, Dasein. Whether coaching executives or helping companies change, he believes that lasting change only occurs from the inside out allowing embedded behaviour patterns to become visible and transparent. He sees his role as a catalyst to facilitate and support this process to create the opportunity for learning, development, and higher levels of achievement.

Monica Lee is Visiting Professor at Northumbria University, and is based at Lancaster University, UK. She is a Chartered Psychologist, and is a Fellow of CIPD, and Associate Fellow of the British Psychological Society. She is Editor in Chief of *Human Resource Development International* and Editor of the Routledge monograph series *Studies in HRD*. She came to academe from the business world where she was Managing Director of a development consultancy. She has worked extensively in Central Europe, CIS and the USA coordinating and collaborating in research and teaching initiatives. She is now concentrating on mentoring senior managers. She is intrigued by the dynamics around individuals and organisations, and most of her work is about trying to make sense of these. This can be seen in recent publications in *Human Relations, Human Resource Development International, Management Learning* and *Personnel Review*.

Christina Mary MacNeil is a Senior Lecturer in Human Resource Management in the Business School at Oxford Brookes University. Her current research interests are: the role of the line manager as a facilitator supporting knowledge sharing in teams; informal workplace learning; the line manager as a change agent in organisations; and the influence of the line manager on employees changing career patterns. Christina has worked as an HRM professional in both private and public sector organisations for ten years before entering higher education, and is currently a member of the Chartered Institute of Personnel and Development.

Carole McKenzie is a leader in her field of strategic consulting and coaching. Her success lies in her diversity of academic foundation: a PhD in cybernetics; systemic therapy; Chinese energy-based techniques; combined with a track record of business transformation in organisations ranging from the public sector to large blue-chip multinationals. Carole's major accomplishment has been to apply the laws of complexity in a practical way to enable individuals and teams to achieve extraordinary levels of creativity and collaboration. Her main professional contribution has been the development of tools, proven over twenty years and based on exhaustive research into the facilitation of the creative processes, which pinpoint the optimal conditions for organisations to motivate and realise the full value of their employees, measurable in bottom-line business performance.

Clare Rigg is Lecturer in Change Management and Organisation Development at the School of Public Policy, the University of Birmingham. She has thirteen years' experience of management development and research, particularly using action learning and action research approaches. Her current research interests include relations between individual learning and organisational development, inter-agency working, the use of action learning and action research for individual and organisation development, and the application of a discourse perspective to organisation analysis.

Jim Stewart has taught in universities for sixteen years following careers in retail and in local government. He has worked at Nottingham Business School for ten years and has held his present position of Professor of HRD for the last four years. An active researcher and writer, Jim is the author or editor/co-editor of seven books, including two others in the Routledge series on HRD, as well as numerous reports, articles and conference papers. Jim is also Chair of the University Forum for HRD.

Kiran Trehan is Head of the Department of Management and Human Resourcing at the University of Central England, where she undertakes research, teaching and consultancy with a variety of public and private sector organisations in the area of human resource/organisational development. Her fields of interest include critical approaches to human resource development, management learning, and power and emotions in learning communities and organisational development. Her current research interests include critical thinking in human resource development and critical reflection with particular reference to power, knowledge and control.

Sharon Turnbull joined Lancaster University Management School in 1994 after a fifteen-year career in HRM and management development in various companies including Dan-Air, Manchester Airport, Pilkington, Woolworths and two human resource consultancies. Since being at Lancaster University, she has directed the Executive MBA and Bass MBA and taught and tutored on many corporate programmes. She currently co-directs the MPhil/PhD in Critical Management. Sharon's research interests include critical perspectives of HRD, management fads, and emotion and change in organisations. She gained her PhD in 2000 from Lancaster University.

David Weir is Professor of Intercultural Management at Ceram in Sophia Antipolis, France where he directs the Euromed project. He was formerly Professor of Organisational Behaviour at Glasgow University and Director of the Bradford University School of Management, where he created and directed the Arab Management Conference. He has researched and written on many aspects of business and management in the Arab Middle East; he is an associate of Gulf National Consultants, and gave the keynote address at the Gulf Co-operation Council Economic Summit in 2002.

Maurice Yolles is a Reader in Management Systems at the Faculty of Business and Law, Liverpool John Moores University and a Visiting Professor at the Technical University of Ostrava, Czech Republic and the University of Baotou, Inner Mongolia, China. He is also Vice President for Research and Publications of the International Society of Systems Science. His research interests are in viable systems theory, knowledge management and organisational change. He is the author of numerous articles in scholarly journals and several books, including *Management Systems: A viable approach*, Pitmans/FT, 1999.

Together, Paul Iles and Maurice Yolles have written several recent articles on knowledge management for *Human Resource Development International* and the *Journal of Research and Practice in HRM*, on international joint ventures for the *International Journal of HRM* and on HRD alliances for *Human Resource Development International*. They have recently acted as consultants to change projects in the Czech Republic with the Technical University of Ostrava and with Bulgarian National Radio and Television, and in 2002 with the Everbright Bank and Baosteel in China. In 2002 they gave invited keynote addresses to the Fourth Conference on Management Innovation in China sponsored by the UN Development Programme.

Acknowledgements

The authors and publishers would like to thank *Human Resource Development International* (see http://www.tandf.co.uk) for permission to publish Chapters 4 and 7, by Heather Höpfl, and Carole Elliott and Sharon Turnbull. Both chapters were previously published in Volumes 5 and 6 respectively.

Introduction

Background to the book

This book arises out of a scholarly seminar on complexity and human resource development that I chaired at Lancaster University. This was one of a series of six seminars that were held in the UK over a twelve-month period from October 2000. They were funded by a competitive award from the Economic and Social Research Council and were jointly convened by myself and Jean Woodall (Kingston University) and Jim Stewart (Nottingham Trent University).

The aim of the seminar series was to provide an opportunity for HRD scholars and scholar-practitioners to debate leading-edge research in HRD outside of the normally hectic academic conference timetable, and thus in a relaxed atmosphere with ample opportunity for discussion and reflection. For this reason, each seminar lasted a whole day and considered only a few papers. All seminar papers were written in advance and circulated on the day. In consequence the quality of work presented and the debate was of a high standard. In particular, many of the papers presented new work that either challenged established assumptions underlying the field of HRD, or added new empirical insights.

Over the past ten years notions of complexity have emerged from the hard sciences and these are now being applied to the social sciences. As applied to the social sciences, these notions are varied and open to interpretation, and the area is still nascent. What is clear, however, is that the notions and language of complexity offer the chance to reinterpret traditional views of theory and practice. Much of HRD remains rooted in traditional approaches, and the seminar on HRD in a Complex World offered the opportunity for attendees from across the world to discuss alternative approaches to their theory and practice and to use complexity as a springboard or metaphor by which HRD can be examined.

Six papers were presented at the seminar, and they form the core of this book. They generated detailed discussion and inspired further papers. The most appropriate of these were selected for inclusion here. It was difficult to decide upon what was 'appropriate' as all were good, but in the end the choice revolved around those that addressed the key themes which emerged from the seminar and subsequent discussions. This book, therefore, presents sixteen different perspectives and represents the current state of the art, as portrayed by twenty of the international group of academics and practitioners who attended the seminar or became involved in the discussion of complexity in relation to HRD.

Each of these perspectives highlights a different aspect of the whole – some address aspects of complexity theory directly, others only by implication; some focus on theory, others on practice; some talk globally, others locally; some address issues critically, others present them as they are – but in each case, the main message is that as the world changes and our understandings of the world develop, so must the theory and practice of HRD expand. We can no longer live and work in a non-complex world, and if we choose to do so we are in danger of blindfolding ourselves and simplifying our existence to the point of impotence.

I shall present a brief overview of the contributions here, and also at the start of each section in order to help you, the reader, orientate yourself amongst these many perspectives – but I would much prefer to let the authors speak for themselves. I beg you, therefore, not to take my word for it, but to read through and engage in the debates directly.

Overview of the structure

The book is divided into four sections of four papers each – these four sections offer the main structure and are roughly based upon level of analysis. They are presented in this order because, conventionally, theory is presented first – this is not intended to indicate that they are superior in any way. Indeed, if you are interested in practical implications, you might wish to read the book from back to front!

The first section is called 'Reviewing the bases of HR: the depth' and the chapters here each address the issue from a more theoretical perspective, exploring the roots of the debate more deeply. Those in the second section 'Reflections of HR: the width' build on these and widen the debate. In the third section 'Realising HR: applying the theories' the chapters each extend the previous debates to introduce possible tools for practice. The fourth section 'Realities of HR: aspects of practice' looks directly at the implications these debates hold for practice.

Each of the sections has four chapters within it, and these are also 'themed' as can be seen in Figure A.1. The four main themes that arose from discussion relate both to the focus and to the way in which the issues are handled by the authors. I hasten to add, however, that these themes are not exclusive – other themes emerge through the chapters and there is quite a degree of crossover between these themes. For example, many of the chapters address issues of emotion and ethics, yet I have not placed these as core themes, although I could easily have done so. A matrix, however, as of that presented in Figure A.1, demands delineation – and so we have the imposition of false boundaries in order to enhance clarity.

Having taken this qualification (or excuse for arbitrary imposition) on board, the four main themes are as follows. First, 'questioning the remit'. The chapters in this group each attempt, in some way, to lay out the field, to establish theoretical or practical boundaries, and to suggest where the current boundaries need to be reviewed. Second, 'questioning divisions'. These chapters each focus on particular

	Questioning the remit	*Questioning divisions*	*Questioning the social*	*Questioning the thinking*
Section 1 *Reviewing the bases of HR: the depth*	1 Lee	2 Iles and Yolles	3 Hatcher	4 Höpfl
Section 2 *Reflections of HR: the width*	5 Weir	6 Stewart	7 Elliott and Turnbull	8 James
Section 3 *Realising HR: applying the theories*	9 Callahan and Gračanin	10 Yolles and Iles	11 McKenzie	12 Davies and Kraus
Section 4 *Realities of HR: aspects of practice*	13 Fraser	14 Trehan and Rigg	15 MacNeil	16 Hill

Figure A.1 The structure of the book.

areas of the field and counterpoise areas that are conventionally disparate, seeking synergy from diversity. The third theme is that of 'questioning the social' or critiquing the relationship between HR theory and practice and our social world. Finally, the fourth theme, 'questioning the thinking', revolves around different ways of thinking and being as emerging from new understandings of the complex world that we live in.

Each of the chapters addresses each of these themes to some extent – thus each theme pervades all the chapters by implication, and so is not unique to any one particular group of chapters – perhaps each theme is just more prominent in some than in others. I will not elaborate further, but just wish you joy in reading the book. I have certainly enjoyed being party to the development of these ideas, and I hope that they spark further discussion and development of the field.

Monica Lee,
Lancaster University

Part I

Reviewing the bases of HR

The depth

The four chapters in this section each question conventional thinking on the theoretical roots of HR. Monica Lee argues that there are processes underlying our normal conception of HRD (and humanity) and that conventional conceptualisations of the human condition are lacking, such that it can be better understood or viewed through the lens of complexity. Paul Iles and Maurice Yolles take the particular case of organisation development (OD) to make a similar argument. In each case, the authors are arguing for a shift in worldview, and Tim Hatcher addresses this directly, proposing the need for more socially responsible alternative worldviews. The final chapter in this section is by Heather Höpfl, who uses the text itself to illustrate the bounded nature of conventional approaches.

Each of these chapters stands on its own, and also links to others. The notions of alternative worldviews, ethicality and the aesthetic permeate the book. Monica Lee's chapter sets out a 'grand vision' – a synergy of theories and approaches, some of which are picked up, in particular by Carole McKenzie and Rosemary Hill, in later chapters. Paul Iles and Maurice Yolles pick up their own work in a later chapter in which they expand upon practical implications of their theoretical approach. The position established by Tim Hatcher resonates with that discussed by Carole Elliott and Sharon Turnbull, as well as that of Jim Stewart. David Weir's chapter presents a strong example of a different worldview – one that is little considered or understood in Western-based management theory and practice. The notions of emotion and the aesthetic, introduced by Heather Höpfl, are picked up throughout the book, but particularly by Kim James, Jamie Callahan and Denis Gračanin, as well as by Lloyd Davies and Paul Kraus. The practical implications of the notion of unravelling theoretical boundaries (that is addressed by all authors in this section in one way or another) are explored, in particular by Sarah Fraser, Christina MacNeil, and Kiran Trehan and Clare Rigg in the final section of this book.

1   The complex roots of HRD

Monica Lee

Social science and complexity

As the various branches of social science have developed the way in which they build accounts for the world and our existence within it, they have moved away from each other and from the natural sciences. Barklow, Cosmides and Tooby (1992) note that the natural sciences have retained a common root in their development, such that any move forward needs to fit with both its 'home' discipline, and also be concurrent with all others in order to be accepted. This has not happened in a consistent way within the social sciences. In adopting a post-scientific perspective, postmodernism has challenged many of the contradictory yet self-sustaining frameworks that have developed. Yet in creating a world that is devoid of structure other than our own unique and individual structuring of it, postmodernism is actively engaged in preventing constructive (or 'with structure') dialogue between the various disciplines of the social sciences (though see Cilliers, 1998). In contrast to this, the notions of complexity provide the ideal vehicle by which a meta-view of human existence can be established within which apparently contradictory worldviews can be accommodated.

Central to complexity theory is the idea that a complex system is more than 'just' a complicated system. A complicated system or a problem might be very complicated indeed, but with time and effort, all its parts, and its whole, can be measured and understood. In contrast, a complex system might be quite simple, yet its parameters cannot be measured or quantified (in the normal sense) and the whole is more than the sum of the parts. However much we atomise the different parts we can never get to the essence of the whole. In this there is similarity between postmodernism and complexity theory. Unlike postmodernism, however, complexity theory suggests that whilst aspects of complex systems cannot be measured in the normal sense, we can infer relationships between the constituent parts and subsystems, and we can deduce global underlying principles. Put another way, however we choose to view the world, there exist processes that underlie all of humanity, and the principles of complexity theory might provide a language by which we can get closer to an appreciation of them (Tsoukas and Hatch, 2001).

There is no requirement that a complex system be uniform in nature. It may have sub-systems that appear in structure and function to be significantly different to each other and to the whole, yet each is in relationship to the others and to the 'environment' of the whole, and the whole is in relation to the wider environment. This relationship might be one that is in a state of 'far from equilibrium' (Stacey, 1993) yet the system maintains dynamic coherence through autopiotic processes, and adheres to its global underlying principles.

The following sections of this chapter suggest that there exist processes that underlie 'the human condition' and mechanisms by which these are transferred across generations. Further, the diversity apparent between individuals and nations is indicative of self-generating and autopiotic sub-systems that might be complex in their own right, but which are still parts of the whole, as each derives its identy or being from its opposite (as perceived from the whole) and 'development' in any of these sub-systems is synonomous with interaction with the whole.

Underlying processes

In this section I shall explore what these processes might be through illustration. I do this to emphasise their metaphorical or representational nature. The words employed are used to represent concepts which are themselves socially constructed representations – in other words, whilst there might be some commonality of language between the various constructions discussed here, it must be remembered that the meanings behind the words are dynamic, situated and ephemeral. One word may mean different things in different contexts and different things to different people (Jankowicz, 1994). I am therefore trying to explore the parameters of the concepts or meanings behind the words, whilst acknowledging that these concepts are also socially constructed and essentially undefinable.

Four main views of 'management' can be identified: the classical, scientific, processual and phenomenological (Lee, 1997a). Managers, within the *classical* view, must be able to create appropriate rules and procedures for others to follow, they must be good judges of people and able to take independent action as and when required. Good managers are assumed to be 'born' rather than 'made' – and so management development is a matter of selecting the 'right' people with leadership potential. The *scientific* view assumes that human behaviour is rational, and that people are motivated by economic criteria (Taylor, 1947). Within this view 'correct' decisions can be identified and implemented appropriately through scientific analysis, and thus good management techniques can be acquired by anyone with the right training. 'Training departments' systematically identify and fill the 'training gap'. Both of these approaches assume a structured and known world based upon rational principles and in which rationality leads to success.

The other two approaches to management assume a world in which agency (rather then structure) is the predominant force. The *processual* view of management assumes that economic advantage will come to those who are best able to spot opportunities, to learn rapidly, and to create appropriate commitment amongst colleagues. HRD is seen to help managers develop leadership and inter-

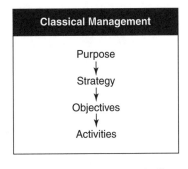
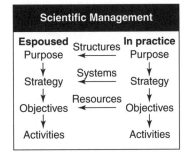
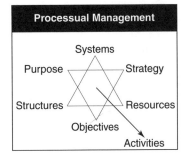
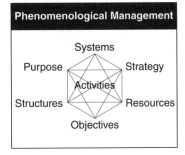

Figure 1.1 Four approaches to management (after Lee, 1997a).

personal skills, creativity, self reliance and the ability to work in different cultures. Although the individual is the main stakeholder in his or her own development, the direction of the organisation (and thus of an individual's development) remains at the behest of senior management who, through initiatives such as business process re-engineering (BPR), aspire to mould the organisation and the people within it. *Phenomenological* management, differs from processual management in the way in which the activities drive the functions, strategies and even leadership of the organisation. For many, management is about 'purpose' and 'doing' whilst phenomenology is about the 'study' of 'being'. All individuals are seen to collude with their situation and, through that collusion, are 'together' responsible for the running and development of the organisation (despite some being 'senior management' and others being from the shop floor). 'Management' is about being part of a system whose activities change as a function of the system and of its relationship to its environment.

These four approaches link quite closely to the four ways in which the word 'development' is used in the literature, as delineated through an entirely different line of research (Lee, 1997b). 'Development' was used to indicate a form of *maturation* – the (inevitable or natural) progression through a series of stages in a life cycle. When used to indicate *shaping* it similarly implied a known endpoint to which the individual or organisation was steered by the application of various tools within a known, quantifiable and manageable environment. In contrast, the

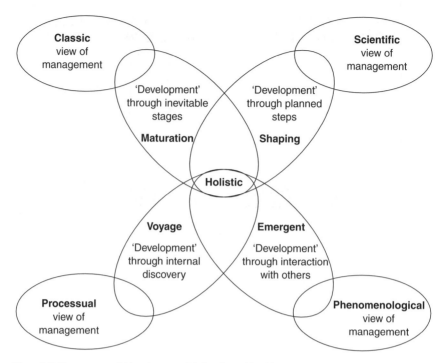

Figure 1.2 Four types of 'development' (after Lee, 1977b).

other two uses of the word 'development' that were identified did not have a known endpoint. Development as a *voyage* was evident in literature about personal development – in which the self was the agent and the object – and development as *emergent* was evident in social science literature particularly, in which the lines between the individual and the organisation became blurred and the focus was upon co-development and co-regulation.

Figure 1.2 shows a representation of these four forms of development, presented as a typology (in which the boundary lines of the figure indicate the strength of spheres of influence, and not delineations or divisive categories) and maps onto this the four views of management discussed earlier.

This latter point is important and worth emphasising. I am *not* here discussing 'real' differences and saying that there exist four ways of 'doing' management or development – or that management or development are 'things' that can be 'done', or can be 'done to'. In contrast, I am saying that there appear to be differences in the way that people talk about, or enact, whatever it is that constitutes 'development' or 'management' in their eyes, and that there appears to be some consistency within the realisation of those differences. These points of similarity could, of course, merely be a product of my imagination – my own research being the common factor between the two; however, others have reached the same conclusion.

Parallels to these notions can be seen in the work of Carl Jung (1964, 1971). Jung suggested that whilst everyone seeks to make sense of the world around them, they do not focus on the same things. He suggested that there exist two processes (perception and judgement) which are independent of each other, and both are bi-polar. Perception is the process by which individuals make sense (consciously or sub-consciously, or in Jungian terms, unconsciously) of their surroundings, and is thus mediated by previous understandings, expectation and anticipations, memory and unconscious influences (from the 'promissary notes' of metaphore, myth and rhetoric (Soyland, 1994) to primal drives). When gathering information people *prefer* to focus either on the 'here-and-now' information from their senses, *or* on the 'what-if' information they 'intuit' from the possibilities and patterns they see developing. Judgement is the process of deciding which of the many alternative perceptival interpretations available at any one instant to adopt as 'reality'. Judgement is influenced by previous understandings and is more likely to be based upon *post hoc* rationalisation than the traditionally accepted approach of 'scientifically' weighing up the alternatives and rationally choosing the best option in advance of the final decision. When deciding about the information they have gathered, people *prefer* to make decisions based on objective thinking, by analysing and weighing the alternatives from a wide perspective, *or* to make decisions based on their feelings for each particular situation in an individualised manner.

There is strong evidence of individual variation in preferred perceptual and judgemental styles (see, for example, Mitroff and Kilmann, 1978 and Reason, 1981). Such variation forms the basic premise of the Myers Briggs Type Indicator (MBTI), a management assessment and development tool for individuals and organisations that is being increasingly used world-wide. It is beyond the remit of this chapter to go into the MBTI-based literature in any depth, though see Briggs Myers and McCaulley (1985) and Krebs Hirsh and Kummerow (1987) for more detail. I raise the issue here to record general acceptance of the MBTI tool, and thus (by implication) the assumptions on which the tool is based. Other researchers have used Jungian dimensions as a basis upon which to build an analysis of their area, for example Tufts-Richardson (1996) links Jungian typology to individual spirituality by mapping four types of spiritual path, whilst McWhinney (1992) maps four paths of change, or choice, for organisations and society. Similarly, as can be seen in Figure 1.3, the work of other researchers who make no claim to root their work in Jungian typology, such as that of Hofstede (1991), can also be mapped onto these dimensions.

I have included different approaches to learning in this figure as I shall refer to them in the next section. Before moving on, however, I wish to emphasise that we cannot label the dimensions in a fixed and unique manner, but we do need to understand their qualia better if they are fundamental to our way of describing and enacting self and society. In the following section I shall explore the underlying dimensions of these quaternities further by positing their evolutionary basis, and the way in which they might be promulgated.

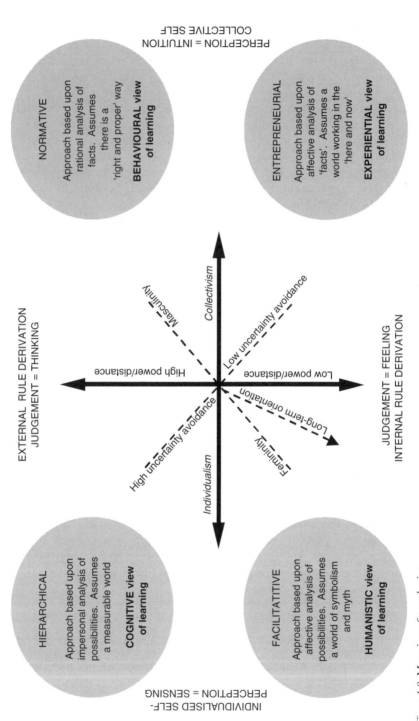

Figure 1.3 Mapping of typologies.

An evolutionary basis?

Research into evolutionary psychology and psychiatry (Barklow, Cosmides and Tooby, 1992; Bradshaw, 1997) suggests that human (and primate) affectional development progresses through the maturation of specific affectional systems, and that 'All major psychiatric syndromes may thus be conceived as inappropriate expressions of evolved propensities concerned with adaptive behaviour in the domains of group membership (…), group exclusion (…), and mating (…).' (Stevens and Price, 1996: 29). They argue that there exist two 'great archetypal systems'. The first formative experience faced by our proto-human ancestors would be that associated with parenting and family. As our ancestors developed the pattern of bearing live young who needed parental care for survival, they also developed the pattern of behaviours and emotions that bonded parent and child in a dependant relationship. Thus their first great archetypal system has to do with attachment, affiliation, care giving, care receiving and altruism. As the child grew, was replaced by other children, and eventually became a parent themselves, so 'self' – and as a necessary and integral part of that process, 'not-self', or the 'other' – emerged. Therefore, the first fundamental dynamic played out in each person's life is that of self and other. This pervades the whole of our existence and is the core of self-development literature.

The second formative experience was that of collectivity. For ninety-nine per cent of its existence, humanity has lived in 'extended organic kinship groups' of about forty to fifty individuals, comprising six to ten adult males, twelve to twenty child-bearing females, and about twenty juveniles and infants (Fox, 1989). As predators, they were sufficiently effective not to need to develop large aggregations, flocking behaviour and high sensitivity to others in the group in order to survive, but they were sufficiently weak that they could only exceptionally survive as solitary individuals. We are therefore left with an awareness of society and its necessary structures and hierarchy, and also of individual agency. This equates to Stevens and Price's second great archetypal system, namely that concerned with rank, status, discipline, law and order, territory and possessions.

Stevens and Price posit that the search for achievement of archetypal goals occurs throughout the whole of the life cycle, though the presenting face of the goals we seek changes as our circumstances change with age. These dual aspects of our collective psyche (self and other, and the structured law and the anarchic body (Höpfl, 1995)) can be seen mirrored in the tensions between sociology and psychology, or between structure and agency, as elucidated by Giddens (1976).

In other words, we can identify two fundamental processes derived from our evolutionary history that continue to affect our humanity and our enactment of our existence. I want to make a clear distinction between the discussion here about the existence of fundamental or underlying processes and our day-to-day appreciation of them. Our daily lives and how we see them are framed by our sense-making of our past and by our anticipation of the future – we each live in our own self-constructed worlds. The surface diversity of our own worlds does not, however, detract from the existence of underlying processes. Our existence is interpreted differently across the spread of our civilisations, but that is a matter of the ways in which we choose to make sense of our existence.

Autopiotic mechanism for promulgation of the sub-sets

Socialisation can be seen as a mechanism by which the tensions and their resolution between self and other, and between structure and agency, are promulgated and emphasised through succeeding generations. I base my argument on the view that social development is a process of creative interaction in which 'individuals dynamically alter their actions with respect to the ongoing and anticipated actions of their partners' (Fogel, 1993:34; Smith, 1992; McWhinney, 1992; Lee, 1994). Relationships exist within mutually constructed conventions or frames of reference (Kelly 1955; Duncan 1991:345; Moreland and Levine, 1989), and a dynamic view of culture is facilitated (Hatch, 1993).

'Society' exists in so far as people agree to its existence – and could be a family unit or a nation. In some way (whether by being born into and thus socialised within it – as in a family or nation; through meeting like-minded people and thus forming friendship groups; or formally through induction into an organisation) individuals come to identify (and be identified by others) as part of a community. In doing so they help create and collude with underlying values and norms. This process starts at birth and is a basal acculturation mechanism in which the underlying processes are the same whether the focus is upon family and friendship groupings, temporary 'micro-cultures', small or large organisations, or national culture (Burns, 1977). There is empirical evidence of correlation between form of parenting and the child's life stance (Baumrind, 1973; Bee, 1985), and between career and family history (Cromie, Callaghan and Jansen, 1992). Similarly, there is evidence that choice of curricula, methodological approach and course design are partially governed by the value base of the providers, and thus perpetuate that value base (Ashton, 1988; Boyacigiller and Adler, 1991). Thus the approach to learning adopted by each society has a fundamental effect upon the continuation of the parameters of that particular society (Lee, 1996).

In Figure 1.3 different forms of learning were mapped against the archetypal parameters of self and other, and of structure and agency. In practical terms, the 'cognitive' environment carries with it group norms about received wisdom and the value of qualifications. Power is vested in those who have achieved qualifications and those who can give them. Cogent argument carries more importance than does applicability or individual difference. The 'problem' student (or heretic, Harshbarger, 1973) would be someone who lacked sufficient intelligence to master the required concepts. The 'behavioural' environment focuses upon activity, functionalism and the importance of the end result. Norms involve identifying competence, and filling the 'training gap' to achieve appropriate levels of competence. The heretic is someone unable to demonstrate the required competence. The 'humanistic' environment focuses upon difference and equality. Received wisdom (in so far as it epitomises a particular view of reality) is inappropriate, as are identifiable and assessable 'competencies' (in so far as they epitomise a 'right'

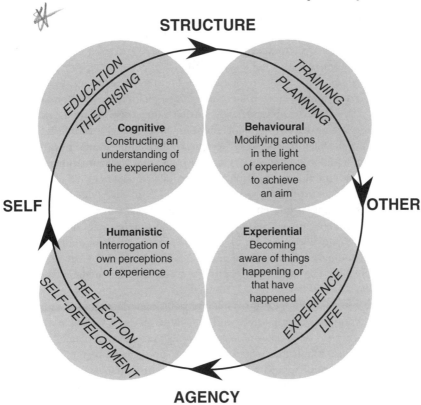

Figure 1.4 Movement through typologies (after Lee, 1996).

way of doing things). The problem participant is unwilling to explore and share their affective and attitudinal aspects. In the 'experiential' environment the focus is on actionable outcomes – the end justifies the means. The heretic is someone who questions the route, or prefers inactivity. ('The confidence to act is a prerequisite for learning', Blackler, 1993.)

It is rare, in 'real life', that 'learning' only occurs within one approach. Instead, it is much more likely that in any situation one learns more 'holistically' (Lee, 1996). Honey and Mumford (1989) suggest that 'experience' plays a part in any learning, regardless of whether or not it is acknowledged or focused upon within the educational process. One of the best-known models of experiential learning is that of Kolb (1974, 1984) who suggests that the process of learning is cyclical, revolving through experience, reflection, theorising and planning. In Figure 1.4 this is represented by the large (arrowed) circle. From this perspective, we learn only by engaging in all aspects of the activity.

Transformative experiences, therefore, appear to be those that force us to (re-) examine our worldview (Emery and Trist, 1965; Pascale, 1990). Any 'experience' is an opportunity for learning, however, as Dewey (1938) pointed out: 'It is not enough to insist upon the necessity of experience, nor even of activity in experience. Everything depends upon the quality of experience which is had ... every experience lives in further experiences'. Vasilyuk (1984) takes it further, building the case that all learning that has a transformative effect upon us is derived from a clash between our understanding of the world and our experience, to the extent that learning and change are painful processes of redefinition, and Romanelli and Tushman (1994) offer empirical evidence for rapid, discontinuous change in organisations being driven by major environmental changes. Similarly, Stevens and Price argue that our changing lives necessitate re-negotiating our position with respect to the great archetypal systems, and that 'Psychopathology results when the environment fails, either partially or totally, to meet one (or more) archetypal need(s) in the developing individual' (1966:34). In the terms of complexity theory, transformative experiences occur at bifurcation points, when the system and the environment impact in such a way that the system can either continue in its current, well-travelled pattern, or shift to some way of being that is new and unpredicted (though not necessarily unpredictable). Indeed, the current analysis would suggest that the system is likely to shift to incorporate qualia of a different world view.

I have argued that there exist two main bi-polar underlying processes by which the human condition is structured, and that these give rise to four main archetypes. The processes of socialisation, or learning, emphasise particular aspects of our worldview, such that the various systems or sub-systems, be they individuals, organisations or nations, have a tendency to enact the qualia of a single archetype. However, although I have talked of the qualia of the archetypes, I have deliberately failed to define them other than by example. Archetypes, by their nature, are undefinable in the scientific sense, and also, as discussed above, the qualia are unmeasurable other than dialectically (Pascale, 1990) by reference to their 'opposite'. Furthermore, that 'opposite' might be different under different occasions or interpretations. For example, in one situation it was found that the word 'conflict' was interpreted by some people to be 'contested negotiation' whilst others saw it as 'a fight to the death', and acted accordingly with misunderstanding on both sides (Lee, 1998). We could extrapolate that for these people the opposite to their views of conflict would be the similar but subtly different qualities of 'easy negotiation' and 'peaceful life'. We live within our own worldview yet, in order to understand or even describe it we need to compare it with that of others in a dialectic manner. In other words – to know what we are, we also have to know what we are not. We cannot categorise the human condition in a positivistic, mutually exclusive sense, but we can use the arguments above to develop a dialectically based typology.

A wheel of typologies

Figure 1.5 shows a typology of typologies of the human condition, constructed by plotting the axes of the great archetypal systems against typologies of individual, organisational and governmental approach and those of individual influence,

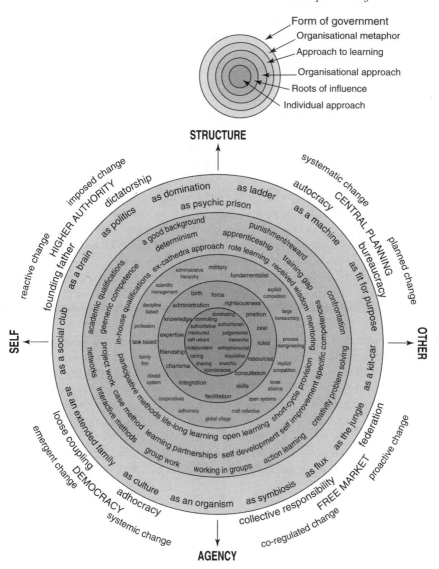

Figure 1.5 A typology of typologies (note: the words are indicative, not definitional).

education and metaphor (as a form of organisational glue, after Morgan, 1986). This is not intended as a categorisation. Each spoke of the wheel supports the others with no clear distinction between neighbouring typologies, and each is validated dialectically by the qualia of the spoke opposite it. Thus an archetypal individual and organisational approach is represented as if it were located in a radial segment of the wheel (the width of which would depend upon the diversity of the element in question), and the probability of identifying an approach typified by other segments or individual parts of the wheel would be negatively correlated with distance from the primal segment. If this meta-typology is imagined in three dimensions, with the centre forming the tip of a cone, the third dimension represents a continuum moving from micro variables at the apex towards macro variables at the base. In other words, the tip of the cone might represent degrees of aggregation, and the base might represent large aggregates of elements, yet each has influence upon the other.

For example, recent work exploring gene-culture co-evolution indicates the potential for rapid genetically-linked cultural change linked to choice of mate (Laland, 1993; Richerson and Boyd, 1989). This example also indicates the complexity of the distinction. Individuals might be actively choosing a mate (though sub-conscious factors of background and parenting are likely to mediate in such choice (Duck, 1986)), but they are unlikely to be doing so in order actively to influence societal form. The distinction does, however, emphasise both the unpredictable influence of individual factors (cf. Gleick, 1987, and chaos theory) and the speed with which such 'inactive' change might occur.

Examination of the meta-typology could be limited to positive correlation with existing typologies along a single axis. For example, Handy's (1981) typology of organisation culture (Power, Role, Task, Person) shows some similarity to the vertical axis. Debates about field dependence/independence in cognitive style (Hayes and Allison, 1994) appear to fit more closely to the horizontal axis, whilst those about the way in which individuals and societies are interconnected and mutually influencing are represented by the third-dimensional axis. Similarly, Rasheed and Prescott's (1992) dimensions of complexity and dynamism in the classification of organisational task environments show some similarity to the two diagonal axes. Thus the meta-typology can be linked to one-dimensional measures, such as equity sensitivity (King and Miles, 1994), interpersonal orientation (Swap and Rubin, 1983), or Machiavellianism (Robinson and Shaver, 1973), and is potentially testable in its prediction of relationships between such measures.

When visualised as a cone, however, the meta-typology represents three dimensions each of which possess a pole that focuses upon 'individuality', though the import of this is different in each case. This generates multiple layers of meaning that are sacrificed if a one-dimensional form of analysis is adopted. Each segment and type is interpretable in the light of its archetypal opposites within these multiple layers, thus analysis of the meta-typology is richer if a dialectic perspective is adopted. Organisations comprise multifaceted membership and are likely to contain dissidents who might be expected to voice an approach at the polar opposite to that held by the organisation (heresy) or to work outside the accepted bounds of the segment (deviance). Inconsistency of approach might also be found across the levels and/or functions of the organisation (Demirag and Tylecote, 1992), and within the individual (leading to analysis within psychodynamic frameworks) (Parsons, 1951). It can be speculated that level of conflict will be positively correlated with degree of inconsistency both between individual approaches and within aspects of an approach.

There is little probability of any organisation or individual demonstrating all the qualia of a particular typology. As a complex system the individual might demonstrate forms of behaviour akin to one segment of the wheel (espousing an approach similar to that of the free market), whilst the observer notes aspects of behaviour that are located within another segment (working within traditional educational methodology and reinforcing respect for position and rules – theory in practice), yet the individual voices a preference for a third segment (one that respects 'human values') (cf. Argyris, 1990; Bate, 1990; Papula, 1993). The exploration of inconsistency might lead to greater understanding of organisations in practice (Schein, 1985) and point to areas of knowledge that are, at present, underexplored. For example, the form of the model suggests an expansion of Morgan's (1986) typology of organisational metaphor, it supports Buchanan's (1991) call for alternative accounts of change, and it might provide insight into the problems encountered when applying Western-style bureaucracy to African culture (Hyden, 1983), or help contextualise inconsistencies in research findings (cf. Judge and Watanabe, 1994).

Different parts of the system might well adopt different configurations, and configurations might change as 'needed'. The activities of the system are emergent and feed back into it (Weick, 1977), they can influence all other aspects of the system, and the system itself can be 'far-from-equilibrium' (Stacey, 1993). This approach, therefore, denies the ability to 'plan' or 'control' organisational development – it argues for a resource-based view of the organisation in which the role of 'managing' is fragmentary (i.e. Mintzberg, 1979) and offers a valuable critique of the established 'discipline' of strategy. In addition, because this view eschews ideas of (real) control by a hierarchy, as well as questioning the ability of the organisation to (truly) predict or plan, it is more in tune with work that questions the serial and causal nature of our existence (Lee and Flatau, 1996).

The three-dimensional interpretation of the wheel presents a holistic and interactive overview of the meta-typology that is, in essence, static. Given the notion that individuals and organisations, despite their 'presenting approach', will possess hidden qualia of their opposites, and that it is the conflict between these, which are themselves part of the environment, or with other aspects of the environment that generates creative tension and transformation, then it is necessary to introduce a fourth dimension to the meta-typology – that of transformation over time, or dynamism.

From Hereclites onwards (*circa* 500 BC) it has been suggested that humanity is in a state of always 'becoming' despite the appearance of structured categorisation and 'being' fostered by Western scientism (Lee, 2001; Stacey, Griffin and Shaw, 2000). In other words, our lives are dynamic, and in a state of constant change. Fixed goals, known end points, and clear delineations are tools that we use to provide a sense of stability, but that sense is merely a mechanism and is false with respect to the wider reality of existence. The meta-typology, presented here with lines and detail, is merely an attempt to indicate underlying structures. Those structures exist, however, not as things in themselves but they are presented as a possible pattern of relationships – a representation of the relationships between other representations. As noted above, even the terminology used is just a representation. For example, Campbell and Muncer (1987) show that both occupational role and gender are indicative of whether a person views 'aggression' as a functional act aimed at imposing control over other people, or in expressive terms as a breakdown of self control over anger. Thus understanding of the word 'aggression' co-varies with the axes and will be interpreted by different readers in different ways.

HRD as the relationship between representations

As illustrated in Figures 1.1 and 1.2 above, one's view of the nature and role of HRD is dependent upon one's worldview. This chapter, however, suggests that, regardless of one's 'understanding', or the terminology used, that which might be called the development of human resources is actually located at the dynamic and co-creative interface between the elements of the system, and between sub-systems, such that in interacting, they become more than the sum of the parts. Thus the business of HRD, in so far as it exists as a concept and a practice, is concerned with the relationship between the representations. Research into HRD is, in effect, research into the processes that underlie the human condition, and the practice of HRD is about influencing the relationships that comprise the glue of the human condition.

As we research into HRD, this insight means that we need to be aware that we are researching the intangible and un-measurable. We can catch glimpses of what we are looking for and we can try to represent or model it – but we need to avoid the temptation to overly objectify or embody that which we research. The 'individual' and the 'organisation' are not unitary bounded concepts – they are part of a whole and are identifiable by their relationship to the whole. It is the interactions that are of importance, rather than descriptions of 'purpose'. Similarly, a change in approach requires a change in the language and meaning that is used. For example, it would be inappropriate to talk of 'organisations' as if they had a body and could be anthropomorphised, or of 'people' as if they were machine cogs within 'the organisation' whose function was to 'operate' if we were to adopt a loosely bounded or relativistic view of these elements of the system.

As practitioners of HRD we intervene in the human condition with some aim in mind, yet both the '*outcomes*' and the 'value' of them are subject to interpretation. There is no longer necessarily a clear and obvious route between cause and effect – and one person's preferred 'outcome' might be someone else's feared possibility/cause. In both theorising about HRD and in the practice of HRD we can no longer assume that a particular intervention at a particular time will produce a known effect. We lose the gloss of certainty that many HRD professionals feel is necessary for their work as academics, consultants, trainers etc. HRD and learning are becoming more central to the needs of the nation (as in Watson, 1994) and this shift in provision further increases the complexity and uncertainty of inquiry into the nature (and practice) of HRD.

In conclusion

I have suggested that there exist 'great archetypal structures' that underlie the human condition, and that these can be identified by their effect upon it, such that human society and thought clusters into four main archetypal worldviews, termed here, for the sake of convenience and bearing in mind the fragility of language, hierarchical, normative, entrepreneurial and facilitative. The axes by which these are located are bi-polar and termed, again, for convenience, self and other, and structure and agency. I suggest that these great systems and their products are most fruitfully discussed using the language (and thus concepts) of complexity. This recognises that whilst the whole system cannot be pulled apart and understood, it can be accessed by examining the relationships between the multiplicity of representations that are located within it. Thus the study of the system is the study of the relationships within it, and that study is what we might commonly call HRD. It follows from this that the practice of HRD is about *agency* in a pluralistic, relativistic and interpretative world. This involves the search for the patterning of the whole, for dynamic structures, an understanding of the possibilities and their links – a *holistic* approach. Holistic agency (Lee, 1996) is therefore about individual action (or non-action) within a relativistic yet structured world, and thus is about the 'doing' and 'becoming' of HRD.

References

Argyris, (C. 1990) *Overcoming Organisational Defences*, Boston, MA: Allyn and Bacon

Ashton, D. J. L. (1988) 'Are business schools good learning organisations?: Institutional values and their effects in management education', *Personnel Review*, 17(4): 6–14

Barklow, J. H., Cosmides, L. and Tooby, J., (Eds) (1992) *The Adapted Mind: Evolutionary psychology and the generation of culture*, New York: Oxford University Press

Bate, P. (1990) 'Using the culture concept in an organisation development setting', *Journal of Applied Behavioural Science*, 26: 83–106

Baumrind, D. (1973) 'The development of instrumental competence through socialisation', in A. D. Pick (Ed.), *Minnesota Symposium on Child Psychology (Vol. 7)*, Minneapolis: University of Minnesota Press

Bee, H. (1985) *The Developing Child*, New York: Harper & Row

Blackler, F. 1993, 'Knowledge and the theory of organisations: Organisations as activity systems and the reframing of management', *Journal of Management Studies*, 30: 863–884

Boyacigiller, N. and Adler, N. J. (1991) 'The parochial dinosaur: Organisational science in a global context', *Academy of Management Review*, 16(2): 262–290

Bradshaw, J. L. (1997) *Human Evolution: A neuropsychological perspective*, Hove: Psychology Press

Briggs Myers, I. and McCaulley, M. H. (1985) *A Guide to the Development and Use of the Myers Briggs Type Indicator*, Palo Alto: Consulting Psychologists Press

Buchanan, D. A. (1991) 'Vulnerability and agenda: Context and process in project management, *British Journal of Management*, 2: 121–132

Burns, T. (1977) *The BBC: Public institution and private world*, New York: Holmes & Meier Publishers

Campbell, A. and Muncer, S. (1987) 'Models of anger and aggression in the social talk of women and men', *Journal of the Theory of Social Behaviour*, 17: 489–511

Cilliers, P. (1998) *Complexity and Postmodernism: Understanding complex systems*, London: Routledge

Cromie, S., Callaghan, I. and Jansen, M. (1992) 'The entrepreneurial tendencies of managers: A research note', *British Journal of Management*, 3: 1–5

Demirag, I. and Tylecote, A. (1992) 'The effects of organisational culture, structure and market expectations on technological innovation: A hypothesis', *British Journal of Management*, 3: 7–20

Dewey, J. (1938) *Experience and Education*, New York: Kappa Delta (then Collier)

Duck, S. (1986) *Human Relationships*, London: Sage

Duncan, S. (1991) 'Convention and conflict in the child's interraction with others', *Developmental Review*, 11: 337–367

Emery, F. E. and Trist, E. L. (1965) 'The causal texture of organisational environments', *Human Relations*, 18: 21–32

Fogel, A., (1993) *Developing Through Relationships: Origins of communication, self and culture*, Hemel Hempstead: Harvester Wheatsheaf

Fox, R., (1989) *The Search for Society: Quest for a biosocial science and morality*, London: Rutgers University Press

Giddens, A. (1976) *New Rules of Sociological Method: A positive critique of interpretive sociologies*, London: Hutchinson

Gleick, J. (1987) *Chaos*, New York: Viking

Handy, C. B. (1981) *Understanding Organisations*, Harmondsworth: Penguin

Harshbarger, D. (1973) 'The individual and the social order: Notes on the management of heresy and deviance in complex organisations', *Human Relations*, 26(2): 251–269

Hatch, M. J. (1993) 'The dynamics of organisational culture', *Academy of Management Review*, 18: 657–693

Hayes, J. and Allison, C. W. (1994) 'Cognitive style and its relevance for management practice', *British Journal of Management*, 5: 53–71

Hofstede, G. (1991) *Cultures and Organisations, Software of the Mind: Intercultural cooperation and its importance for survival*, London: McGraw-Hill

Honey, P. and Mumford, A (1989) *The Manual of Learning Opportunities*, Maidenhead: Peter Honey

Höpfl, H. (1995) 'Organisational rhetoric and the threat of ambivalence', *Studies in Cultures, Organisations and Societies*, 1(2): 175–188

Hyden, G. (1983) *No Shortcuts to Progress: African development management in perspective*, Berkeley: University of California Press

Jankowicz, A. D. (1994) 'Parcels from abroad: The transfer of meaning to Eastern Europe', *Journal of European Business Education*

Judge, T. A. and Watanabe, S. (1994) 'Individual differences in the nature of the relationship between job and life satisfaction', *Journal of Occupational and Organisational Psychology*, 76: 101–107

Jung, C. G. (1964) *Man and his Symbols*, London: W. H. Allen

Jung, C. G. (1971) *Collected Works* (R. F. C. Hull, revised translation), Vol. 6, 'Psychological Types', Princeton, NJ: Princeton University Press

Kelly, G. (1955) *A Theory of Personality: The psychology of personal constructs*, New York: Norton

King, W. C. and Miles, E. W. 1994, 'The measurement of equity sensitivity', *Journal of Occupational and Organisational Psychology*, 67: 133–142

Kolb, D. (1974) 'On management and the learning process', in D. A. Kolb, I. M. Rubin and J. M. McIntyre (Eds) *Organisational Psychology*, (2nd edition), Englewood Cliffs, NJ: Prentice Hall

Kolb, D. (1984) *Experiential Learning*, Englewood Cliffs, NJ: Prentice Hall

Krebs Hirsh, S. and Kummerow, J. (1987) *Introduction to Types in Organisational Settings*, Palo Alto, CA: Consulting Psychologists Press

Laland, K. N. (1993) 'The mathematical modelling of human culture and its implications for psychology and the human sciences', *British Journal of Psychology*, 84: 145–169

Lee, M. M. (1994) 'The isolated manager: Walking the boundaries of the micro-culture', *Proceedings of the British Academy of Management Conference*, Lancaster: 111–128

Lee, M. M. (1997a) 'Strategic human resource development: A conceptual exploration', *Academy of Human Resource Development Conference Proceedings* R. Torraco (Ed.), 92–99, Baton Rouge, LA: Academy of HRD

Lee, M. M. (1997b) 'The developmental approach: A critical reconsideration' in J. Burgoyne and M. Reynolds (Eds) *Management Learning*, 199–214, London: Sage

Lee, M. M. (1998) 'Understandings of conflict: A cross-cultural investigation', *Personnel Review*, 27(3): 227–224

Lee, M. M. (2001) 'A refusal to define HRD', *Human Resource Development International*, 4(3): 327–341

Lee, M. M. (1996) 'Holistic learning in the new Europe' in M. M. Lee, H. Letiche, R. Crawshaw and M. Thomas (Eds) *Management Education in the New Europe*, London: International Thomson Publishing

Lee, M. M. and Flatau, M. (1996) 'Serial logic in a parallel world', in Mitzla, M. (Ed.) *Facilitating ISO900 training: Report for the European Commission*, Brussels: EC

McWhinney, W. (1992) *Paths of Change*, California: Sage

Mintzberg, H. (1979) *The Structuring of Organisations*, Englewood Cliffe, NJ: Prentice Hall

Mitroff I. I. and Kilmann, R. H. (1978) *Methodological Approaches to Social Science: Integrating divergent concepts and theories*, San Francisco: Jossey-Bass

Moreland, R. L. and Levine, J. M. (1989) 'Newcomers and Oldtimers in small groups', in P. Paulus (Ed.) *Psychology of Group Influence*, 2nd edition, 143–186, Hillsdale, NJ: Erlbaum

Morgan, G. (1986) *Images of Organisation*, London: Sage

Papula, J. (1993) 'The development of management education in Slovakia', paper presented at TEMPUS: Central European Management Development Programme, Vienna

Parsons, T. (1951) *The Social System*. London: Routledge & Kegan Paul Ltd

Pascale, R. T. (1990) *Managing on the Edge: How successful companies use conflict to stay ahead*, London: Viking, Penguin.

Rasheed, A. M. A. and Prescott, J. (1992) 'Towards an objective classification scheme for organisational task environments', *British Journal of Management*, 3: 197–206

Reason, P. (1981) ' "Methodological approaches to social science" by Ian Mitroff and Ralph Killman: an appreciation', in *Human Inquiry: A source book of new paradigm research*, P. Reason and J. Rowan (Eds), 43–51, Chichester: John Wiley and Sons Ltd

Richerson, P. J and Boyd, R. (1989) 'The role of evolved predispositions in cultural evolution: Or human sociobiology meets Pascal's Wager, *Ethology and socio-biology*, 10: 195–219

Robinson, J. P. and Shaver, P. R. (1973) *Measures of Social Psychological Attitudes*, Ann Arbor, MI: Institute for Social Research

Romanelli, E. and Tushman, M. L. (1994) 'Organisational transformation as punctuated equilibrium: An empirical test', *Academy of Management Journal*, 37: 1,141–1,166

Schein, E. H. (1985) *Organisational Culture and Leadership: A dynamic view*, San Francisco: Jossey-Bass

Smith, P. B. (1992) 'Organisational behaviour and national cultures', *British Journal of Management*, 3: 39–51

Soyland, A. J. (1994) *Psychology as Metaphor*, London: Sage

Stacey, R. D. 1993, *Strategic Management and Organisational Dynamics*, London: Pitman

Stacey, R., Griffin, D. and Shaw, P. (2000) *Complexity and Management: Fad or radical challenge to systems thinking?* London: Routledge

Stevens, A. and Price J. (1996) *Evolutionary Psychiatry: A new beginning*, London: Routledge

Swap, W. C. and Rubin, J. Z. 1983, 'Measure of interpersonal orientation', *Journal of Personality and Social Psychology*, 44: 208–219

Taylor, F. W. (1947) *Scientific Management*, London: Harper & Row

Tsoukas, H. and Hatch, M-J. (2001) 'Complex thinking, complex practice: The case for a narrative approach to organisational complexity', *Human Relations*, 54(8), 979–1,014

Tufts-Richardson, P. (1996) *Four Spiritualities: Expressions of self, expressions of spirit*, Palo Alto, California: Davies-Black Publishing

Vasilyuk, F. (1984) *The Psychology of Experiencing: The resolution of life's critical situations*, English translation, 1991, Hemel Hempstead: Harvester Wheatsheaf

Watson, J. (1994) *Management Development to the Millennium: The new challenges*, London: Institute of Management

Weick, K. (1977) 'Organisational design: Organisations as self-organising systems', *Organisational Dynamics*, Autumn, 31–67

2 Complexity, HRD and organisation development

Towards a viable systems approach to learning, development and change

Paul Iles and Maurice Yolles

Introduction: HRD, strategy and complexity

Much interest in the late 1980s and early 1990s was expressed in the notion of 'strategic HRD'; HRD was prescribed to be 'vertically integrated' or subject to 'external fit' with business strategy, as well as 'horizontally integrated' or subject to 'internal fit' with other aspects of HRM. However, much theorising in this tradition has been naïve, unitarist, apolitical and over-rational, often urging the 'matching' of HRD with competitive strategy, organisational life cycle or strategic type.

Such prescriptions have come under increasing challenge from complexity and soft systems theories. Complex systems such as organisations and networks can be seen as having a very large number of interacting parts, the interactions of which are non-linear in the sense that, if the systems are to be understood and decision-making facilitated, the behaviour of the system cannot be predicted simply by understanding the behaviour of the component parts.

The increasing complexity of social and economic organisation, incapable of single, all-embracing strategic solutions, has challenged the dominant paradigm in strategic HRD, namely that of managers as strategic actors providing leadership and managing change in a planned way, based on rational analysis and strategic choice. This paradigm is based on a closed system model of organisations, universalistic in nature and assuming the need for formal strategy to optimise the fit between the organisation and its environment. Complexity theories with roots in chaos theory and non-linear dynamics have recently emerged to challenge this view (e.g. Stacey 2001, Stacey *et al.* 2000). For example, Wheatley (1994) has discussed how our understanding of the universe has been radically altered by the 'new sciences' of quantum physics, chaos theory and systems theories, and that these provide powerful insights for understanding leadership and organisations. Organisational designs and practices have often been based on Newtonian mechanics, whilst quantum physics 'challenges our thinking about observation and perception, participation and relationships, and the influences and connections that are created across large and complex systems' (Wheatley 1994, xl). Theories of self-organising or dissipative structures, for example, introduce new ways of understanding disequilibrium, change and transformation (e.g. Prigogine and Stengers 1984). Complex systems question standard positivist concerns with description, prediction and explanation, as their behaviour results from dynamic interaction between component parts over time, emerging as the holistic sum of these interactions. Increasing structural complexity can mean that in certain circumstances organisations and networks may undergo rapid transformational change (morphogenesis). Processes of informal feedback loops and emergent self-organisation have become important foci of study, as simple causal models appear inadequate to model systems with complex interconnections and feedback loops. Our contention is that complexity is better addressed through viable systems perspectives (e.g. Beer 1979, 1985, Yolles 1999).

The aims of this chapter are to:

- assess the impact of complexity on current models of HRD and strategic HRD;
- explore the potential contribution of OD to a reconceptualised HRD, often unrecognised in current frameworks;
- assess the appropriateness of input-transformation-output models currently underpinning much OD theory and practice;
- begin to develop a more appropriate viable systems model of HRD as a more adequate response to the challenges of complexity.

Complexity in organisations and HRD

Complex situations are particularly susceptible to examination by methodologies from management systems, as they represent structured approaches to inquiry capable of reducing complexity (Yolles 1999). Complexity theory therefore encourages us to look away from 'hard' systems and causalities towards other perspectives. Checkland and Scholes (1990) have drawn attention to the potential of soft systems methodology in analysing purposeful activities, introducing notions of inquiry into and intervention into real-world situations as processes of learning. The approach developed here is connected to viable systems theory, itself a development from soft systems methodologies (Beer 1979, 1985) – soft systems, in that it is connected to critical theory. It implicitly supports the theory of complexity, and is sufficiently rich to enable organisations to be modelled in such a way as to explore how they might 'successfully' operate in complex dynamic environments.

The influence of systems theory on HRD is sometimes acknowledged in the HRD literature. For example, Swanson (1999: 2–3) argues that HRD's theoretical foundations lie in psychological, economics and systems theories, and also points to its connection with organisation development (OD). Similarly, Jacobs (1989) has called for a unifying theory of HRD, based on systems theory, whilst McLean (1999: 6) considers anthropology to be another foundational area of HRD as it is 'a field that is often suggested as a core contributor to organisation development', particularly in terms of its understanding of culture (e.g. Burke 1994, Cummings and Worley 1997, French and Bell 1995).

Swanson (2001) develops these ideas further in attempting to articulate the theoretical foundations of HRD, especially its roots in systems theory (e.g. Gradous 1989). He sees this as at the core of HRD in focussing on both understanding the system and on its potential for change. Swanson (2001: 303) argues in favour of 'having the system theory and tools' and in favour of 'rigorous system analysis'. HRD is defined as 'a process of developing and/or unleashing human expertise through organisation development (OD) and personnel training and development (T and D) for the purpose of improving performance' (Swanson 2001: 304). HRM, career development and quality improvement are regarded as key application areas. HRD is seen as 'a process or system [sic] within the larger organisational and environmental system. As such, it has the potential of harmonising, supporting and/or shaping the larger systems' (Swanson 2001: 304). Systems theory is able to capture the complex and dynamic interaction of environments, organisations and work process, and group/individual variables operating over time. General systems theory (e.g. how HRD and other subsystems connect and disconnect), chaos theory (helping the organisation retain its purpose and effectiveness in the face of chaos) and futures theory (helping the host organisation shape alternative futures) are seen as important in developing systems theory principles that require 'sound theory building; research and the utilisation of new tools for sound practice' (Swanson 2001: 309).

This chapter is an attempt to contribute to the development of theorising about HRD, acknowledging Swanson's (2001) recognition of the importance of systems theory to HRD whilst not necessarily endorsing his definition or his prescription for its future development. However, it argues that the system worldview model of HRD as a process within the organisation and its environment presented in Swanson (2001: 305, Figure 1) itself adopts a simple input-transformation-output (process) systems model which requires rethinking. This is particularly relevant in the light of his acknowledgement of chaos and futures theory and the dynamic and complex interactions that need to be analysed and understood by HRD theory. It is the contention of this chapter that viable systems theory provides a more adequate model for HRD theory research and practice.

OD and HRD

In recent years, attempts to define and characterise the emerging field of HRD have increasingly acknowledged the influence of OD on HRD's development, to the extent that HRD may be seen as 'living in the shadow of OD' (Grieves and Redman 1999: 82). In the US, HRD is often seen as encompassing OD, career development and individual training and development (e.g. Swanson 1995). Grieves and Redman (1999) draw attention to HRD's role in organisational solutions to strategic issues, focussing on identifying the core skills and knowledge of the HRD professional by comparing the roles of HRD and OD practitioners as internal change agents. They see OD as informed by six essential characteristics: a methodology informed by action research; a recognition of the need for participation through stakeholder approaches to collaborative action; the adoption of a pluralist framework that takes account of political processes; an increased emphasis on personal and organisational learning; an appreciation of organisational culture; and an embrace of humanistic values. OD has been a continuous influence (though not always a recognised one) on HRD in the UK, especially in promoting the idea of the learning company or organisation as a challenge to traditional training solutions (e.g. Mumford 1991, Pedlar *et al.* 1991). For example, the OD tradition has stressed the use of reflexive, self-analytic methods of organisational intervention and the need to institutionalise and legitimise the examination of organisational processes to develop an organisation's capacities for self-renewal (e.g. Burke 1994). Our focus here is on the need to re-conceptualise OD and HRD in the context of the rise in the importance of complexity theories. We also consider that recent developments in OD and its systemic underpinnings can make useful contributions to developing HRD's theoretical reach in responding appropriately to complexity.

Traditional OD, systems theory and complexity

Many limitations of current OD (e.g. its cultural bias, its emphasis on consensus and participation, its narrow view of effectiveness, its inability to address issues of power, politics and culture, its ethnocentrism and cultural bias) stem from reliance on an outdated simple systems model of input-output transformation. We therefore propose to reconceptualise traditional OD in the light of current systems thinking based on viable systems theory (e.g. Beer 1985, Yolles 1999, Iles *et al.* 2001, Iles and Yolles 2002).

Many authors have stressed the neglect of and naïveté about power and politics in OD. For example, Walumbura (1999) argues that the field of OD has been very slow in addressing the dimensions of power and politics in organisational change (e.g. Cummings and Worley 1997). Walumbura's interest is in drawing out the practical implications of power and politics for OD professional practice. Our interest here is somewhat different, as we consider that OD (and therefore HRD) are based on outdated, simplistic systems thinking based on early input-transformation-output systems models, rendering them incapable of dealing adequately with complexity, power and change.

However, despite developments in 'whole systems change' methodologies (e.g. Williams 1979, Rosen 1996, Weisbord 1987, Weisbord and Janoff 1996, Bunker and Alban 1997), the predominant 'systems' models in use in OD and HRD remain rooted in rather simple 'input-transformation-output' systems models, and OD (and HRD) remain vulnerable to the charges often levied against them of commitment to 'planned' rather than 'emergent' change, to top-down change, to a unitarist and managerialist view of organisations in which 'win-win' gains are possible, and to a rather naïve, rationalistic and apolitical view of change that finds it difficult to deal with power in organisations.

In the case of OD, some of its ideas still remain embedded in concepts that were at one time prominent systems theory conceptualisations, but which have no

Table 2.1 Steps of the traditional OD methodological cycle

Phases	Steps
0 Introduction and pre-evaluation (scouting)	0 Getting acquainted with clients; introduction to client organisation; introduction to problem situation; pre-analysis; client expectations defined; contract agreement
1 Diagnosis	1 Confrontation with environmental changes, problems and opportunities
	2 Identification of implications for organisation
2 Involvement and detailed diagnosis	3 Education to obtain understanding of implications for organisation
	4 Obtaining involvement in project
	5 Identification of targets for change
3 Action evaluation and reinforcement	6 Change and development activities
	7 Evaluation of project and programme in current environment and reinforcement

place in modern paradigms. Two concepts for example that can be identified as having this status are based on the ideas of Ashby: stepwise change from one steady state to another as used by Lewin (1951), and ultrastability as used by Pugh (1993).

Traditional OD methodology involves three phases (Lewin 1951) combining to produce seven stages as depicted in Table 2.1 (Mabey, 1995). The introductory and pre-evaluation (scouting) stage is identified by Harrison (1994).

More recently, Mabey (1995a) has proposed an alternative to traditional OD shown in Table 2.2. This sets up the phases in a new way, and establishes inquiry into the future state as the first step. In addition, it involves the initial step 0 as part of the pre-evaluation phase. The new form addresses the consultation process perceived to lie at the centre of the methodology, which is seen as a consensus-building process. The contexts of step 2 relate to the work of Pettigrew (1988) on

Table 2.2 New version of OD (Mabey, 1995a)

Phases	Steps
1 Determine the future state (where do we want to be?)	1 Agree on organisational purpose/mission
2 Diagnose the present state (where are we now?)	2 Assess outer/inner contexts
3 Manage the transition	3 Gather data
	4 Gain involvement
	5 Set targets for change
	6 Implement change and development activities
	7 Evaluate and reinforce changes

Table 2.3 The diagnosis phases of Harrison

Step	Attributes
1 Inputs	• Problems • Prior findings • Models
2 Choose fits	• Level • System elements, subcomponents
3 Design study, gather data	• Research design • Methods • Data collection
4 Assess degree of fit	• Needs of units, system parts • Conflicts, tensions • Actual versus official practices • Organisational design methods
5 Assess impacts	• Negative • Positive • Loose coupling

outer contexts (the socio-political, economic, legal, technological and business competitive factors in the external environment, identified through, say, a SWOT analysis) and inner contexts (the internal capacity for change, including concepts of leadership, organisation structure and culture, personalities of key people, primary tasks and emergent technologies).

Harrison (1994), in the development of aspects of traditional OD, discusses *system fits*, where the open system model is fitted to the perceived reality of a situation. Thus, a system fit is a description of the situation and its context. System fit diagnosis represents the core of Harrison's perspectives, defining an approach to inquiry shown in Table 2.3. Operating as a cycle of sequential stages that begins with inputs, it involves a set of four phases, and then feeds back into the OD cycle. Diagnosis involves more developed systems thinking than traditional OD, in that not only does it adopt an open system model, but in addition explicitly highlights the focus of the system.

Reconceptualising HRD and its ability to address complexity as methodological enquiry

The basic form of traditional OD (Figure 2.1), based on Mabey (1995) and defined in Table 2.1 is a sequential process that defines a cycle of inquiry. According to Harrison (1994), OD inquiry should, however, begin with a prior introduction and pre-evaluation stage. It supposes feedback between steps 6 to 3 in the event that the change and development activities are not seen to be satisfactory. The cycle then continues to step 4 and onwards.

The more recent form of the OD cycle (from Table 2.2) is presented in Figure 2.2 (Mabey 1995: 335), loosely based on the work of Beckhard (1969) and

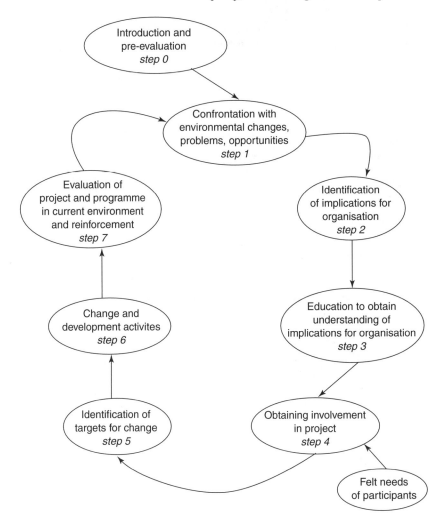

Figure 2.1 The OD cycle, based on Mabey (1986).

Beckhard and Harris (1977) on transformational change. In any organisation there are perceived to be three 'states': the future state, the present state, and the transition state that identifies how to move between the current and future states. We have amended this by including the pre-evaluation step 0 and the link between steps 1 and 2 to ensure that this is seen as a cycle of inquiry. Comparing this to the original version of the traditional OD cycle, we note that steps 2 to 4 of the diagnosis phase have been redefined in Figure 2.2, while steps 5 to 7 remain principally the same.

Another paradigmatically commensurable form of inquiry to this recent form of OD is Harrison's diagnosis (Figure 2.3).

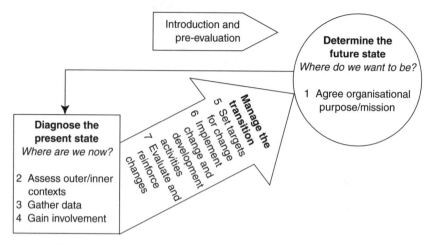

Figure 2.2 More recent form of OD (Mabey 1995a).

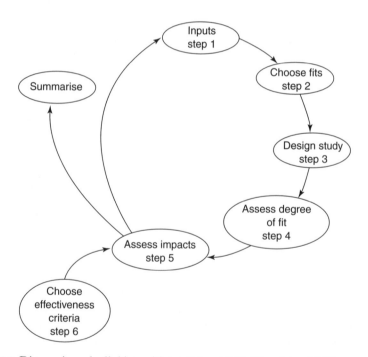

Figure 2.3 Diagnosis cycle, linking with traditional OD (Harrison, 1994).

We can develop a more appropriate viable systems theory of HRD by building on the work of Harrison (1994), Mabey (1995, 1995a) and Yolles (1999) in developing a more sophisticated model of OD. In Table 2.4, we summarise HRD methodology in more appropriate viable systems terms. This terminology arises from Yolles

Table 2.4 Definition of the system and metasystem for HRD

Methodology

The System

Step 1:   Three foci of the system are considered; the organisational, the group, and the individual. The system is defined with respect to the relative and sometimes contradictory views of stakeholders. Metapurposes will be determined by consensus view, or from the primary stakeholders/clients to whom consultants have responsibility

Cognitive purposes

Mission and goals

The overall methodological metapurpose is to manage learning and development. The mission-related *goals* determine what is meant by and what the strategy for learning and development is. These are:

m1:   *Political power* – concerned with ensuring that a learning strategy cannot be sabotaged through power conflicts

m2:   *Control* – which must be ensured if a strategy for learning is to progress in the face of potential conflicts

m3:   *Resistance to change* – which must be addressed in order to ensure that stakeholders are able to accept learning and development.

Inquiry aims

These are determined by an inquirer in relation to the situation and relate to the creation of effective strategies for learning and development.

(1999): in the same way that organisations operate out of paradigms and group world views that make the propositions which direct the organisation more or less explicitly, so too do methodologies. As with organisations, methodologies need to

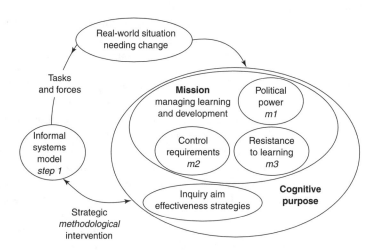

Figure 2.4 Influence diagram: cognitive purpose of HRD.

define their missions and goals to make their paradigms more transparent. However, missions and goals are part of a paradigmatic 'cognitive purpose' linking to the way the methodology is applied. This contrasts with the environment in which the tools are applied, referred to as the methodology's 'system' (Yolles 1999).

In order to develop this further, we need to construct an influence diagram depicting the cognitive purpose of HRD (Figure 2.4).

The overall (methodological) purpose of inquiry is to facilitate learning and development to ensure a new relationship with the environment of the system (im1). The nature of im1 will depend upon the world view of inquirers and stakeholders. No formalised system model is generally produced; they are normally informal. The impact of the real world on the informal system models produced is identified in terms of tasks and forces from the environment that generate the need for learning and development. The system models are not separated out from the real world; rather, the models emerge from the interactions that occur with stakeholders.

The concept of 'stakeholder' has been subject to critical analysis, most notably by Winstanley (e.g. Winstanley and Stuart-Smith 1996, Stoney and Winstanley 2001). Winstanley and Stuart-Smith (1996) attempt to clarify the literature by analysing the conceptual confusion, underlying pluralist assumptions, problems of implementation, and debatable impact on business performance and competitiveness in the stakeholder literature. Such conceptual confusion and inconsistency is seen as mystifying the intellectual terrain, rendering practical application implausible if not impossible, and marginalising questions of power, structure, conflict and resistance – all key issues identified as central issues for HRD in Table 2.4 and Figure 2.4.

In our conceptual framework developed here, we take a pluralist perspective on organisations for analytical and intervention purposes, and argue that our particular stakeholder perspective is valuable in providing a route to increased organisational effectiveness at the 'corporate governance' level. However, we argue that the approach adopted here allows us to address more rigorously the questions of power, structure, conflict and resistance identified as crucial by Stoney and Winstanley (2001) and developed more fully in Table 2.4 and Figure 2.4, which outline our viable systems-based approach to HRD.

Two forms of traditional OD have previously been identified: Mabey (1995) and Mabey (1995a). The two forms differ both in the first three steps and in presentation. We have taken the steps of the second to represent traditional OD. In addition, diagnosis has been analysed further in Table 2.6. Since these two approaches are based on a similar paradigm and are not incommensurable with the HRD paradigm developed here, they can be combined to generate a new specification which provides the basis of a new form of HRD methodological cycle of inquiry that takes advantage of both approaches (Table 2.5).

Methodologies of organisational inquiry can therefore be linked to incorporate the concepts of traditional OD with the broader advantages of diagnosis, making it possible to generate a form of HRD inquiry according to Table 2.5. This is re-presented in Table 2.6, with an explanation relating to Mabey (1995) of what the steps involve, and the possible HRD tools that can be used. These steps are shown graphically in Figure 2.5.

Table 2.5 Methodological inquiry in a reconceptualised HRD

Steps of traditional OD	Steps of Diagnosis	Proposed steps of reconceptualised viable systems HRD
1 Agree organisational purposes, identifying environmental change, problems and opportunities	1 Inputs: problems, prior findings, models	1 Exploration of situation and define purposes
2 Gather information for organisational understanding	2 Choose fits: level, system elements, subcomponents	2 Define relevant system
3 Assess inner/outer contexts and identify meaning for organisation		3 Assess contexts
4 Gain involvement in project		4 Confirm stakeholder participation and relevant system
5 Identification of targets for change	3 Design study, gather data: research design, methods, data collection	5 Identify targets and design models of learning and development
	4 Assess degree of fit	6 Evaluation and selection of models of learning and development
	5 Assess impacts	
6 Change and development activities		7 Learning and development activities
7 Evaluation of project and programme in current environment and reinforcement		8 Evaluation of project and programme in current environment and reinforcement

Conclusions

So, to conclude, we can present a more adequate viable systems model of HRD (shown in Table 2.6), one that is more able to deal with complex systems.

The structural inquiry represented in Table 2.6 can be shown as a cycle. Here, control aspects of the cycle occur to determine the stability of the action stage. If this is not stable, recursion occurs and the cycle is continued from there (Figure 2.6).

Inquiry workshops, whether or not they are client-centred, and workshops can be part of the HRD process. For instance in steps 1, 3 and 5, the cycle with embedded themes can also be used, making HRD a recursive methodology more suited to complexity. Thus it can be more appropriate as a contribution to strategic HRD, enabling it to manage more adequately complex systems and change than the simple, outdated, input-transformation-output system models currently in use.

Table 2.6 Steps of a reconceptualised HRD model and action tools

Phase	Step	Action and context	Explanation and tools
Current/ future state	1 Explore situation and purposes	Exploration of organisational mission. Consultation process. Identifying where the organisation is going and what it wants to achieve	Interaction with clients. Awareness of power, control and possible resistance to learning aspects of situation
Diagnosis	2 Define relevant system	Gather data. Identify stakeholders. Explore perspectives of the situation to create system representations. Identify structures and processes	Interviews and use of diagramming techniques (systems maps, power context diagrams, activity sequence diagrams, organisation matrix)
	3 Assess contexts	*Outer contexts* *Inner contexts* Identify commodities of power, control mechanisms/ and input constraints	Brainstorming. SWOT analysis. Force field diagrams. Mind maps. Multiple-cause diagrams
	4 Confirmation of participation and relevant system	Strategic learning and development requires different views to be heard as part of the process to win support and commitment. Ensure participation of appropriate stakeholders and confirm relevant systems	Stakeholder consultation. Techniques to encourage participation. Exploration of resistance to learning and development
Facilitative learning and development	5 Identify targets and design learning models	Learning and development can cause confusion about roles, responsibilities and decision-making channels. Public models can be instrumental in reducing this, and meaningful targets and reinforcing milestones derive from these. Explore designs for *de-regularising* patterns of behaviour	Scan for targets and milestones. Consider needs of components of system. Evaluate conflicts and tensions. Actual against official practices. Define effectiveness criteria. Use control diagrams
	6 Evaluation/ selection of learning models	Evaluate learning models and associated targets, and confirm selection with stakeholders/clients	Consultation with stakeholders/ clients
	7 Learning and development activities	Re-regularising patterns of behaviour to *reinforce* learning and change helped through (1) individuals having a personal stake and being accountable for learning and change; (2) new working relationships and boundaries between work groups negotiated; (3) finding ways of recognising and rewarding desirable behaviours.	Tabulate activities.

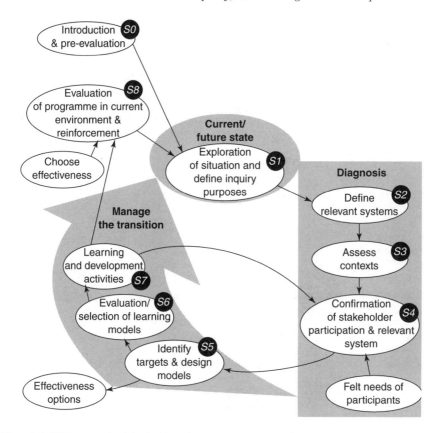

Figure 2.5 HRD as methodological inquiry.

Methodologies of organisational inquiry based on viable systems theory can therefore be extended to include the concepts of traditional OD with the broader advantages of diagnosis, making it possible to generate a reconceptualised form of traditional OD and diagnosis according to Table 2.6. This is re-presented in Table 2.7, with an explanation relating to Mabey (1995) of what the steps involve, and the possible tools that can be used at each step.

A new approach to OD and HRD is proposed that is evolutionary because it seeks to build on the deviations made by Mabey (1995, 1995a) and Harrison (1994) from traditional OD. It derives from the thinking of cybernetically-based viable systems theory, from which our interest is derived in how cybernetic feedback methodological principles are engaged. Indeed, its cybernetic aspects can be enhanced, but there is no space here to discuss how and why that should occur. However, our reconceptualisation of HRD points towards how such a model can be developed (see also Yolles and Iles 2002). Table 2.7 has, as part of its representation, a set of phases that are generic features of scientific enquiry (Yolles 1999). It is here that the control aspects of a methodology can be clearly highlighted.

Table 2.7 HRD methodology – complex systems model

Entity/Process	HRD paradigm Explanation	Step
Pre-analysis	Introduction and pre-evaluation	S0
Analysis	Exploration of situation and definition of purposes	S1 Current/future state
	Defining relevant systems	S2 Diagnosis
	Assess inner/outer contexts	S3
Control	Confirmation of stakeholder participation and relevant system	S4
Conceptualisation		
Synthesis	Identify targets and design learning models	S5 Manage transition
Constraint	Felt needs of participants Choose effectiveness	
Choice	Evaluation of models	S6
Action	Learning and developmental activities	S7
Control	Evaluate if *action* is stable *stable*: continue *unstable*: refer back to S4	
Control	Evaluation of project and programme	S8

This evolutionary development of a model of HRD as methodological enquiry from earlier systems insights in the OD tradition is an improvement on the simple input-transformation-output models on which much HRD is based (often without recognition or acknowledgement). It seeks to build on the modifications to OD methodology developed by Mabey (1995a) and Harrison (1994) by orienting the HRD paradigm towards a viable systems approach that clearly illustrates its cybernetic properties.

The implications for research include evaluating the application of such a model to understanding and managing change in complex systems. Such systems will include not only the focal organisation, as is the case with traditional OD, but the whole system in which it is embedded (depending on level of focus) including its stakeholders. The framework may be of particular utility in understanding and

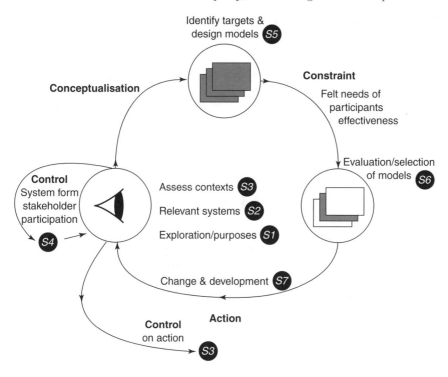

Figure 2.6 Evolving model of HRD.

analysing partnerships and alliances and in inter-organisation, rather than organisation, development (e.g. Iles and Yolles 2001, Iles *et al.* 2001). In terms of implications for practice, OD and HRD practitioners and consultants, whether external or internal, are recommended to abandon simple, outdated input-transformation-output systems models underpinning much traditional OD and HRD as being inappropriate to understanding and managing change and complexity, and in particular transformational change. Adopting a recursive, viable systems model of HRD will, it is contended, lead to a more comprehensive mapping of the dynamics of change. In particular, for both research and practitioner groups, it should be stressed that the framework developed is not prescriptive. Table 2.7 lists some tools and techniques that could be used at each stage, but the list is not intended to be exhaustive or prescriptive. Other tools and techniques might be useful, depending on the purposes of the study or intervention. The relative usefulness of various tools and techniques at each stage is, of course, a further matter for empirical research (Yolles and Iles 2002).

References

Beckhard, R. (1969) *Organisation Development: Strategies and models*, Reading, MA: Addison-Wesley

Beckhard R. and Harris R. T. (1977) *Organisational Transitions: Managing complex change*, New York: Addison-Wesley

Beer, S. (1979) *The Heart of Enterprise*, Chichester: Wiley

Beer, S. (1985) *Diagnosing the System for Organisations*, Chichester: Wiley

Bunker, B. B. and Alban, B. T. (1997) *Large Group Interventions: Engaging the whole system for rapid change*, San Francisco: Jossey-Bass

Burke, W. W. (1994) *Organisation Development: A process of learning and changing*, 2nd edition, Reading, MA: Addison-Wesley

Checkland, P. B. and Scholes, J. (1990) *Soft Systems Methodology in Action*, Chichester: John Wiley and Sons

Cummings, T. G. and Worley, C. G. (1997) *Organisation Development and Change*, 6th edition, Cincinnati, OH: South-Western College Publishing

French, L. W. and Bell, H. C. (1995) *Organisation Development: Behavioural science interventions for organisation improvement*, 5th edition, Englewood Cliffe, NJ: Prentice Hall

Gradous, D. D. (Ed.) (1989) *Systems Theory Applied to Human Resource Development*, Alexandra, VA: ASTD Press

Grieves, T. and Redman, T. (1999) 'Living in the shadow of OD: HRD and the search for identity', *Human Resource Development International*, 2(2): 81–102

Harrison, I. H. (1994) *Diagnosing Organisations: Methods, models and processes*, Thousand Oaks, CA: Sage

Iles, P. A., Yolles, M. I. and Altman, Y. (2001) 'HRM and knowledge management: responding to the challenge', *Journal of Research and Practice in HRM*, special issue on Knowledge Management, 9(1): 3–33

Iles, P. A. and Yolles, M. I. (2003) 'International HRD alliances in viable knowledge migration and development: The Czech Academic Link Project', *Human Resource Development International* (forthcoming)

Jacobs, R. (1989) 'Systems theory applied to human resource development', in D. Gradous (Ed.) *Systems Theory Applied to Human Resource Development, Theory to Practice Monograph*, Alexandria, VA: ASTD Press, 27–60

Lewin, K. (1951) *Field Theory in Social Science*, New York: Harper & Row

McLean, G. N. (1999) 'Get out the drill, glue and more legs', *Human Resource Development International*, 2(1): 6–7

Mabey, C. (1995) *Managing Development and Change*, Open University Course B751, following Mayon-White

Mabey, C. (1995a) 'Managing strategic change successfully', *Business Growth & Profitability*, 1(4): 353–362

Mumford, A. (1991) 'Individual and organisational learning: the pursuit of change', *Industrial and Commercial Training*, 23(6): 24–31

Pedlar, M., Burgoyne, J. and Boydell, J. (1991) *The Learning Company*, London: McGraw-Hill

Pettigrew, A. (1988) *The Management of Strategic Change*, Oxford: Blackwell

Prigogine, I. and Stengers, I. (1984), *Order out of Chaos*, New York: Bantam Books

Pugh, D (1993) 'Understanding and managing organisational change', in Mabey, C., Mayon-White, B., *Managing Change*, 108–112, London: Paul Chapman Publishing Co., originally in *London Business School Journal*, 1978, 3(2): 29–34

Rosen, A. (1996) *A Future Search Conference: Creating a new culture in a merged organisation*, AMED R and D conference, 'Visions, Values and the Virtual Organisation', August 1996

Stacey, R. D. (2001) *Complex Responsive Processes in Organizations: Learning and knowledge creation*, London: Routledge

Stacey, R. D., Griffin, D. and Shaw, P. (2000) *Complexity and Management: Fad or radical challenge to systems thinking?*, London: Routledge

Stoney, C. and Winstanley, D. (2001) 'Stakeholding: confusion or Utopia? Mapping the conceptual terrain', *Journal of Management Studies*, 38(5): July, 603–626

Swanson, R. A. (1995) 'Human resource development: performance is the key', *Human Resource Development Quarterly*, 6(2): 207–213

Swanson, R. A. (1999) 'HRD Theory: real or imagined?', *Human Resource Development International*, 2(1): 2–5

Swanson, R. A. (2001) 'Human resource development and its underlying theory', *Human Resource Development International*, 4(3): 299–312

Walumbura, F. (1999) 'Power and politics in organisations: implications for OD professional practice', *Human Resource Development International*, 2(3): 205–216

Weisbord, M. (1987) *Productive Workplaces: Organizing and managing for dignity, meaning and community*, San Francisco: Jossey-Bass

Weisbord, M. R., Janoff, S. (1996) 'Future search: finding common ground in organisations and communities', *Systems Practice*, 9(1): 71–84

Wheatley, M. J. (1994) *Leadership and the New Science: Learning about organizations from an orderly universe*, San Francisco CA: Berrett-Koehler

Williams, T. A. (1979) 'The Search Conference in active adaptive planning', *Journal of Applied Behavioural Science*, 470–483

Winstanley, D. and Stuart-Smith, K. (1996,) 'Policing performance: the ethics of performance management', *Personnel Review*, 25(6): 66–83

Yolles, M. I. (1999) *Management Systems: A viable approach*, London: Financial Times/Pitman

Yolles, M. I. and Iles P. A. (2002) 'Complexifying OD and HRD', in M. Lee (Ed.), *HRD in a Complex World*, London: Routledge

3 Worldviews that enhance and inhibit HRD's social responsibility

Timothy G. Hatcher

Introduction

A profession is more than an occupation. It is more than a simple collection of skills. A profession includes extensive intellectual knowledge and the provision of products and/or services which are important to the functioning of society (Callahan, 1988). HRD as a field of practice has recognized collections of competencies that identify extensive intellectual knowledge such as competencies developed by the American Society for Training & Development, and in the UK, the National Vocational Qualifications administered by the National Council for Vocational Qualifications and the competency standards of the Chartered Institute for Personnel. But what the HRD profession has yet fully to acknowledge and resolve is its inability to enhance global sustainability and its fundamental responsibility to society.

Professionals' worldviews, or the lens through which reality is viewed, colors how a profession understands itself and influences its actions. As a multidisciplinary and emerging field, HRD draws on many different disciplines as its theoretical foundations, yet economics and psychology have been predominantly influential (Swanson, 1999; Hatcher and Brooks, 2000; Hatcher, 2002). Discussions are needed to assess critically certain worldviews in which HRD as a profession is currently embedded and to understand better how such worldviews continue to bind and limit its social responsiveness. The outcome of this discussion is to enhance the likelihood that as a profession HRD will act consciously on issues of social responsibility within complex work environments. Thus, the purpose of this chapter is to examine critically the assumptions underlying HRD's over-reliance on economics and psychology as theoretical foundations, the limitations imposed by unbalanced and mechanistic worldviews, and to explore more socially responsible alternatives within a context of global complexity.

To begin this discussion it is important to characterize the theoretical foundations of HRD. Once we have identified the theoretical underpinnings of HRD, and to acquire a better understanding of social responsibility as a proposed outcome, it is important to define social responsibility. The context of HRD within a complex world as the theme for this book is grounded in various theories and worldviews. Complexity theory in particular seems relevant within the context of the world as a complex system, yet few discussions and no publications are available within recognized and popular HRD literature about complexity theory as an HRD worldview. If we are to understand better HRD within our complex world then emerging and relevant worldviews such as complexity theory need to be discussed.

Theoretical foundations of HRD

HRD is a multidisciplinary field. Thus, its underlying theoretical foundations are derived from multiple theories/disciplines. Several disciplines or theories have been identified as contributing to the knowledgebase of HRD to varying degrees, namely education, general systems theory, economics, psychology, sociology and organizational behavior (Hatcher, 2000a, 2002). Disciplines such as anthropology and management have also been mentioned (Chalofsky and Lincoln, 1983). Jacobs (1990) indicated five bodies of knowledge: education, systems theory, economics, psychology and organizational behavior. Swanson (1999) said there are three primary disciplinary bases, namely economics, general systems theory and psychology. The works of Jacobs (1990), Swanson (1999), Hatcher (2000a, 2002) and others indicated that although various bodies of knowledge had influenced HRD, its primary focus should be on *economic, psychological, systems theory, social* benefits, and *ethics*.

Few publications have discussed the theoretical foundations of HRD and little empirical research has been published. Yet these disciplines are the theoretical underpinnings of the profession; all HRD research is dependent upon sound theory. Hatcher (2000a) queried HRD professionals, scholars and practitioners in the US as to their opinions on which of the theoretical foundations were most important to research and practice. Not surprisingly, and mirroring Swanson's (1999) suggestions, results indicated that *psychology* and *economics* had the greatest current impact.

In a profession that espouses the enhancement of learning, human potential and high performance in work-related systems (Bates, Hatcher, Holton and Chalofsky, 2001), and has aspirations such as individual growth and positive organizational change, a focus on economics and psychology seems prima facie limiting in its ability to create ethical organizations, a healthy society or a sustainable ecosystem. A better understanding of the construct of corporate social responsibility helps to address this dilemma.

Social responsibility

To value the relationship between HRD, its theoretical foundations and social responsibility it is crucial to recognize social responsibility as a construct. Being socially responsible as HRD professionals has at least two possible meanings. The first, a rational economic one, says that we have no moral responsibility beyond helping our own organization increase profits. Because rational economics is presumed to be morally neutral and human beings to be either amoral or immoral without outside control, morality is enforced through laws, contracts and rules such as employment laws and codes of ethics. The second meaning says that we do indeed have a moral responsibility to address the needs and problems of the larger community beyond those of our own organizations. Morality arises from an understanding of the interconnectedness of all entities in the world and beyond to transcendence. The first meaning, a rational economic one, implies that organizations are bounded entities dedicated to increasing profits through interactions with other bounded entities in society. The second is more fluid and suggests that the realities we construct and the boundaries we set are artificial, and we cannot profit if other stakeholders do not profit as well.

Social responsibility under the rational economic worldview suggests that we either justify what appears to be a moral action taken beyond the bounds of our own organizations as 'good for business', or take the radical step of going beyond the boundaries of our organizations to include stakeholders with no direct or obvious link to what we do. The first is reflected in the tax deductions allowed to both organizations and individuals for philanthropic contributions and the current appearance of philanthropic foundations sponsored by companies such as Microsoft and Wal-Mart in order to improve their corporate image. Similarly, we regularly see advertisements by oil and tobacco companies showing how they 'care' for either the environment or our children. One method that HRD professionals have used to show concern for the bottom line in a socially responsible manner has been to contribute to recruitment and educational improvement of diverse and traditionally under-represented groups. However, many of the community issues that require attention are not readily or directly linked to a company's bottom line. Devoting time and resources to them as HRD professionals within an organization cannot be justified in terms of rational economics. For example, other than what is regulated and required by law, companies have been little concerned with the Earth's ecosystem, and thus no rational justification related to the bottom line exists for HRD professionals to address this crucial issue. It is little wonder then that social responsibility for HRD professionals is viewed as either calculated or cynical or a fringe preoccupation of a marginalized minority.

The second meaning of social responsibility suggests that a profession such as HRD *does* have a responsibility to communities beyond its employing organization's boundaries. It implies that organizations and professional groups are social institutions and have a social contract with society. Social responsibility under this precept suggests that HRD has a moral obligation to use resources for the common good as well as obligations to groups such as stakeholders, consumers, employers, clients and creditors (Tomer, 1994). In this worldview, we construct reality with each action we take, all living and non-living entities are interconnected and interdependent, rationality is holistic and non-linear, and each of us (like organizations and communities) is defined by our relationships. Morality issues from recognition of our fundamental interdependence.

While an understanding of social responsibility offers us a new and different way to view the outcomes of HRD beyond the instrumental, it is critical that this

view be expanded to include a better understanding of the theoretical foundations of HRD that have interfered with our ability to achieve social
responsiveness.

'Irresponsible' paradigms: economics and psychology

As a multidisciplinary field, HRD is influenced not only by individual, organizational and societal needs, but also by several underlying disciplines; namely,
education, economics, psychology, organizational behavior, general systems,
ethics and sociology, among others (Jacobs, 1990; Hatcher, 2002). Arguably, most
of the organizations in which HRD professionals work are economically-driven,
meaning that HRD is infused with the economic/capitalist ethos of a post-
capitalist society (Drucker, 1993). Historically, the disciplines of economics and
psychology (especially through industrial and organizational psychology) have
been capitalism's handmaiden in developing ever-better ways to adapt employees
to this economic/capitalist worldview, and appear to be important to HRD professionals (Hatcher, 2000b).

Economics and development

Even though economics, through an intense focus on return on investment and
value-add, is the driving force behind much of the current success of the practice
of HRD, researchers and practitioners have not embraced it as a basis for
research and practice in ways that would benefit the HRD field (Passmore, 1997)
or society (Hatcher, 2002). Scholars and practitioners have made few attempts to
study the relationship between economic theory and HRD research and practice
or to apply various economic theories to research and practice. The assumed economic belief system of HRD professionals is that the purpose of HRD
interventions is to provide financial benefit to the organization, people are economic capital, and organizations are economic entities (Swanson, 1999). This
economic ideology is consistent with widespread *neoclassical economic thought* and the
notion of *development*.

Neoclassical economics explains the free-market capitalist system and suggests,
starting from zero consumption, that individuals strive to consume goods and services without limit (Burk, 1994). However, in a finite system there are always
limits. Scarce resource economic theory implies that 'decision makers choose
between options based on their forecasted return on investment' (Swanson, 1999:
13). The problem is that most decision makers in today's complex organizations
neither understand nor acknowledge that organizations are not only engines of
economic growth but also critical agents of social and political integration (Tichy,
McGill and St. Clair, 1997). Thus, decisions are made using myopic economic
models such as the Gross Domestic Product (GDP) in the US, the UK and most
other Western economies that wreak havoc on the environment and have been
linked to violence in the workplace and bad judgment by corporate leaders. For
example, the devastating Alaskan oil spill of the *Exxon Valdez* in 1989 actually *added*

to the US GDP. The brilliant economist E.F. Schumacher said that the modern economic system was a path to resource depletion, environmental degradation, worker alienation and violence (Schumacher, 1979).

Closely related to neoclassical economics is the notion of *development*. Development is synonymous with economic and technological growth, where bigger is always better and more is the desirable outcome. Development is 'economics fueled by corporate growth, productivity, efficiency, and profit' (Hatcher, 2002: 155). This over-reliance on development as economic output forces organizations and the people within them to make decisions based solely on economic rationality. According to Harman and Horman (1990), there is no reason to assume that economic rationality will lead to decisions that are wise from human, ecological, compassionate and spiritual standpoints. The recent ethics debacle of Enron, WorldCom and other large US corporations well illustrates the financial and social fallout of a myopic focus on economic rationality.

The current discontent with privileging economics and development over human and social issues is exposing the weaknesses of neoclassical economic theory and development as well as limitations of a rational scientific worldview. Both the ideology of capitalism and the culture of consumerism need to be fundamentally reassessed (Welford, 1995; Korten, 1995; Hatcher, 1999, 2002). Based on exploitation of valuable and non-renewable resources and characterized by individualism rather than collectivism, orthodox, short-term and linear economic models and the overall notion of development fall short when addressing systemic societal and global environmental dilemmas (Hatcher, 2002). The profession of HRD, inherent even in the name, contributes to this dilemma. The word 'development is a clear signal that HRD adds not only to individual but also to economic growth' (Hatcher, 2002: 157).

Traditional capitalist economies are mechanistic, static and atomistic, and view technical growth as the way to make our resources endlessly sustainable. The ability of the environment to continue to support life is increasingly undermined by the same neoclassical economic approaches subscribed to (consciously or unconsciously) by many HRD professionals. The obstacles preventing sustainability, i.e. depletion of natural resources, increasing population, workplace violence and environmental degradation, show little sign of diminishing. The awareness of the planetary life support system's deterioration is forcing the realization that decisions made on the basis of short-term economic criteria can have far-reaching and disastrous results. The challenge is to strengthen the interdependence between economic development and environmental and social sustainability by embracing theories that actively support this interaction.

The call for alternative economic theories based on society and the ecosystem has gone ignored for too long. Flawed theories such as the GDP, that fails to view the ecosystem as value, must be replaced with economics that provide for and value human, social and environmental wealth. Other economic models such as steady-state economic theory of Herman Daly, Hicksian Income proposed by Sir John Hicks and the Genuine Progress Indicator developed by Halstead and Cobb (1996) offer us a way to calculate and assign value to biological diversity, cultural autonomy and ecosystem sustainability; to make corporations responsible for environmental sustainability rather than allowing them to externalize such costs to an unwitting public mired in overflowing landfills and witness to a staggering decline of indigenous cultures and biodiversity in general.

Economics and development are not only overt processes but also ways of viewing the world. Seeing HRD through an economic lens forces us to make decisions about interventions, such as training based more on economic value than on the extent to which people grow as individuals or our organizations add value to global sustainability. Our ability to understand how economics and development impact HRD is based largely on cognition. The study of cognition, or psychology, drives much of the current theory and practice of HRD and thus deserves further consideration.

Psychology

The field of psychology and learning as a subset has provided the basis for much of the organizational impact and current success of HRD. For example, behavioral psychology spawned competency-based training, behavioral and performance objectives and the four levels of evaluation; psychologist Kurt Lewin's input/output model of organizational change and psychoanalytic and Gestalt theories dominate organizational development theory and practice; developmental psychology provides a foundation for career development, and cognitive models prescribe current approaches to learning, both individual and organizational.

However, neither as a worldview nor as a discipline of study does psychology provide a good model for social responsibility. Psychology is in continual conflict between freedom to pursue science on the one hand and ethical/social responsibility on the other, all the while adhering to rigid rules of empirical science and ignoring ecological generalization. And its history is one of strong commitment to the tenets of scientific rationalism. It is only now reassessing the serious limitations of historical alliances that were established in order to gain legitimacy as a scientific field and to secure prestige and funding for research (Hatcher and Brooks, 2000). Psychology as a field has used its skills to further the interests of society's dominant groups and thus has often failed to act on behalf of those who are oppressed. It has even been accused of ignoring anti-racism (Henwood, 1994). Clinical psychology pathologized those who fail to conform. Organizational psychology medicalized dysfunctional organizations and learning psychology problematized recalcitrant learners as simply having learning disabilities (Hatcher and Brooks, 2000).

Much of this history has been incorporated into HRD practice in the name of increased efficiency, management development, competency-based training, performance appraisals, organizational development, and even team building and some types of action research (Hatcher and Brooks, 2000). In fact, even when we choose to view our organizations from beyond a company's walls, we still focus on our own psychological and economic well-being by asking questions such as 'How am I doing in relation to the company's margins, the success of its products or services, and its customer satisfaction ratings?'

Divergent and emerging psychological theories are addressing many of the aforementioned negative traits of conventional psychology. New theories emphasize the inseparable nature of the individual and society (Bruner, 1996; Gergen, 1994), the ways in which we use narrative to construct our realities (Bruner, 1990), the ways in which we define ourselves by our relationships (Mitchell, 1988), the co-construction of ourselves and our understandings of reality (Gergen, 1994; Brooks and Edwards, 1997), the emergence of the ecological self and a growing understanding that the deepest levels of the psyche merge with the biological body (Freudian), the physical and non-physical world (Jungian), and the cosmos (ecopsychology). They also emphasise the increasingly complex cognitive demands our environment places on us (Roszak, Gomes, and Kanner, 1995; Kegan, 1994). These theories help us to construct a systemic worldview. They ask that we take responsibility for the world beyond our organizations and ourselves, and recognize that with each interaction we have and each action we take, we are co-constructing a new organization within an ever more important realization of the larger ecosystem. They require us to take a perspective and develop the ability to enact our professional skills in a way that is non-linear, non-reductionistic and thus more holistic and transcendental. Does competency-based training develop people who can understand their interdependence with all stakeholders? Does the development of organizations encourage us to focus on our interrelatedness with affected cultures, the ecosystem or the cosmos? With a new understanding of interrelatedness and existential choice, new theories of psychology have engaged the possibility of diminishing the isolation of individuals within Western society and establishing a basis for responsible social action (Hatcher and Brooks, 2000), thus helping to answer such questions.

With psychology's current movement toward holism and sustainability, HRD finally has the opportunity to interact with a discipline that provides theoretical clarity for carrying out research and practice that is potentially socially responsible. HRD can and should lead organizations to an ever-deeper psychological understanding that social responsibility is no longer an option or financial burden, but a necessity for individual, organizational and societal survival (Hatcher and Brooks, 2000; Hatcher, 2002). This understanding should be the foundation for our worldviews.

Bounded and unbounded worldviews

Taking for granted the rational scientific assumptions of neoclassical economics and development and of traditional psychology has resulted in the lens through which HRD views reality being bounded by both reductionism and predictability in a variable, limitless and increasingly complex world. The importance of viewing HRD through diverse worldviews including logical positivism, critical theory, hermeneutics, and systems thinking, deep ecology and complexity theory, for example, requires further discussion. While there are many related theoretical

Table 3.1 Bounded and unbounded worldviews

Bounded	Unbounded
Logical positivism	Systems thinking
Anthropocentrism	Deep ecology
Reductionism	Autopoiesis
Determinism	Complexity theory
Mechanistic paradigm	Naturalism
Scientific management	Holistic paradigm
	Gaia

and philosophical approaches (see Table 3.1, for purposes of brevity a discussion of the bounded worldview of *logical positivism*, and several unbounded worldviews such as *systems theories, deep ecology,* and *complexity theory* are offered. The intent of this discussion is to clarify why HRD has struggled with and has been ineffective in its social responsibility and how it may, through adoption of unbounded world-views, such as deep ecology and complexity theory, emerge as a more socially responsive profession.

Bounded theory: logical positivism

According to Lincoln and Guba (1985) logical positivism is a philosophy with an extremely positive evaluation of scientific methodologies. As a worldview, it limits our approach to individuals, organizations and even societies to one of control, efficiency, rule-based predictability, two-dimensional thinking, anthropocentric-orientation, and cause-effect relationships (Hatcher and Brooks, 2000). Logical positivism is an outdated worldview, a perception of reality that is inadequate to deal with our globally connected world (Capra, 1996). Positivism as the dominant worldview of business and industry is passé. It is the product of small, bewildered minds that are drawn to it because they lack any other viable alternatives (Lincoln and Guba, 1985).

Two consequences of positivism, namely determinism and reductionism, are negative to professions like HRD and unfounded as a viable way of viewing today's organizations and society. Determinism negates human free will to change social mores and networks or to establish new social interconnections (Hatcher and Brooks, 2000). Reductionism makes all phenomena, including ethics and social responsibility, subject to a single set of laws (Lincoln and Guba, 1985), undesirable and limiting in complex social systems.

HRD's ability to be socially responsible is impacted by the worldview of logical positivism. When we choose to view our reality as deterministic, we negate our ability to regenerate and legitimate HRD as a profession. And when we believe that there is a single tangible reality that can be reduced to a series of parts to be studied independently, and that the whole is simply the sum of those parts, we are unable to grasp the utter simplicity that our profession is part of society and the ecosystem (Hatcher and Brooks, 2000; Hatcher, 2002). Similarly, when we are unable or unwilling to accept our part in the web of life, we are sentencing our profession to second-class status as the slave of a paternalistic economic/management system. A system that is dedicated to profit at any cost is blind to the disastrous effects that uncontrolled capitalism is having on our social and ecosystems and ultimately, the capitalist organization itself (Capra, 1996; Fox, 1994; Hatcher, 1999, 2002). Bounded frameworks such as logical positivism offer nothing new or constructive for an emerging profession like HRD. To evolve into a profession that can add value equally to organizations, people and the ecosystem requires a fundamental shift in the way its professionals view the world. Theories and worldviews that shift our focus beyond monetary gain require our cognitive and affective consideration.

Unbounded theory: systems theories, deep ecology and complexity theory

Systems theories allow us to change our frame of reference (Kuhn, 1962). Systems theory is a recognized theoretical foundation for HRD, unlike logical positivism, which is likely to be a less familiar worldview to HRD professionals. General systems theory enables us to transfer the principles of one field to another (von Bertalanffy, 1968). Organizations and societies are complex, three dimensional, cosmological, open systems with interdependent subsystems working together to achieve the goal of the whole system (Capra, 1996; Wimbiscus, 1995). Yet, compared to rational ideas like economics, general systems theory represents a relatively modest body of knowledge (Swanson, 1999).

Recent concerns with the lack of a positive relationship between society and organizations such as Enron and WorldCom that represent a flawed economic system have illuminated the relevance of related and contemporary systems theories such as *autopoiesis* or self-regulating systems (Maturana and Varela, 1980), *deep ecology* (Capra, 1996), and the *Gaia* hypothesis (Lovelock, 1979, 1988). Each systems theory is briefly discussed.

Autopoiesis, also known as self-regulating or self-producing systems, is concerned with two hypotheses: first, all living systems are organized in a closed circular process, and second, all living systems are cognitive systems, and living is a cognitive process (Maturana and Varela, 1980). Physical laws govern behavior in the physical domain while behavior in a social system is governed by norms and rules, which can be broken (Capra, 1996). Luhmann (1990) developed the concept of social autopoiesis as a process or network of communication. Since social systems are language-bound, i.e. symbolic/metaphoric, they are self-produced by non-physical boundaries of expectations, loyalty, confidentiality and so on (Capra, 1996). This system's worldview implies that organizations and societies are living systems and as part of the physical world are self-regulating and thus capable of continual change while preserving a pattern of organization.

Capra's concept of *deep ecology* is a broad-based, holistic worldview: a way of seeing the world as an integrated whole rather than a detached collection of parts.

Deep ecology recognizes the fundamental interdependence of all phenomena and the fact that we are all embedded in and dependent on nature's cyclical processes (Capra, 1996). Thus, humans, communities, organizations and societies are simply strands in a web of life (Capra, 1996).

Perhaps the most enchanted example of systems theory is *Gaia*, the notion that the planet Earth is a living system. Gaia is an ancient and organic, *mother-earth* metaphor, drawn from the process of life; mechanistic thinking depends on metaphors drawn from man-made machines (Sheldrake, 1991). Gaia as a mother-earth metaphor is evidenced in cultures worldwide. Mother earth was accepted as a sacred belief until the Protestant Reformation in the sixteenth century when humanity's fear of wild, untamed nature reinforced its desire to subdue her. A worldview where nature was no longer acknowledged as mother or deemed sacred, and no longer considered alive, finally evolved out of the desacralized scientific and industrial revolutions. Shifting focus from ecosystems to the planet as a whole, Gaia is a system of three layers (metaphorically): (a) Earth's biosphere, a thin layer of living things; (b) the inanimate Earth itself, and (c) a protective layer of atmosphere surrounding the biosphere. Gaia is considered autopoietic, i.e. it is self-bounded, self-generating and self-perpetuating (Capra, 1996).

Systems theories have evolved from a mechanistic general systems theory to the organismic philosophy of Gaia. Mechanistic science rejects the idea that Gaia is alive, yet morphogenesis, instinctive behavior, learning and memory are still among our most pressing unsolved problems. The very nature of life itself remains an unanswered question (Sheldrake, 1991). Unlike scientific systems thinking, Gaia reflects the fact that humankind's actions cannot be separated from the Earth, and like the great mother of ancient mythology, that Earth has a reciprocal aspect that cannot be ignored.

Our worldviews must begin to reflect contemporary needs for explanations that are applied, holistic, social and ecologically benevolent. Wheatley (1994) suggested that if nature uses certain principles to create infinite diversity, it is highly probable that those principles apply equally to human organizations. Modifying theories and our worldviews without concurrent shifts in practice seals the fate of HRD as a second-rate and continuously dependent discipline and most certainly obscures its role in enhancing social responsibility. Continuously reviewing, revising and utilizing theories and diverse worldviews, such as systems theories and complexity theory that affect the ability of HRD to play a decisive role in building a sustainable future, is both judicious and moral.

Complexity theory suggests that we are co-creators of our world and that attempts at control, especially organizational control, are antithetical to creativity and innovation. Similar to the notion of interconnectivity in systems thinking, complexity reveals that organizations are in a dynamic reaction with the environment and that we are co-creators of the systems of which we are a part. Emerging from the natural sciences, complexity has recently been applied by Stacey (1996), Frederick (1998) and others to human organizations. Complex systems use a diverse and often obscure language that includes exotic terms such as fitness landscapes, autocatalysis, strange attractors, and edge of chaos (EOC). Although authors differ on complexities' makeup, Frederick (1998) offered a comprehensive and clear explanation of the core tenets of complexity: (1) self-organization, (2) autocatalysis, (3) complex adaptive systems (CAS) and edge of chaos (EOC), and (4) fitness landscape. A generic and abbreviated account of each is presented here.

Self-organization is spontaneous self-assembly, the hallmark of all living systems. An interaction of cells at the molecular level somehow enables a seed to self-organize into a tree or a frog to develop from a tadpole. Similar to the idea of autopoiesis, self-organization is a tendency in all forms of human organization, including corporations (Frederick, 1998; Kauffman, 1995).

Like a catalyst in chemical reactions, *autocatalysis* accelerates the self-assembly, self-organization process. This feedback process makes very rapid rates of change and varying directions of change possible in organizations (Frederick, 1998).

A *complex adaptive system* is any complex living system, including a corporation, that has the ability to interact with and adapt to its environment. CASs exhibit certain principles such as being at risk when in equilibrium, being self-organizing, tending to move towards the *edge of chaos* (EOC) through catalysis, and being easily disturbed by what is best defined for our purposes as leverage points. EOC implies that organizations, due to their instability and tendency for rapid evolution through the introduction of one or more autocatalytic influences, may self-destruct. Autocatalytic abilities enable an organization to push competitors out of an environmental niche and enter a zone of random-like behavior verging on chaos, i.e. the edge of chaos. However, being chaotic does not mean out of control. Underneath, what appears as randomness is actually hidden order. The trick for companies or professions like HRD is to find the balance between too rapid, directionless change where it is susceptible to hostile environmental forces and equilibrium, the precursor to stagnation and ultimate death. If a company or a profession can step up to the edge of chaos without self-destructing it gives its autocatalytic forces an opportunity to create new adaptive skills like technological innovations (Frederick, 1998) or socially responsive behaviors.

Complex adaptive systems do not succeed or fail in a vacuum; they maneuver and seek niches within an environment called the *fitness landscape*. Finding a home, a 'safe harbor' within the environment, a niche where an organization can fit in or adapt determines its life or death. If an organization or profession loses its niche or fails to fit into its landscape, like a mouse getting too close to an eagle in flight or a company failing to organize around learning, it soon becomes prey to those who do.

What these unbounded theories have in common is a view of organizations and ourselves within a naturalistic paradigm, away from the Newtonian, machine-oriented metaphors that have plagued us well into the early twenty-first century. They offer us a new way to see the profession and to understand how we can add real and sustainable value in a complex world. HRD as a field of study and a profession should always reflect only those theories and worldviews that can truly enhance its ability to create a better world for individuals, organizations and society.

Concluding thoughts

As an organizational function and as a profession HRD plays a principal role in enhancing the long-term sustainability of organizations and has the potential to help cultivate organizations and people that positively influence communities, society and the environment (Hatcher, 2002). The power that economic and psychological theories have had over HRD and the worldviews that have influenced the profession and its professionals required review and discussion so that we might clarify and better understand their impact on our potential contributions and ultimate responsibility to society.

Today, we must view organizations as part of the ecosystem; society must be served through organizations not ruled by them. As organizations become more influential they become either instruments of destruction of the environment and society or tools for sustainability of communities, the ecology and humanity. As an integral part of today's organizations, there is no doubt that HRD has an economic responsibility to the organizations that employ its professionals and methods. However, the HRD profession also has a moral responsibility to individuals, organizations, societies and the ecosystem it influences. HRD has a responsibility to create a profession that is morally responsible beyond short-sighted economic gain, behaviorally-oriented psychological fulfillment or bounded and limited worldviews. Rational economic and traditional psychological theory and obsolete and restrictive worldviews are faithful to short-term returns and disjointed approaches to sustained change. Such theories trample on morality and hamper socially responsive organizational and societal changes. There could be no greater folly than to manage the economy *or a profession* as though its sole relationship to Earth is that of exploiter – as though the planet Earth could be viewed as an unlimited fund of resources and a dumping ground for our wastes (Harman and Porter, 1997).

Shifts in the way we view our world (reality) are catalysts for progress toward sustainable development of the environment and humanity. What we believe is important, what we choose to notice creates our view of the world. We then 'see' the world through this self which we have created (Wheatley and Kellner-Rogers, 1996: 49). Disciplines such as HRD, dedicated to individual and organizational transformation, must systematically review their assumptions and worldviews to insure they are valid and worthwhile. This chapter outlined several theories and worldviews that either maintain the current unsustainable status quo or facilitate a new and hopefully more sustainable and responsible way for us to view the world and the profession of HRD. It seems axiomatic that shifting our worldviews away from those that are bounded and limiting to those that afford us insight, and promise organizational and ecological sustainability, are necessary in such an economically-driven and increasingly complex world.

References

Bates, R. Hatcher, T., Holton, E., and Chalofsky, N. (2001) 'Redefining human resource development: An integration of the learning, performance, and spirituality of work perspectives', *Proceedings of The Academy of Human Resource Development Annual Research Conference*, Feb. 28–March 4, 2001, Tulsa, OK

Bertalanffy, von L. (1968) *General Systems Theory*, New York: Braziller

Brooks, A. K. and Edwards, K. A. (1997) 'Transgressing the boundaries of social discourse: Narratives of women's sexual identity development', *Proceedings of the SCUTREA Conference*, 1997, London

Bruner, J. (1990) *Acts of Meaning*, Cambridge, MA: Harvard University Press

Bruner, J. (1996) *The Culture of Education*, Cambridge, MA: Harvard University Press

Burk, M. (1994) 'Ideology and morality in economics theory', in A. Lewis and K-E. Warneryd (Eds), *Ethics and Economic Affairs*, 311–333, London: Routledge

Callahan, J. C. (1988) 'Kinds of moral principles', in J. C. Callahan (Ed.), *Ethical Issues in Professional Life*, 19–20, San Francisco: Jossey-Bass

Capra, F. (1996) *The Web of Life: A new scientific understanding of living systems*, New York: Anchor Books

Chalofsky, N. and Lincoln, C. (1983) *Up the HRD Ladder: A guide for professional growth*, Cambridge, MA: Perseus Books

Drucker, P. F. (1993) *Post-capitalist Society*, New York: HarperCollins Publishers

Fox, M. (1994) *The Reinvention of Work: A new vision of livelihood for our time*, San Francisco: HarperSanFrancisco

Frederick, W. C. (1998) 'Creatures, corporations, communities, chaos, complexity', *Business and Society*, 37, 358–389

Gergen, K. (1994) *Realities and Relationships*, Cambridge, MA: Harvard University Press

Halstead, T. and Cobb, C. (1996) 'The need for new measurements of progress', in J. Mander and E. Goldsmith (Eds.), *The Case against the Global Economy: And a turn toward the local*, 197–206, San Francisco: Sierra Club Books

Harman, W. and Horman, J. (1990) *Creative Work: The constructive role of business in a transforming society*, Indianapolis, IN: Knowledge Systems

Harman, W. and Porter, M. (Eds) (1997) *The New Business of Business: Sharing responsibility for a positive global future*, San Francisco: Berrett-Koehler.

Hatcher, T. G. (1999) 'Reorienting the theoretical foundations of human resource development: Building a sustainable profession and society', in K. P. Kuchinke (Ed.), *Academy of Human Resource Development 1999 International Conference Proceedings*, 202–208, Arlington, VA: Academy of Human Resource Development

Hatcher. T. G. (2000a) 'A study of the influence of the theoretical foundations of human resource development on research and practice', *Academy of Human Resource Development 2000 International Conference Proceedings*, NC: Research Triangle

Hatcher, T. G. (2000b) 'The social responsibility performance outcomes model',. in K. P. Kuchinke (Ed.) *Academy of Human Resource Development 2000 International Conference Proceedings*, Raleigh, NC: Academy of Human Resource Development

Hatcher, T. G. (2002) *Ethics and HRD: A new approach to leading responsible organizations*, Cambridge, MA: Perseus Publishing

Hatcher, T. G. and Brooks, A. (2000) 'Social responsibility of human resource development: How our definitions and worldviews impact our leadership role', *Academy of Human Resource Development 2000 International Conference Proceedings*, N.C.: Research Triangle

Henwood, K. L. (1994) 'Resisting racism and sexism in academic psychology: A personal/political view', *Feminism & Psychology*, 4(1): 41–62

Jacobs, R. (1990) 'Human resource development as an interdisciplinary body of knowledge', *Human Resource Development Quarterly*, 1(1), 65–71

Kauffman, S. (1995) *At Home in the Universe: The search for the laws of self organization and complexity*, New York: Oxford University Press

Kegan, R. (1994) *In Over Our Heads: The mental demands of modern life*, Cambridge, MA: Harvard University Press

Korten, D. C. (1995) *When Corporations Rule the World*, San Francisco, CA: Berrett-Koehler Publishers

Kuhn, T. (1962) *The Structure of Scientific Revolutions*, Chicago: University of Chicago Press

Lincoln, Y. S. and Guba, E. G. (1985) *Naturalistic Inquiry*, Newbury Park, CA: Sage

Lovelock, J. (1979) *Gaia: A new look at life on earth*, Oxford: Oxford University Press

Lovelock, J. (1988) *The Ages of Gaia: A biography of our living earth*, Oxford: Oxford University Press

Luhmann, N. (1990) 'The autopoiesis of social systems', in N. Luhmann (Ed.), *Essays on Self-reference*, New York: Columbia University Press

Maturana, H. and Varela, F. (1980) *Autopoiesis and Cognition*, Holland: D .Reidel, Dordrecht

Mitchell, S. A. (1988) *Relational Concepts in Psychoanalysis*, Cambridge, MA: Harvard University Press

Passmore, D. L. (1997) 'Ways of seeing: Disciplinary bases of research in HRD', in R. A. Swanson and E. F. Holton (Eds), *Human Resource Development Research Handbook*, 199–214, San Francisco: Berrett-Koehler

Roszak, T., Gomes, M. E. and Kanner, A. D. (Eds) (1995) *Ecopsychology: Restoring the Earth, healing the mind*, San Francisco: Sierra Club Books

Schumacher, E. F. (1979) *Good Work*, New York: Harper & Row

Sheldrake, R. (1991) *The Rebirth of Nature: The greening of science and God*, Rochester, VT: Park Street Press

Stacey, R. D. (1996) *Complexity and Creativity in Organizations*, San Francisco: Berrett-Koehler

Swanson, R. (1999) 'Foundations of performance improvement and implications for practice', in R. J. Torraco (Ed.), *Performance Improvement Theory and Practice*, 1–25, Baton Rouge, LA: The Academy of Human Resource Development

Tichy, N. M., McGill, A. R. and St. Clair, L. (1997) *Corporate Global Citizenship: Doing business in the public eye*, San Francisco, CA: The New Lexington Press

Tomer, J. F. (1994) 'Social responsibility in the human firm: Towards a new theory of the firm's external relationships', in A. Lewis, and K-E. Warneryd, K-E. (Eds). *Ethics and Economic Affairs*, 125–147, London: Routledge

Welford, R. (1995) *Environmental Strategy and Sustainable Development: The corporate challenge for the twenty-first century*, London: Routledge

Wheately, M. J. (1994) *Leadership and the New Science: Learning about organizations from an orderly universe*, San Francisco: Berrett-Koehler

Wheately, M. J. and Kellner-Rogers, M. (1996) *A Simpler Way*, San Francisco: Berrett-Koehler

Wimbiscus, J. J. (1995) 'A classification and description of human resource development and performance improvement scholars', *Human Resource Development Quarterly*, 6 (1): 5–34

4 Strategic quest and the search for the primal mother

Heather Höpfl

Continuous improvement and the desire to engage in heroic quest

The argument presented here is concerned with the way in which organisations produce and reproduce themselves as texts. As such, it seeks to give some attention to the ways in which strategic planning can be related to a disregard of the moment in favour of some hypothetical future state which is invariably preferable to the present. This concern for futurity not only involves a vicarious engagement with the present but also, by an emphasis on progress and improvement, leads to a concern with measurement and a desire for well-defined means of determining whether or not any achievement towards future goals has been made. The concept of benchmarking typifies this need for performance measures and suggests a fundamental need for reassurance that the organisation is, after all, moving in the right direction. Of course, the trajectory of strategic development is not only about parameters of normality but also about improvement. Organisational life is replete with the exhortation to improve and, moreover, to continue endlessly to improve. So, all aspects of organisational life are subjected to the 'totalising discourse' (Knights and McCabe, 1997) of quality management, culture change or whatever is the current vogue in change terminology.

HRM style practices involve:

- Personnel or human resource issues becoming the *concern of all managers* (as opposed to being delegated to a personnel function).
- Human resourcing issues becoming central to all strategic-level deliberations in the organisation.
- The development of a strong culture encouraging employees to be highly committed to the organisation and its *continuous improvement*.

Account of high commitment HR practices, (Leopold, Harris and Watson, 1999: 30)

This chapter attempts to explore the meaning of this behaviour and to examine what it might mean in relation to the feminine. Inevitably, this type of argument always leads to a simplistic equation of the feminine with women and masculine with men. This is not the case here. The intention is to examine feminine and masculine aspects of consciousness and to see how they are played out in organisational life. Moreover, and it is important to identify this from the outset, the chapter seeks to identify even these dynamics as being subject to definition and categorisation by the phallocentric discourse and, therefore, notions of masculine and feminine have to be carefully mediated within prevailing constructions.

The cup and completion

Probably one of the most enduring myths of questing is to be found in the Grail legend. This is pertinent to the discovery of the meaning of questing behaviour and to some speculations about the object of the quest. Rosander (1989) and Webb (1991) demonstrate the link between questing and strategic issues very clearly. The intention in this section of the chapter is to identify some of the strands of the mythology of the Grail and to consider these in relation to the role of the goddess in myth and symbol. The symbol of the Holy Grail as the object of quest is simultaneously religious relic, and talisman. Adolf (1960) traces the etymology of *talisman* as being derived from the Greek word τελος meaning *completion* and τελεσμα meaning *a charm* and refers to the Grail as 'a charm leading man [sic] to completion' (Adolf, 1960: 156). Even in this elementary definition, the feminine aspect of the Grail is made transparent. The Grail is the emblem of completion. The Grail symbolises the lost feminine which has to be restored in order to achieve completion. Indeed, the Grail imagery is feminine. The Grail as a symbolic vessel is a container. In religious symbolism it is sometimes the cup of the Last Supper or else it holds the Precious Blood. The *quest* for the Grail, on the other hand, and the desire for perfection, is masculine, and carries with it imagery of conquest and capture.

Various theorists have attempted to come to grips with the meaning of the Grail mythology (Jung and von Franz, 1960; Whitmont, 1983; Adolf, 1960) and a number of common characteristics emerge. Adolf has identified what he terms the 'lotus-like' symbol of the Grail legend (Adolf, 1960: 163). By this, he refers to a number of common characteristics of the Grail stories. These are the notion of the wasteland or the 'Stricken Society; the Hidden Community of the Blessed, the Talisman, the symbol of Deus and anima, of the Divine and of our own Integrity, the Quest, the Quester' (Adolf, 1960: 163). Whitmont (1983) attempts to locate the dynamics of the Grail legend within the conditions of failed modernity, failure, collapse and despair. This analysis causes him to look at the role of and need for the feminine principle against a background of failure and despair (Whitmont, 1983: 153).

'Carlo De Benedetti has pulled off a *near-miraculous* change in the fortunes of Olivetti, the Italian office-equipment company. He not only saved Olivetti from almost certain bankruptcy but made it the second largest microcomputer manufacturer in the world and a *symbol* of entrepreneurial success ... "We were full of debt – we were losing something like ten million dollars a month." In *a situation so desperate*, he explained, "The real problem is defining reality". [italics added].'

(Waterman, 1988: 111)

The krater of the great goddess

Whitmont considers the Grail myth from the late Middle Ages to the present, what he terms 'post Christian' times, and argues that the Grail mythology serves an important psychological function in combining the symbol of the great goddess, the cauldron or krater or bowl, with the Grail which is filled with the blood of Christ as symbols defining the object of quest. Emma Jung makes a detailed study of the role and function of the symbolic vessel. She points to the vessel of the *corpus hermeticum*, a bowl filled with νοῦς, that is to say, with understanding and consciousness. The *corpus hermeticum* was sent from heaven so that men might immerse themselves in it and understand the reason for which they were created (Jung, 1960: 135). It was thought to be the uterus of spiritual rebirth. Jung continues this discussion with an account of the part played by the krater in gnostic mystery celebrations and refers to the beliefs of the Gnostic Naassenes and the cup of Anacreon which was thought to produce a similar gnosis or knowledge of God. The Naassenes believed in an androgynous original being whom the Greeks called 'the heavenly horn of the moon'. The Gnostic alchemist Zosimos of Panopolis in third-century Egypt writes of the krater of Poimandres in which his *soror mystica* is to immerse herself. The krater according to Jung is 'a font or piscina, in which the immersion takes place and transformation into a spiritual being is effected. It is the vas Hermetis of later alchemy ... uterus of spiritual renewal or rebirth' (Jung, 1960: 142). The krater, the vessel, the cup, is also the 'matrix or uterus in which the *filius philosophorum* (son of the philosophers) is born' (Jung, 1960: 142), and, at the same time, it is container and contents. As such, it is conceptually both the container and the thing contained: matrix as container and matrix as contents are one. This is where the completion is to be found: in the matrix as symbolic container and as the feminine as knowledge. This difficult notion of simultaneity of vessel and contents works better in the original translation because in German the notion of a concept uses the masculine noun *Begriff* while what is comprehended comes from the transitive verb *begreifen*, or as might be said in English 'to grasp' an idea. Both of these terms, concept and to comprehend, have their root in *Griff* or grip, but take a different term, *Verständnis*, as comprehension, which is a masculine noun, or as wisdom, *Weisheit*, which is feminine.

The uterus of Christ and the second birth

The German mystics use the word *Vaz* (vase) to signify the individual. This word expresses a conception of the individual as the vessel that finds completion when it is filled with comprehension and, ultimately, with spiritual understanding or wisdom. So, for example, Theobald de Hoghelande in the sixteenth century argues for the quest of *the vision* of the hermetic vessel for the attainment of higher consciousness, νους.

'We said we needed to create a vision for people in the organisation which was something they could aspire to and supporting that vision a set of values, and what we wanted to do was to change both employee behaviour and management behaviour using the old language.'

Quality Manager (Knights and McCabe, 1997)

Hence, in this line of thinking, the vessel that is the object of the quest is a uterus for spiritual renewal or *rebirth*. Indeed, a fifteenth-century woodcut shows precisely this understanding of the mystical role of the vessel in spiritual rebirth by depicting the crucified Christ with a bleeding uterus. What is unmistakably Christ's heart in the woodcut is placed in the position of uterus. His heart, his uterus of rebirth, bleeds into a cup held by two angels. This bleeding from the uterus imitates the bleeding of the physical matrix. It symbolises the power to reproduce and the cycle of reproduction. But, the uterus of spiritual rebirth is a metaphysical *Vaz*: concept and not conception. In the peculiarly male notion that the metaphysical takes precedence over the physical, the power of the matrix is superseded by the power of the concept of the matrix.

There is a relationship here with the idea that the vessel, as Grail or as krater, is the philosophical pelican (Jung, *Theatrum chemicum*, IV, 698, cited in Jung, 1960: 144). The pelican is the symbol of sacrifice. This symbol, which is common in Catholic imagery, comes from accounts of the behaviour of the mother pelican in protecting her young. It is said that the mother pelican pecks at her own breast until it bleeds in order to feed her young. Jung says that the feminine and maternal symbol of the vessel is that of the womb where ideas are conceived and become vital: '*a matrix in which the archetype of the Self is transformed*' (original italics) (Jung, 1960: 145). Jung continues this argument by referring to the medieval mystics whom she says understood the richness and intensity of human experience 'in this sense [that] the vessel ... signifies the whole psychic man *(not his ego)* [sic] as a realization of divinity reaching right down into matter' (Jung, 1960: 159).

The primal mother

This relates to what Adolf (1960) has referred to in her discussion of the Grail as a talisman, as a charm leading to completeness. The stone (the lapis), or the vessel (the krater), indicates what is to be achieved to bring about the completion of the *whole* individual, conscious and unconscious. The stone is the favoured object of alchemy in the sense that the medieval alchemists were trying to grasp content and matter, whereas the medieval poets favoured the notion of the vessel, the container, the feminine symbol with its emphasis on the emotions and holding and shaping. Consequently, it is in the maternal domain that the story of the Grail finds its meaning. The quest for the Grail is a quest into the outer darkness, in symbolic terms into the feminine, and into the development of consciousness. It is concerned with the pursuit of wisdom. The quest, as for example in the story of Perceval's quest for the Grail, is a journey to find the primal image of the mother, the vessel of birth.

In this respect, the work of Gustav Jung on the nature of the Holy Trinity provides a basis for understanding the need for the restoration of the goddess (Dourley, 1990: 45–53) for completion of the emblem and as an emblem of completion. In his later works, Jung came to describe the collective unconscious as the 'matrix mind' (Dourley, 1990: 45) and, in doing so, he sought to restore the maternal and the creative to a profound status within the psyche. For Jung, the matrix mind is the creative inspiration for mythologies, religions, art, literature and expressions of humanity. This is the notion of the mind as mother, fertile and wise.

Indeed, for Jung the *prima materia*, the matter from which all consciousness arises, is feminine. The ego and the creative matrix produce what he terms the 'golden consciousness' which arises when matter is made incarnate via consciousness. The mother is both consciousness itself and its continuity. Hence, as Dourley puts it, 'the mother of consciousness creates consciousness in order to become real in it … to become real in each individual centre of consciousness in a process of mutual completion' (Dourley, 1990: 46). This is no mere metaphysical reproduction. It is body and mind in the process of becoming, *mater materia*.

In contrast to this maternal process, Jung challenges what he terms 'patriarchal consciousness' with its preference for rationality and the direction of the will. He seeks to reintroduce the mother of consciousness to the structure of consciousness, by restoring a fourth element to the Holy Trinity: the divine creatrix. However, there is a further implication in this. In asserting that the relationship between consciousness and the divine matrix is one of organic continuity (Dourley, 1990: 49), Jung introduces human consciousness into the construction of the deity. In doing so, he implicitly cancels the notion of ordering, sequence and succession, that is to say, of father and son; of dialectical progression, that is, of son and Holy Spirit, and what he refers to as the 'patriarchal order of society' (Dourley, 1990: 50) and goes further to identify 'sterile perfection in the divine as a hallmark of patriarchal consciousness' (Dourley, 1990: 51) 'which could easily have been avoided by paying attention to the feminine idea of completeness' (Dourley, 1990: 50).

Compare: The Boston Consulting Group Matrix
(Boseman 1988)
(the contents of this matrix are not reproduced)

So taking all this together, there is a recurrent theme in the literature of the Grail that concerns itself with the notion of the Grail as a container of feminine knowledge and wisdom. There is also a concern with the idea that this knowledge is lost and needs to be restored to consciousness in order restore the organic unity of mind and body, masculine and feminine, text and experience, abstraction and physicality in the *mater materia*. In this respect, this chapter is concerned with the purposive rationality of organisations and, in particular, with the ways in which organisations reproduce themselves in writing. It is concerned with the relationship between the purposive and questing behaviour of organisations as expressed in the literature of strategy, total quality management, business process re-engineering and such like as a primarily masculine enterprise and with the object of quest, the lost object of consciousness, the sublime object of desire, the Grail.

In this context, the Grail symbolises the lost feminine, the mother, physical reproduction, embodied experience and all that is alienated from experience by the pursuit of abstract notions of the future, and a belief in textual reproduction. The notion of continuous improvement can only operate from a position of defined inadequacy. However, it is worse than that. By invoking notions of quality as a mountain without a plateau, the total quality movement has given no possibility that this work of redemption will ever be complete. We are always unworthy under this exhortation and will ever remain so. There is no promise of the acquisition of wisdom or the restoration of the mother. This is the pursuit of 'sterile perfection' which Jung identifies as the hallmark of patriarchal consciousness. The totalising discourses of the organisation are precisely totalising because they can never offer completion. They need to be totalising so as to preclude the possibility of otherness. Therefore, they seek to exclude and, more precisely, they seek to exclude the possibility of the feminine. This is because the feminine implicitly rejects the sterility of the patriarchal logos. The feminine, by its nature, offers completion and so poses a threat to the logic of self-serving and totalising narratives of the organisation. At a simplistic level, this is one reason why organisations have been keen to turn women into homologues of men. By containing women within the purposive logic of futurity, organisations as directive entities have sought to defend themselves against the threat posed by their very presence, ambivalence, physicality and knowledge. Yet, the result of this purposive striving is, nonetheless, an inevitable sterility. This is because the patriarchal logic substitutes words and exhortations and their reproduction as text for bodies, physicality and embodied reproduction. In privileging constructions over experiences, organisations lose contact with their physicality. Consequently, it is not the writer of this who reifies the organisation but the organisation that reifies itself by constructing itself as an abstraction and, via strategy formulation moreover, as a sublime abstraction. In other words, the organisation comes to reproduce itself as text and understand itself in metaphysical terms as the product of that process of reproduction.

In this context, it is not surprising that organisations function at variance to the bodies who work in and for them. Consequently, people in organisations are always struggling with issues that arise from the substitution of textual matrices for physical ones. They are dehumanised by loss of contact with their physicality, as organisations reduce them to categories and metrics. But, from a feminist point of view, the position is more serious. In the relentless pursuit of future states, organisations as purposive entities seek to construct for themselves the empty emblems of the object of the quest. In part, this is because the purposiveness is without end and, therefore, the notion of any real completion is antithetical to the idea of trajectory. Strategy gives birth to more strategy, and so on. The sublime is never attained. The individual in the organisation is always constituted in unworthiness, always deficient in relation to the constructed sublime. This means that for this questing to continue, the organisation must construct an emblem of the lost object of consciousness.

This melancholic gesture restores the illusion of completion but, of course, cannot satisfy and is not intended to satisfy. It is intended to console like the photograph of a loved one who is overseas. The emblem functions as an anamnesis to register the loss in representational form. For this reason alone the emblem of loss is melancholic and pervades the organisation with melancholy. It cannot offer consolation because ironically it can only recall the loss. So, the emblem of the lost object provides a false reassurance that completion can also arise from a construction. Let me say this more precisely. It cannot reassure because it arises from an erection. This is the constructed feminine and it is a travesty. It is the feminine constructed in the image of masculine desire to meet the needs of sterile perfectionism. It is a feminine which is tidy, logical, entirely representation and without power, ambivalence and sexuality. Indeed, it is merely the speculum of the feminine (Irigaray, 1974).

This is precisely the argument used by Kristeva to explain the Roman Catholic doctrine of the Assumption in which there are parallels with the homologation of the 'other'/'the feminine' into the symbolic order (Kristeva, 1986: 175). The doctrine of the Assumption is, hence, an *Aufhebung*, simultaneously an elevation and a cancellation. The Virgin Mother is a contradiction in terms and constructed as a steril-*ised* representation of the body of the mother now made safe and deprived of power (Höpfl, 2001). In other words, the Virgin Mother, as representation, is the law and, as Eagleton argues, 'The law is male, but hegemony is a woman; this transvestite law, which decks itself out in female drapery is in danger of having its phallus exposed', (Eagleton, 1990: 58). This is apparent in the ways in which organisations seek to create the feminine in notions of care and satisfaction: customer care, client satisfaction and emotional intelligence. So, the organisation constructs itself in diagrams and charts, texts and metrics which seek to uphold the representation of the body but which inevitably achieve a cancellation. It is little wonder, therefore, that notions of quality and care, the ubiquitous valorisation of staff, have more in them of melancholy than of matter. These are Eagleton's transvestite manifestations of the law attempting to present themselves as concerns of the body: the phallus under the skirt.

These are gross substitutes for the power of the feminine in the structure of consciousness. Feminists should not be hostile to the equation of the feminine with care. The pejorative connotation of 'care' which many feminists equate with service and seek to reject, is itself a seduction to aid the construction of homologues. Elsewhere (Höpfl, 2000), The author has consistently substituted the word 'erection' for 'construction' because it is by erecting categories and their definition that feminine power becomes subjected to interpretations which dismiss its significance. The derogation of notions of care serves to define and to diminish the power of reproduction and the embodied matrix. It is a means of subjecting the matrix to a mere metaphysical and male reproduction.

'A consultant puts his career on the line by talking about love; tough love perhaps, but lifts the quality issues on to the highest ethical level.' (Wille, E. 1992) (italics added)

(Harrison, 1987)

Embodied reproduction is then replaced by the reproduction of concepts and the fertility of the site is surrendered to the fertility of concepts and theoria. So, the matrix is an instrument of regulation which locates and characterises relationships on the basis of power. The physical matrix reproduces from itself and matter is made incarnate. The appropriated matrix, however, deals on the level of the abstract alone. It is not sufficient but seeks to construct for itself icons of what it experiences as lack. For the masculine matrix, perfection comes from striving. Consequently, the matrix gives birth into a world of obsessive reproduction and insatiable desire. Masculine reproduction arises from the sense of lack that only the acknowledgement of the unconscious, of the maternal matrix could satisfy and give a sense of completion. Hence, the masculine matrix is concerned with logic and order and rationality, with location and hierarchy, with allocation and definition. The maternal matrix *knows* in embodied experience and this knowledge is sufficient to itself when it finds expression in embodied action.

That the masculine matrix orders and captures in its quest for the perfect is obvious by recourse to any textbook drawing of matrix relationships. In this chapter, the construction of 'text boxes' throughout the text is likewise a stylistic device to demonstrate the capture of these cells of text within the 'body' of the chapter. The cells of the matrix are precisely cells. Order and the quest find expression through the logic of male reproduction. At the same time, the maternal matrix threatens to disrupt the secure ordering of the rational. Consequently, it is the regulation of the matrix and the appropriation of its space which is the agonistic site, the contested space which is the object of the quest. Here is the site of fertility (from the Greek word to bear, *pherein*): the site of growth and fruitfulness. This is the quest and the Grail the reward. Yet the fruits of the quest and the fruits of the womb may find similar expression. The bleeding uterus of Christ in the fifteenth-century woodcut fills the cup in the symbolic representation of new birth. At the heart of the quest is the goddess whose menstrual blood was both feared and revered as the symbol of fertility and feminine power. Organisations, as collectivities, have understood the sense of loss of the feminine and have tried to construct it in symbolic and in representational terms. This is a profound conceit as is evidenced by the contradictions of contemporary organisational life and the pervasive melancholy that arises from the knowledge of an ill-defined loss.

> 'Hear me a few minutes longer. I wanted to tell you of my mother, and how she keeps her fingers round my heart. For years I longed to carve my mother's statue, it seemed most splendid of my dreams ... Even a short while ago I should have thought it unbearable to die without having carved my mother's image. My life would have seemed so useless ... I can see it still, and would carve it, if I had any strength left in my hands. But she will not have it so. She will never have me disclose her secret ... And yet, I am glad to die, she makes it so easy for me.'
>
> (Hesse, 1971: 300)

The expression of the embodied feminine cannot be excluded by caricatures of experience, nor by imitations which, like the tribesmen described by Bettleheim (1955) who at puberty slit open their penises to create the resemblance of a bleeding vulva, seek to mimic feminine power. The quest for the Grail, therefore, can be seen as a desire for the recovery of the feminine, for the knowledge of the mother. However, it must be conceded that this argument is at once romantic and idealistic. After all, it seeks to find the object of the Grail quest in the union of body and mind. As Eagleton puts it, 'a fantasy of mother and father in one, of love and law commingled' (Eagleton, 1990: 263).

Having said this, my purpose in writing this chapter is two-fold. First, to give attention to the loss of humanity in organisational life in favour of the veneration of the text and, secondly, to expose the phallus of the representation which organisations erect to pretend that this humanity is still there. That I have chosen to equate humanity with the feminine is largely to do with more familiar arguments about the relationship between the body and the law (Kristeva, 1983). From the melancholy of the various simulacra of caring comes a move to restore the body. However, it is important to ensure that the body is not simply re-presented as text as a further substitution of bodily reproduction with textual reproduction, elevated in order to be cancelled. As the vessel or repository of wisdom, νους, the feminine then might be seen as the possibility of the 'ideal of compassionate community, of altruism and natural affection, ... which represents a threat to rationalism ... (but where) the political consequences ... are ambivalent', (Eagleton, 1990: 60). This then is the completion desired in the Grail legend, and the implications of it are not ambivalent but *ambivalence*. The argument presented here seeks to call to mind the desire for higher knowledge, understanding, meaning which can be set against the totalising discourses which regulate contemporary lives. Hence, this is not simply a romantic view of re-union of body and law which, I fear still, makes the body subject to the law. It is a device to explore the nature of what is excluded, to give emphasis to *otherness* since, 'What we designate as "feminine", far from being a primeval essence, (is the) "other" without a name', (Kristeva, 1982: 58).

References

Adolf, H. (1960) *Visio Pacis, Holy City and Grail*, Pennsylvania: Penn State University Press

Bettleheim, B. (1955) *Symbolic Wounds, Puberty Rites and the Envious Male*, London: Thames and Hudson

Boseman, G. (1988) *Cases in Strategic Management*, London: Wiley

Dourley, J. P. (1990) *The Goddess, Mother of the Trinity*, Lewiston: The Edwin Mellen Press

Eagleton, T. (1990) *The Ideology of the Aesthetic*, Oxford: Blackwell

Hesse, H. (1971) *Narziss and Goldmund*, Harmondsworth: Penguin

Höpfl, H. (1994) 'Learning by heart: The rules of rhetoric and the poetics of experience', *Management Learning*, September 1994

Höpfl, H. (2000) 'Falling from grace in Las vegas', in J. Biberman and A. Alkhafaji (Eds) *Global Perspectives on Business, Business Research Year Book*, Vol 7, 662–666, Michegan: IABD

Höpfl, H. (2001) 'The mystery of the Assumption: Mothers and measures', in N. Lee and R. Monroe (Eds) *The Consumption of the Mass*, Oxford: Blackwell

Irigaray, L. (1985) *Speculum of the Other Woman*, translated G. Gill, Ithaca: Cornell University Press

Jung, E. and von Franz M.L. (1960) *The Grail Legend*, London: Hodder and Stoughton

Knights, D. and McCabe, D. (1997) *Innovate to subjugate: The self-reconstituting manager and the reconstitution of employees in a motor manufacturing company*, proceedings of the EIASM Conference, Organizing in a Multi-Voiced World, Leuven, Belgium

Kristeva, J. (1983) 'Stabat Mater', in T. Moi (Ed.) 1986, *The Kristeva Reader*, Oxford: Blackwell (for Leon Roudiez' translation of Kristeva's Stabat Mater)

Kristeva, J. (1982) *Powers of Horror*, translated Leon Roudiez, New York: Columbia University Press

Kundera, M. (1985) *The Unbearable Lightness of Being*, translated M. H. Heim, London: Faber

Leopold, J., Harris, L. and Watson, T. (1999) *Strategic Human Resourcing, Principles, Perspectives and Practices*, London: Pitman Publishing

Moi, T. (Ed.) (1986) *The Kristeva Reader*, Oxford: Blackwell

Rosander, A.C. (1989) *The Quest for Quality in Services*, Milwaukee: American Society for Quality Control

Webb, I. (1991) *The Quest for Quality*, London: Industrial Society

Whitmont, E .C. (1983) *Return of the Goddess*, London: Routledge and Kegan Paul

Wille, E. (1992) *Quality: Achieving excellence*, London: BCA

Part II

Reflections of HR

The width

The four chapters in this section each broaden the conventional notion of HRD. David Weir starts this section by arguing that HR is normally seen through three different lenses – the most dominant being that of the West, but that there is a fourth, largely ignored paradigm, that of the Arab Middle East. Jim Stewart introduces ethics as an often overlooked core of HR theory and practice. Carole Elliott and Sharon Turnbull take up the debate, and introduce the discourses of citizenship and spirituality as a way of reconciling tensions between the performative needs of the organisation and the identity needs of individuals. The final chapter in this section is that by Kim James who launches a passionate plea for the incorporation of creativity and aesthetics into the HR agenda, as a necessary means of moving forwards.

As in the previous section, each chapter stands on its own, but also links to others in the book. David Weir's fourth paradigm complements Monica Lee's argument, presenting a detailed case study of a much neglected quaternity. His description of the Arab Middle East also resonates with Sarah Fraser's principles for effective leadership in the health service and Kiran Trehan's and Clare Rigg's discussion of changes that are needed in current pedagogy. Jim Stewart's thesis resonates with many of the chapters in the book, particularly those of Tim Hatcher, Lloyd Davies and Paul Kraus, and Rosemary Hill. Similar links occur with Carole Elliott's and Sharon Turnbull's chapter, which also links to Paul Iles's and Maurice Yolles's work in the way in which it seeks to expose an area to wider debate, and, through the introduction of alternative perspectives, address fragility, or certain lack of coherence, in the area itself. Finally, Kim James's chapter links directly into that of Carole McKenzie, and resonates particularly with those by Heather Höpfl, and Lloyd Davies and Paul Kraus.

5 Human resource development in the Arab Middle East

A 'fourth paradigm'

David Weir

Introduction

We can distinguish at least four culturally distinct master types or 'paradigms' of management: the Anglo-American, the Japanese, the European and the Arab (AMC; Weir, 2000a, b, c; 2003). In this chapter we shall argue that 'HRD' is normally seen as a simplistic concept, derived from the first paradigm. If HRD is seen as in a complex world, however, it needs to be able to address more than this one world view.

The language of HRD is a multiply problematic feature of one aspect of the discourse of 'management'. While we use the language and special terminologies of natural science, what we describe is a culturally determined phenomenon. The field of discourse contains many aspects that are subject to professional regulation and strong commercial interests. So the discourse becomes complicated and expressions of value become conflated with issues of empirical reality.

A representative definition of HRD is:

> HRD is an integrated area of study of the developmental practices of organizations so that they may accomplish higher levels of individual and organizational effectiveness.

> HRD uses training and development to identify, assure, and help develop the key competencies that enable individuals to perform current or future jobs with planned individual learning accomplished through training, on-the-job learning, coaching or other means.

> HRD uses organization development as a focus for assuring healthy inter- and intra-unit relationships and helping groups initiate and manage change by facilitating individuals and groups to effectively impact on organization as a system.

> (AHRD, 2002)

Lee however argues that the 'dynamic, ambiguous, and ill-determined' nature of HRD as a process makes precise definition unhelpful and that we need to understand HRD as a 'thing of becoming' rather than as a 'thing of being'.

She also notes that 'the bulk of early management research was done on (and in) white US bureaucratic organisations and our current understandings of management theory and practice are derived from this culturally specific and non-representational sample, and the very nature of this compounded the bias. Early research was assumed to apply to all management, and assumed that management was a singular global concept without national or situation-specific boundaries, that there were right and wrong ways of managing and that it was possible to derive a single global set of tenets for best practice.'(Lee 1999)

Even in the West HRD is a late development in a line of intellectual ancestry that stretches back through HRM, OD, management development, personnel management, staff and payroll management to the simplicities of Taylorism and scientific management. There are an implicit set of characteristics that comprise the following assumptions as core elements.

People, their growth and development, and the liberation of individual and collective talents and energy are equally significant in organisational goals as are profit and turnover. Equality and fairness in the treatment of staff are touchstones for evaluating organisational success. Participative and consultative styles are more productive than authoritarian and centralised modes of decision-taking as well as being more in accordance with (Western) values of democracy and justice. Co-operative behaviour is more rewarding than competitive behaviour. Information, if not a collective asset, ought to be shared unless there are strong reasons of commercial secrecy to justify a less open stance. Ownership is implicit in membership of a collectivity and absence of a felt sense of ownership inhibits performance. Conflict should be dealt with openly and seriously because unresolved conflicts lead to long-term weakening of collective energy. Rewards should be justified by meritocratic criteria and fairness as between equally contributive participants. Autonomy and freedom of action are pre-requisites of participation and performance. The infusion of value statements, cultural preferences and prejudices in this analysis is evident.

'Development' itself as a concept remains at the heart of this analysis. Lee in the study just mentioned identifies multiple senses of 'development as maturation; shaping, a voyage, and as emergent.' But this whole discourse assumes that for voyages to be described and lives understood, there must be a common pattern of movement from one place to another. These assumptions, however, may lead us to compare the incomparable.

A contemporary example of the error into which even the great may be led is the otherwise excellent book by Bernard Lewis, doyen of Middle East studies, that contains an erudite and committed exegesis of economic and political development in the Arab Middle East from the fifteenth century (Lewis, 2002). But its careful analysis is subverted by the implicit assumption that the course of development is everywhere a river that flows between parallel banks in which some currents run faster because less obstructed, others lethargically, turning into stagnant pools, but both destined to issue in the same broad 'modern' sea of economic prosperity and development.

But this is to oversimplify the reality of history and culture. This fallacy is a version of what Herbert Butterfield famously defined as the 'Whig Interpretation of

History'; a sedulous assumption that what one culture defines as economic progress is the inevitable goal of all histories (Butterfield, 1965). The histories of management are likewise not singular and univocal but may be comprised under a number of historically and culturally specific patterns. In previous writing we have sought to identify four master paradigms of management and its discourses. These may be identified as the Anglo-American or Anglo-Saxon, the Japanese, the European and the Arab. Each is *sui generis* and to a great extent incomparable, even when apparently the same events or processes are being described. Thus the 'right' of management to 'hire and fire', fundamental in the Anglo-American paradigm, hardly exists in the Japanese and is hedged with explicit legal constraints in the European. The very notion of being 'hired' is *per contra* anathema in many Arab practices. The 'right' to organise collectively is enshrined in custom and practice in Europe, non-existent in some other paradigms ; the concept of 'development' as an organisational as well as a personal descriptor is hard to conceptualise in the Arab world, though endemic to the very concept of the enterprise in Japan.

These differences are not coincident or random, nor do they derive from the different stages of development of these societies and their cultures. Four is not a magic number and it is possible to distinguish other variants; we now have to distinguish both a Chinese and a South-East Asian paradigm, significantly different in important respects from the Japanese. There are other ways in which the Islamic cultural matrix infuses the management patterns in countries that are Islamic, but not Arabic, like Indonesia, Pakistan and Bangladesh. But our present concern is with the geographically defined reality centred on the Arabian peninsula and its surrounding environment.

Comparing the incomparable

After September 11, 2001, it is clearly easier to sustain the argument that there are forms of behaviour, derived from patterns of belief and practice, which are alien and incomprehensible to Western commentators. There are mind-sets here we do not comprehend and behaviours not amenable to our rhetorics. But it is important not to see all management as inextricably located in Western thought-patterns and in that historical process characterised as 'the disenchantment of the West'.

The very structuring of historical periods that in Western histories ascribe centrality to 'the Renaissance' contributes to this tendency to see other peoples' pasts through Euro-centric, even xenophobic eyes. For if the 'Renaissance' represented for Christendom the rediscovery of classical knowledge and designs for living, insights, and belief-patterns originated in Greece and Rome, the transition had been mediated through the structures of the Arab and Islamic worlds, their universities, teachings, and the writings of such scholars, as Ibn Khaldun and Ghazali. A Europe striving to crystallise its own identity as indefeasibly Christian under the pressures of the Reformation and incipient rationalism was not anxious to acknowledge its intellectual debts to a tradition that had so recently proved its vitality in military terms by threatening the gates of Vienna.

The media of the transition were the traders, merchants and business people of the Mediterranean basin, the language of the barter of ideas and goods more likely to be Arabic than Latin. The central role of the Eastern Mediterranean in sustaining the classical inheritance of Greece and Rome was only equalled by the importance of the region in mediating new knowledge from the Far East and the Middle Kingdom of China over the same period. It was this region above all that possessed a 'common culture' of religious practice, language and core concepts that was even more tightly integrated than the worlds of Christendom or Confucianism.

Textbooks of the history of 'management' are wont to quote the origins of the practices of general management in the shipyards of Genoa and Venice, and to trace the derivation of the word itself in the Italian *menaggiere*, used of expert horse-trainers. But in the recent past, those techniques and concepts had travelled from East to West, and like the map-making initiatives of Leo Africanus, (otherwise Hasan al Wazan) the first traveller to produce a viable map of Africa, from South to North. By the time Vasco da Gama rounded the Cape of Good Hope to 'discover' the Indies, the Arabs had been trading there for centuries. This is not an exercise in historical one-upmanship, but an argument that the styles, techniques, practices and beliefs of management, and its specialised sub-categories are, as management is everywhere, an aspect of the generic culture of a particular historically-specific society.

If the language and definitions of 'management' did not emerge at the same time and in the same way in this world as in the American mid-West or the manufactories of northern England, this is not prima-facie evidence that there were no managers and no managing, as roles and processes, in the contemporary Arab world.

Islam as a unifying force

The prevailing pattern of belief and the near-universal matrix of explanation within this region derives from the religion of Islam; itself a diverse phenomenon, with at least as many opportunities for sub-categorisation as offered by Christianity, but with salient central features that relate directly to our topic. This is not to say that everyone in this region is a Moslem, or that there are no other cultural traditions, for this region has historically evidenced diversity, tolerance and mutual respect among many religions and schools of belief. Many countries including Lebanon, Palestine, and Iran have strong-stranded histories of religious practice including varieties of Christianity that have co-existed cheek-by-jowl with Islam. Nonetheless, Islam is a religion which claims universal applicability, but is not tethered to some contentious tenets of dogma, for it is a religion of practice rather than of dogma.

The fundamentals are simple and easily codified, consisting of an obligation to pray five times daily, to undertake the pilgrimage to the holy places, the Hajj, to claim that there is one God and that his prophet is Mohammed, to share worldly riches with the poor and to follow the way of life understood to be that of Islam:

the word itself means 'submission'. It is in its universality and simplicity that its behavioural and conceptual power lies, infusing the practices of management as all other aspects of culture. This is not to imply that Islamic principles compel tightly-structured and intractable obligations to manage in a specific way, but that the diversity of behaviours and practices which exist have to be explicable within this framework (see for example: Rahman, 1979).

Science, law, inter-personal behaviours and obligations to others are all understood to be aspects of a fundamental reality, which has to be understood as far as it is practicable, and knowledge and the bearers of knowledge are themselves highly regarded.

Reality is to be respected; rulers to be obeyed and duties to be undertaken. In principle, there is no inescapable conflict between religion and science as, for example, may exist between creationists and Darwinists. This respect extends to the other religions, notably Judaism and Christianity. The followers of these faiths are regarded as 'people of the book' and are understood to share similar fundamental principles, and Moses and Jesus are alike respected as prophets by believers.

These assumptions can of course readily be represented as deriving from habits of mind and behaviour which are 'pre-scientific', even 'irrational' and some politicians, writers and reformers, such as Mustafa Kemal Ataturk in post-World War 1 Turkey, have seen in them barriers to the necessary progress of modernisation and Westernisation. Nor is it reasonable however to ascribe the epithets of 'conservative' or 'fundamentalist' to these beliefs and practices, holus-bolus. That there is reaction, conservatism and fundamentalism in the Arab Middle East cannot be doubted, but these phenomena can equally be found in the West and in the Far East, in Texas and in Tokyo.

That the Arab Middle East can cope with rapid social change without fundamental threat to the underlying structures of Islam, cannot be doubted by anyone who has worked in Dubai or Kuwait. That Islam, as a religion, cannot function outside of its original heartland is belied by the experience of inner-city America, or rural Indonesia. It is nonetheless true, as V. S. Naipaul points out that:

> Islam is in its origins an Arab religion. Everyone not an Arab who is a Muslim is a convert. Islam is not simply a matter of conscience or private belief. It makes imperial demands. A convert's world view alters. His holy places are in Arab lands; his sacred language is Arabic. (Naipaul, 1998)

The gaining of worldly wealth is not understood to be antithetical to the prospects of eternal salvation for the possession of wealth imposes certain specific duties.

Groucho Marx once famously noted that 'I've been rich and I've been poor… and rich is better'. Certainly most Arabs well understand the truth of this maxim. There is no burning desire to embrace unnecessary poverty and irrelevant subordination in the contemporary Arab world. But the strength of Islam lies precisely in its apparent capability to deal with both of these extremes of experience.

A barrier to the ability of many to come to terms with the diversity of the modern world is the implicit assumption that 'modernisation' must inevitably imply 'Americanisation' or at the least 'Westernisation'. This canard has been further generalised by much of the current indolent verbiage of 'globalisation'. But it is a taken-for-granted assumption within most of the Arab Middle East that it will remain possible for choices to continue to be made of the aspects of Western life and culture that are compatible with the culture and traditions of that region, and that it will remain possible to reject those aspects which are perceived as objectionable or unnecessary. The Arab Middle East comprises a wide variety of states and economies, and a diverse terrain containing some of the richest and poorest peoples of the world. No simple formula can possibly do justice to its diversity: nonetheless we attempt to delineate some common features, and identify trends. It must be understood as what it is, rather than as some feeble copy or inadequate representation of some master exemplar, located in the technically more advanced Western world.

The region which we are considering comprises the mainly Arabic-speaking countries of Egypt, Jordan, Palestine, Saudi Arabia, Syria, Yemen, Oman, United Arab Emirates, Bahrain and Kuwait. The countries of the Maghreb, Morocco, Algeria, Tunisia and Libya share many features in common with this region, but their historical, administrative and linguistic traditions are different, so they are excluded. Iran and Iraq have been excluded for similar reasons, though such field research as has been undertaken in recent years supports the view that, despite recent political experience, many underlying features remain comparable.

Within this region it has been historically appropriate to distinguish an Islam of the desert and an Islam of the rivers, an Islam of the rural areas and an Islam of the cities. But one aspect is central to all of these experiences and that is the universal, indeed as Naipaul phrases it, the 'imperial' framework provided by the harsh backdrop of the desert. This master matrix represented in the Quran and the holy writings forms a framework of interpretation and guides to conduct that are intended to direct behaviour and recommend conduct in times of difficulty, where individual choices must always be subordinated to the long-term interests of the collectivity.

This philosophy is based on the experience of surviving hardship and of maintaining social value through periods of threat and challenge, rather than of the calculus of individual choice under conditions of affluence. It is also relatively indifferent to political considerations that are construed as having temporary impact.

The master social structures that are predicated on these elements are those of the web of family and kin obligations sometimes characterised as those of the 'tribe' or 'clan'. Arabic society is by no means the only one to be structured in this way and indeed, many societies bordering the Mediterranean share similar elements. These structures frame life in city and town alike, and are equally powerful elements in family, business and political experience. Works of fiction like the *Cairo Trilogy* of the Egyptian novelist Naguib Mahfouz trace the interpenetration of family and kin obligations through periods of radical political change, the end of colonialism and the upheavals of nationalism (Mahfouz, 1992). In this region political boundaries and the managerial philosophies of governments are surface phenomena compared to the deeper, infra-structures of belief, family, kin and obligation. These may be coterminous with 'markets' which are not easily mapped on to current political boundaries.

The Arab world today

During the period since the mid 1970s there has been a very strong educational trend in which the Arab world has participated more than proportionately. It is now usual for universities and business schools in Western countries to boast a substantial complement of graduate students from the Arab Middle East. Regimes of all political tendencies have provided increased opportunities for the education of their young people. Education and the 'development' of the young is a core value in Islam and the first objective of both individuals and nations on obtaining disposable wealth is to invest in the knowledge assets of the future.

The oil-rich countries of the Gulf states have explicitly set out to turn the short-term surpluses from oil revenues into long-term educational investment. In the mid-1990s a survey of middle and senior managers in Bahrain reported that nearly thirty per cent of them were qualified to Masters degree level; at this period the corresponding percentage in the United Kingdom was less than a third of that level. (Al-Hashemi and Najjar, 1993). The last three decades have also seen a considerable strengthening of the intensity and professionalism of research into management behaviour and attitudes in the region so that it is now possible to build interpretations on an assured basis of empirical fieldwork and comparative methodologies.

Inevitably, much of the early research consisted of the attempt to apply Western models and techniques that had proven their applicability in the West to the newer conditions in the Arab world. Farid Muna's *The Arab Executive* aimed to characterise the region and its managers as a synoptic whole (Muna, 1980). Al-Faleh in Jordan, set out explicitly to map the local organisational terrain and to provide a characterisation of management in transition (Al-Felah, 1987). Hossein Dadfar's characterisation of the different types of manager to be found in Arab organisations leant strongly on interpretations of wider political and social changes. (Dadfar, 1993). Some research clearly started from the assumption that the western model could be 'tested' in alien circumstances, for example Medhat Ali's (1997) account of the introduction of a total quality management regime into a major Saudi company. Others have started from the belief that it would be possible to demonstrate the superiority of an 'Islamic' approach to management. But increasingly it became clear that, whatever the intentions of their sponsors and introducers, whatever the wider objectives of political and administrative reform, the very texture and processes of management in this region remained different from their Western models. There are some often noted cultural features of management in the region, and the cause of much angst among Westerners in trying to interface with management there for the first time. The phrase '*Insha'Allah*'; literally 'If God wills it', can be a simple statement or a form of words covering the strong possibility of inaction or even a negative outcome to apparently agreed courses of action. By its nature, it is an indefeasible expression, for all outcomes represent the will of God and what eventually happens, or does not, is equally an expression of divine will.

This is a hard idea for westerners to grasp or to feel much empathy with, for it seems to counter the concepts of 'control' and 'planning' which are central to the Anglo-American model.

The second is the equally frustrating concept of '*Bukrah*'; literally 'tomorrow', a term which in Western usage implies a definite, but in Arab terms an indefinite, entity. The very concept of time is synchronous rather than monochronous and it is expected that more than one event or type of event can take place in parallel, so a meeting, apparently on one topic, can transmute into another type of encounter, and back again, be curtailed or postponed without stated objectives apparently attained, without any offence being intended. Time is thus polychronous and multilinear.

'*Wasta*', literally 'influence', 'connections', or 'networking' or 'power', is inextricably tied up with personal and positional aspects of the manager's role. It can symbolise the skills of a broker or middleman, an intermediary or agent but also connote formal as well as informal capabilities. Many Western-trained management scholars are highly critical of this phenomenon; indeed some perceive in it an inevitable tendency to inefficiency, corruption and criminality. Certainly it can shade over into these undesirable aspects. Nonetheless it is a near-universal fact of management and business life in this region. Attempts to regulate it by legal or juridical constraint usually fail because it springs from the intrinsic texture of social structures and the clan, tribal and family connections which power the social fabric.

The exchange of gifts which puzzles or offends Western managers is not necessarily to be construed as an attempt to influence or suborn the judgement of the recipient but may be interpreted as a mark of respect, signifying reciprocal acceptance of status and marking the initiation or honouring of an agreed bond.

Bureaucracy, red tape, delay and inefficiency are also widespread in the culture in which managers have to operate: sometimes these may be ascribed to a lack of trained personnel, more often to caution within public bureaucracies, and to the combined impact of *Insha'Allah*, *Bukrah* and *Wasta*.

In a series of publications based on empirical studies of the banking and financial communities in Jordan, Al Rasheed (1996) has identified other generic features of 'traditional business organisation' in the region. The lack of reference to job goals, absence of career planning and systematic performance appraisal are related to a limited orientation toward the future. So this fundamental aspect of HRD as understood in the West is likely to be absent, as is the delegation of authority. Decisions tend to be referred upwards, where authority is concentrated; inevitably this tends to delay decisions and dis-empower all but the most senior managers in the organisation. Relationships between managers, both horizontal and vertical, even within quite formal hierarchical structures, tend to be expressed in personalised, rather than impersonal terms. This brings benefits as well as disadvantages, but the sense of personalisation is unusual and sometimes unwelcome to Western managers. It brings with it connotations of positioning in the wider communities of status, which can offend managers accustomed to expect a strict segmentation of work and non-work roles.

Training can be construed in personal terms and mentoring is an understood and welcomed aspect, as it can be construed as respect for seniority, age and experience. But this often co-exists with a disregard of job-related training and developmental philosophies, thus leading to high levels of felt frustration. In these respects public sector organisations may represent models more sympathetic to Western ideas of training, planning and career development.

Promotion opportunities are not usually perceived as predictable, even in performance terms, so much as dependent on the perceived sponsorship of seniors and the necessity of undertaking those behaviours which make the manager appear worthy in their eyes. This perception leads to much frustration on the part of those who perceive themselves as performing competently and who identify with the advantages of a meritocratic system of advancement. Many of these resentments are expressed by younger, better-qualified and Western-trained managers.

Personnel and human resource departments, where they exist formally, may be concerned with detailed matters of payroll, recruitment, remuneration and discipline within quite explicit constraints, with little discretionary capability and with little or no involvement in strategic issues or even in forward loading and planning matters. Organisation structures may exist on paper, be apparently quite clearly defined and well articulated, however the reality of their operation will normally be mediated by the aspects identified above, and in particular by considerations of *Wasta*.

These phenomena are not specific or restricted to the structures of organisation. It has been argued that the very texture of Arab culture, language and life encourages imprecision, ambiguity and diversity. This is coupled with a cultural tendency to avoid or at least to postpone consideration of contentious issues and to avoid the emergence of potential topics of disagreement, in order to better preserve the fabric of social relationships. Such a philosophy is anathema to Western managers and especially to Americans, whose whole training leads them to focus on the ability to surface issues and resolve them, a process emblematic of the science of management itself.

One important generic aspect of Arab business organisations is the extent to which they tend to be family owned and managed. Even if there exists a tier of professional management, trained, experienced and qualified, family status, power and seniority create expectations of deference and constraint that are hard to ignore, even for otherwise compelling business reasons. Middle managers may tend to be less well qualified than their Western counterparts, although, as noted earlier, that situation is changing.

Many studies have identified the absence of opportunities for women managers. This is undoubtedly a well-taken point, bearing in mind always the profound differences in the gender roles in Arab and Western society. In fact however this phenomenon is not uniform but is quite variable, with Saudi Arabia and

Jordan at opposite extremes of experience. In studies in Palestine during the *intifada* Abuznaid, Salman and others have pointed to the way in which women have increasingly taken the lead in business and management roles (Abuznaid, 1992; Salman, 1996; El Kharouf, 2000).

Benchmark studies reviewing the realities of HRM experience have been completed in several countries, notably in Jordan, Saudi and the GCC states bordering the Gulf; research is currently underway also in Libya.

The future of HRD in the Arab world

It might be understood from the above analysis that prospects for HRD in the sense these approaches are understood in the West are remarkably limited in the Arab world, and there is a sense in which that must be a correct conclusion. What will occur will not be the same as what will happen in the Western organisations. However, there are some important features of business and management in the Arab world in relation to the changing approach to HRD issues in the international scene under the impact of globalisation that modify this judgement.

It is widely accepted, and indeed is clearly a premise of the present book, that it is very timely to rethink urgently the 'traditional' paradigms of HRD in order to comprehend better the increasingly global and technologically sophisticated environments with which individual managers, clients, consultants, HRD specialists and organisations are confronted. Globalisation is clearly not going to represent uncontested terrain, a walk-over for the Western ways of doing business; the existence of other approaches, based on differing cultural paradigms, indicates that many of these represent far more than archaic, pre-scientific survivals.

While it is conventional to depict many aspects of the Arab or the Chinese, or the Japanese ways of management as 'traditional' there is in practice no more or less warrant for this depiction than there is for the Western model itself. What is incontestable is that within each of these three, as well as the European paradigm of management attitudes and behaviour, the past few decades have shown remarkable changes and a marked intensification of the rates of change. But the evidence that they are all converging to the same end-state is remarkably limited, indeed most studies, especially in the Arab world, tend to the reverse conclusion; that the differences remain as salient as the similarities.

But a review of the textbooks, cases and other pedagogic materials on which HRD professionals are trained for the world of international business, and which forms the accepted 'theoretical' backdrop to our endeavours as teachers, indicates that the substance of these topics is based substantially on North American experience. For the rest, the greatest weight of contributions relates to Japan, with Europe trailing behind in third or even fourth place, often behind other 'Far Eastern' or Chinese examples. There is a 'fashion' aspect to these swings in academic interest but the Arab world may be seen to be unreasonably neglected in terms of its relative socio-political significance.

The whole academic enterprise is thus biased towards an implicit agenda that gives priority to issues that may be ethnocentric at best, certainly tendentious and constraining. The extent of this implicit cultural biasing is not always evident from those working inside the received paradigm; the criteria for selection of topics and the treatment may alike be infused with unexamined assumptions and deep-rooted prejudices. The assumption of convergence, of growing similarities of behaviour and practice is one of these.

Implications for HRD

In this section we briefly review some of the current trends in the changing approach to HRD and consider the extent to which the Arab paradigm may prove to be specially advantaged or disadvantaged in facing the challenges of a new era, drawing on the results of empirical research and on considerable experience of consulting and working with organisations in the Middle East.

It would be impossible to claim that all of the features of contemporary HRD are to be found widely represented in HRM practice in a typical organisation in the Arab Middle East. And it would not be realistic either to use the presence or absence of these characteristics as a touchstone of the degree of 'modernisation' to be found. These organisations did not start from these premises and they are not bent on attaining those ideological destinations. But Western organisations are on the move also and there may be opportunities for unanticipated convergence as there are grounds for arguing that the styles and behaviours, the systems and attitudes found in this region are becoming quite well adapted to the emerging realities of international business in the twenty-first century.

Burke offers a summary positioning of the skills for the optimum performance of an HRD consultant. They comprise: the tolerance of ambiguity, the ability to influence, confront difficult issues, to support and nurture others, listen well and empathise, recognise one's own feelings and intuitions quickly, conceptualise, discover and to mobilise human energy, teach and create learning opportunities, and maintain a sense of humour (Burke, 1998). These are represented as attainable aspects for good HRD consultants: they are also, in this literature and generally, portrayed as desirable attributes of the type of manager capable of surviving and flourishing in the new era of global business.

Some structural features of the organisation make a good fit with this array of individual competencies, including flexibility, adaptiveness, speed of response, customer-sensitivity and the syndrome characterised by Peters and Waterman as the simultaneous presentation of 'loose-tight' structural elements (Peters and Waterman, 1988). Together these elements comprise a shorthand of the type of organisation that it is believed will offer superior value-added performance in the new era of high-speed communications, expanding markets and fast-changing technological substructures.

If we review the strengths and weaknesses of the typical business organisation in the Arab Middle East, we see a mixed picture certainly, but one that in some ways represents a pattern that is by no means 'pre-modern' or 'undeveloped': nor do we see a dominance of static, 'traditional' and conservative elements. Quite the contrary; many of these organisations may be more in tune with the proposed future than are some in the apparently more advanced Western world. In terms of structure, the typical Arab organisation is network-based, trans-national, and at least bilingual, for most large organisations are competent first in English, only secondly in Arabic, and will normally be able internally to draw on many other language-competences within their labour forces.

This adaptiveness is normally built on financial structures which permit ready access to disposable investment capital, and banking systems which encouraged measured risk, so decision-taking abilities can mature within reasonably secure, albeit somewhat conservative, environments.

The styles of decision-making do not conform to facile Western specification in terms of 'democratic' or 'authoritarian' but are based on techniques, like those of the *Diwaniah* or *Majlis* which are consultative, open and wide-ranging, while still consolidating ultimate responsibilty for the ownership of a major decision at an appropriately senior level. The designation 'loose-tight' is quite appropriate for this kind of decision-making style.

The development of junior talent by a process of mentoring and sponsorship may not conform to overt Western models of 'even-handedness' or democracy, but neither do the actual processes which operate within large Western organisations. But it creates opportunity for talent to emerge within a structured framework.

Companies such as Emirates Airlines, based in the United Arab Emirates, have become commercially highly successful, operating in highly competitive global environments. They have successfully melded the appropriate elements of contemporary HRM as practised in leading-edge Western organisations to a management matrix that conforms to local customs and expectations. Others, like the Hayel Saeed Anam group, based in the Yemen, have become leading international players in their sector, almost by stealth, without being noticed by the competition and have not compromised their indigenous behavioural heritage, remaining very tightly controlled by family members who see their skill base as less significant than their family positioning and balance. In organisations like this latter there may nonetheless be significant numbers of experienced and well-qualified expatriate managers in key positions, but strategic and group-wide issues are typically reserved to senior members of the family.

In Kuwait, companies like Wataniya Telecom see the introduction of standard procedures of job and task structuring, and performance evaluation as the essential foundations for creating a commercial ethos among managers whose previous experience was dominated by public sector norms. The role of expatriate managers, mainly but by no means exclusively from the Anglo-Saxon West, leavened with well-qualified management professionals from the Indian sub-continent has been widespread. However such organisations are now coming to terms with the need to conform to new constraints imposed by the policies of 'Arabisation' imposed by governments.

Al-Junaibi (2001) has reviewed the growth of the UAE economy and the motivations of managers and professionals from Western cultures in this scene. They are well qualified with high expectations and they bring state-of-the-art skills, which they pass on to their local colleagues, both to improve the levels of organisational performance for which they are responsible and thus their own rewards, and to create an improved set of structures, processes and competencies, knowing that, in principle, they will not be there for the long haul. A striking feature of the past three decades has been the increasing role of the banking sector and in particular of the Islamic banks. A number of misconceptions abound about their role, styles and functioning. These are by no means passive recipients and depositaries of unusable funds but they normally pursue highly commercial and even aggressive policies of expansion and network growth. A recent study by the chief executive of one of the major players in this league has focussed on the role of the Islamic banking sector in promoting corporate recovery and turnaround among entrepreneurial companies in the Gulf region (Al-Janahi, 2002).

These institutions offer a more proactive role than in comparable situations of business failure in a Western environment. The subsequent fates of companies which have got into business difficulties indicates the importance of techniques of succession planning, mentoring, interpersonal networking and introduction of performance measurement, appraisal and other techniques familiar to Western human resource managers.

Conclusion

The goals of HRM as conceived in typical organisations in the West have emerged from a specific historical development, formation and experience. They form part of a paradigm which ascribes particular roles to the legal and juridical structures and the constraints of national and international legislation. These specific histories differ nationally and regionally.

These goals, derived from a specific and recognisable intellectual history, may well be attainable by other means, more empathetic to the traditions and cultures of the Arab Middle East region and its economies, which have themselves survived and prospered through a period of dramatic social, political and economic change, at least as great as that experienced over the same period in the 'developed' world.

The Arab world which boasts the advantages of common culture, language, moral assumptions, financial and economic networks based on trading cultures with generations of network-building and expertise development, and clear survival capability will continue to adjust, learn and prosper within the changing opportunities offered by the twenty-first century, and in so doing it will continue to extend the currently constricting boundaries of that Western-defined envelope we call HRD.

References

Abuznaid, S.(1992) 'Palestinian women: From followers to leaders', *Proceedings of British Academy of Management Conference*: Bradford

Academy of Human Resource Development website 2002 (www.ahrd.org)

Al-Faleh, M. (1987) 'Cultural influences on Arab managerial development' *Journal of Management Development*: 6(3)

Al-Hashemi, I and Najjar, G. (1993) *A Survey of Management and Managers' Qualifications in Bahrain*: (1993) Kingdom of Bahrain: Ministry of Education

Al-Junaibi, Talal (2001) *The Economy of the United Arab Emirates and the Role of Expatriate Managers*, PhD thesis, University of Northumbria

Al-Janahi, A. (2002) *Corporate Turnaround in Companies in the Gulf Region*, PhD thesis, Bradford University

Al-Rasheed, A. M. (1996) *Traditional Arab Management: Evidence from empirical comparative research*, PhD thesis, University of Kent

Ali, Medhat (1997) *Introduction of Total Quality Management into a major Saudi multi-national:* PhD thesis, Bradford University

Burke W. Warner, (1998) *Organizational Development: A process of learning and changing*, New York: Addison-Wesley

Butterfield, Herbert (1965) *The Whig Interpretation of History*, New York: W. W. Norton

Dadfar, Hossein (1993) 'In search of Arab management, direction and identity', *Proceedings of the Arab Management Conference*, Bradford University

El Kharouf, A. E. L. (2000) *Factors Influencing the Employment of Women from the Point of View of Employed and Non-employed Women and Managers in Amman City,* Jordan: Unesco

Lee, Monica (1999) 'A refusal to define HRD', *Human Resource Development International*, 4(3): 327–343

Lewis, Bernard (2002) *What Went Wrong*, London: Weidenfeld and Nicholson

Mahfouz, Naguib (1992) *Palace Walks, Sugar Street, The Palace of Desire* ('The Cairo Trilogy'), New York: Anchor

Muna, Farid (1980) *The Arab Executive*, London: Macmillan

Naipaul, V.S. (1998) *Beyond Belief: Islamic excursions among the converted peoples*, New York: Little Brown

Peters, T. and Waterman, R. (1988) *In Search of Excellence: Lessons from America's best-run companies*, Warner Brothers

Rahman, Fazur (1979) *Islam:* Chicago: University of Chicago Press

Salman, H. K. (1996) *Case Studies in Palestinian Enterprise*, Villanova: Villanova University Press

Weir, David (2000a) 'Management in the Arab Middle East', in Tayeb, Monir, *International Business:* London: Prentice Hall, 501–509.

Weir, David (2000b) 'Management in the Arab World', in Warner, Malcolm, *Management in Emerging Countries*, London: Thomson Learning, 291–301

Weir, David (2000c) 'Management in the Arab World: A fourth paradigm?', in Al-Shamali, Ali and Denton, John, *Arab Business: The globalisation imperative*, London: Kogan Page, 60–76

Weir, David (2003) *Management in the Arab World*, London: Edward Elgar (forthcoming)

6   The ethics of HRD

Jim Stewart

> The difficult part in an argument is not to defend one's opinion, but rather to know it.
>
> (André Maurois, French author and critic, 'Thought for the day', *The Independent*, 12 April 2001)

Introduction

The quote given above suggests that holding and expressing an opinion is a complex matter. Since the purpose of this chapter is to do just that, the previous sentence justifies the chapter's inclusion in a book with this title. There is, though, an additional justification. The opinion I hold and wish to express here is that HRD is, in and of itself, an ethical endeavour. Put another way, I wish to argue that ethical questions are immanent in the practice of HRD. It will I think be accepted that ethical questions are indeed complex questions since they are prompted by and draw on the thinking of philosophers throughout the ages. So, if it is the case that ethical questions are immanent in HRD, and that those questions are complex, it follows that the ethical nature of HRD practice is a source of its complexity. It is because HRD is an ethical endeavour that it is also a complex endeavour. Or, perhaps more accurately, the ethical nature of HRD is one cause of its complexity.

The purpose of this chapter is, then, to demonstrate the truth and validity of the following proposition: 'Human resource development is, in and of itself, an ethical endeavour'.

A few words of explanation on the proposition will be helpful. The word 'endeavour' is chosen to mean 'effort towards a goal'. I am confident that most readers will grant the premise that this is characteristic of HRD. My understanding of the word 'ethical' is that it describes phenomena in which moral values are implicated and in which, therefore, moral choices have to be made. So, I do not use the word 'ethical' to mean moral or good. I use it to describe my view that the practice of HRD requires moral choices to be made.

The proposition represents the main opinion that I wish to express in this chapter. However, additional opinions will be hinted at if not fully argued. A logical approach to the argument will be to say something about HRD, and then something about ethics, and then to bring those together to demonstrate the truth and validity of the argument. Broadly speaking, that will be my approach. I will, though, be saying some things about ethics when the main focus of the discussion is HRD, and vice versa. I want to begin, though, with an additional argument, namely that the ethics of HRD is a neglected field of study, both in the HRD literature and in literature on business ethics.

A neglected field of study

I want to begin this section with a controversial opinion. It is simply that the study of business ethics is certainly wrong, at best confused and at worst just plain daft. My reasons for this opinion can be illustrated by two examples. The following is a quote from one of the early and still leading writers on the subject of business ethics: 'Business is driven by values. Some business values are commercial and technical . . . Often, the values are clearly moral values as when companies declare their policy to be "responsible".' Donaldson (1992: v). The implication of this argument is that it is possible to distinguish between moral and non-moral values in business and management. And, that commercial or technical issues and decisions have no moral dimension. It follows from this that commercial or technical decisions on sourcing manufacturing, for example in third world countries using child labour for less than subsistence wages, have no moral implications. Taken to a logical conclusion, such a position would also endorse working conditions which provide high risk to health, or even life, as similarly not needing to trouble the moral conscience of decision-makers. All of this follows from the view that pursuit of profit is the most fundamental of commercial values in business. According to Donaldson's argument and position, this is not a moral value and so morality need not enter the variables influencing decisions.

Donaldson's position is illustrative of the kind of thinking which leads the literature on business ethics to focus only on some aspects of business and management to the exclusion of others. My second example, from a more recent piece of work (Davies, 1997), is fairly typical of the kinds of issues addressed by the business ethics literature:

- sustainability
- corporate governance
- social responsibility
- whistle blowing.

In my view then, the basic confusion at the heart of current understandings of business ethics – a confusion which makes that understanding wrong and, on occasions, just plain daft – is to view the activities of business, and the decisions and actions of those who manage them, as separable into ethical and non-ethical issues. I personally find it impossible to conceive of any aspect of business and management which does not have a moral dimension. The confusion I see as arising from the opposite view may in part explain why Tom Sorell can make the following observation: 'Business ethics continues to have a marginal status in both the theory and the practice of commercial organisations at the end of the 1990s.' Sorell (1998: 15). According to the moral philosopher, Mary Midgley, who I will return to later, the same might be said of ethics itself as a field of study. It is not just business ethics that is marginalised. Midgley has this to say:

> For many highly educated people, in fact, ethics is enclosed today in a ghetto that shuts it off altogether from the rest of the intellectual scene.
>
> (Midgley 1996: 14)

The views expressed by Midgley and Sorell on ethics in general and business ethics in particular, both support my claim that the ethics of HRD is a neglected field of study. Turning to the specific case of HRD, further support is available. One of the most recent and influential pieces of work was done by Professor Jean Woodall and her colleague Danielle Douglas. They have this to say on the ethics of HRD:

> Training and development activities are perhaps the area of HRM policy and practice that is least likely to come under ethical scrutiny, invariably being presented as intrinsically 'good activities'.
>
> (Woodall and Douglas 2000: 116)

This suggests that the ethics of HRD is indeed a neglected topic. The quote implies a particular reason for that neglect. A conversation I had recently with a senior HRD practitioner suggests a different reason. He offered the following opinion: 'The ethics of HRD isn't it? There aren't any are there?'. When pressed, this practitioner elaborated by arguing that HRD served managerial purposes and therefore adopted whatever approaches or methods worked in particular circumstances without needing to consider ethical implications. These two quotes on the specific case of the ethics of HRD – one from an academic text and one from a practitioner – do, I think, support my claim on neglect, and also illustrate the confusion inherent in current understanding of the topic. Happily, that neglect is beginning to be addressed. I recently received a copy of a book by Tim Hatcher with the title *Ethics and HRD*. I am pleased to say that that book shares much common ground with this chapter.

The foundations of HRD

It is now time to return to the proposition. To demonstrate its truth and validity, I first have to establish what it is I mean by the term 'human resource development'. My starting point here is that there is no theory of HRD. This can easily be established by reference to two recent reviews of the literature of HRD. The first concentrated primarily on the US-based literature and reached the following conclusion:

Without a focus on the theoretical foundations of research and practice, HRD is destined to remain atheoretical in nature.

(Hatcher 2000 quoted in McGoldrick *et al.* 2002)

Working with Professor Jim McGoldrick and Sandra Watson from Napier University, I have recently completed a review of the literature which encompassed both US and European sources. The following two quotes come from that work:

[this] suggests that HRD has not established a distinctive conceptual or theoretical identity. (p. 7);

This variety of perspectives demonstrates vividly that there is no dominant paradigm of HRD research. (p. 4)

(McGoldrick, Stewart and Watson 2002)

As an aside, or hinting at another of my many opinions, it is of interest that we did the work for a book we have recently edited and completed. Following current practice in academia of maximising returns on investment, we have presented slightly different versions of the book chapter at two recent conferences. In each case, the conference papers have been selected for publication in special editions of journals. I could therefore have cited any one of five different sources for the two quotes. We might ask whether behaviour which results in five additions to the CV from one piece of work is ethical. The answer though would require a different chapter.

To reiterate, my main point is that there is no theory of HRD. I want to go further. In my view, there is no possibility of a theory of HRD, at least not in the sense that I understand the concept of theory. More importantly, I also believe that we do not need a theory of HRD, and for a very simple reason. As I intend to show later, HRD is concerned with influencing, some might say shaping, human behaviour. HRD therefore rests on theories which are concerned with understanding and explaining human behaviour. And we have quite enough of those without adding to that confusion!

To justify the previous assertion, I could at this point include an examination of theories of human behaviour by addressing the perennial 'nature versus nurture' debates, and in particular, attempts to produce a unifying theory in what is known as socio-biology. My reasons for adopting that focus are that I have read and been influenced by the science of ethology since the early 1970s, and I am a persuaded evolutionist as well as a social scientist. However, I do not have the space in a single chapter to do justice to those theories and debates. I do, though, want to mention briefly that I fail to be impressed by the latest attempt to unite biological and social explanations of human behaviour through what is termed evolutionary psychology, for two reasons. I am sceptical about either its power to unite the biological and social sciences or its validity in explaining human behaviour. First, it fails to unite biological and social theories since it gives dominance to the former over the latter. In fact, it does nothing to unite the disciplines since it simply provides biological explanations for social behaviour. This leads to my scepticism on its validity which rests on some of those explanations. According to evolutionary psychology, there are valid biological and evolutionary reasons why men do not do housework. It is not our fault, or even our choice apparently; it is genetically determined! Two other examples of male behaviour illustrate what is in my view the absurdity of these arguments. First, that the existence of the 'glass ceiling', which describes men denying women promotion opportunities, is actually the result of Darwinian evolution, and second that men raping women has its cause and explanation in the same process. I have both moral and intellectual reasons for rejecting such arguments, but I will leave readers to ponder what they might be as the chapter and argument develops.

As a long-standing amateur student of ethology, and convinced evolutionist as well as social scientist, I do support the principle and the possibility of a unifying theory of human behaviour. And there is one which I find persuasive, not least because it synthesises much of my own thinking and many of my opinions. The theory has been argued very cogently by Patrick Bateson and Paul Martin, and their argument is represented in Figure 6.1. A number of points need to be made about this diagram. First, it does not appear in the book by Bateson and Martin; it is my interpretation of their arguments. I may have misunderstood them, though if I have, I think my diagram is more valid than their arguments! Second, the diagram is meant to demonstrate a strong and interactive relationship of mutual influence between development and behaviour; a point of obvious significance to HRD. Third, both development and behaviour are influenced by biological factors which create both potentialities and limitations. Fourth, these potentialities and limitations of behaviour and development are influenced by experience of and in both physical and social environments. Fifth, factors unique to the individual organism also influence behaviour and development. Finally, in the case of human beings at least, these individual factors include agency; that is the exercise of choice and free will so that neither behaviour nor development is determined by either biological or environmental factors, nor exclusively by their interaction. Individuals are active agents in their development and behaviour.

I can illustrate these arguments with the simple example of my height. The reason I am five feet five inches tall is because of the complex interaction of the factors in Figure 6.1. Biologically, I was destined to be never less than say four feet eleven inches and never more than say five feet nine inches tall when fully grown. The physical environment influenced my growth through the living conditions, including the availability of food of varying types, I experienced during the development of my height. Of those available, the choice of food I actually consumed was influenced by those in my social environment – parents, siblings, peers, for example. So too were the forms of physical exercise I chose to engage in, or not. In the end, I exercised some choice on food consumed and exercise undertaken and so I exercised agency. All of which lead to me arriving at five feet five inches. My height is an example of physical development. It illustrates,

A developmental biology view of human behaviour

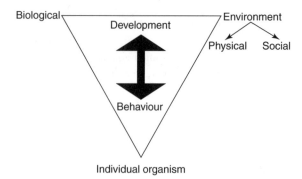

Figure 6.1 An interpretation of Patrick Bateson and Paul Martin (2000) 'Design for a life: how behaviour develops'.

though, that even this aspect of development is influenced by behaviour and agency. Bateson and Martin make the point thus:

> In reality, developing organisms are dynamic systems that play an active role in their own development.
>
> (Bateson and Martin 2000: 238)

This point has obvious implications for ethics. Without agency, the notion of ethics has no meaning or value. Bateson and Martin make an additional important point for my overall argument. It is that, for human beings at least, learning is a critical factor in influencing development and behaviour. And, that learning is both a biological and social phenomenon. They have this to say about learning:

> It seems likely that the initial rules for learning are themselves unlearned, universal and are the product of Darwinian evolution.
>
> (Bateson and Martin 2000: 76)

> Behaviour, in particular, becomes adapted to local conditions during the course of an individual's development, whether through learning by trial and error or through copying others.
>
> (Bateson and Martin 2000: 8)

These two quotes suggest a biological propensity to learn through a process which depends on experiences in a physical and social environment, and which has social outcomes in the form of individual behaviour. This has obvious significance and implications for HRD.

A model of HRD

I have argued so far that HRD is concerned with human behaviour and that developmental biology provides the best understanding of human behaviour that we have to inform the practice of HRD. It is now time to be more precise about what I mean when I use the term 'HRD'. I developed a model of HRD in the early 1990s. Since then, I have discussed the model with many colleagues and students, and I have received many comments and suggestions. So far though, I have not had reason to change the model. It follows from and is based on the following definition.

> Human resource development encompasses activities and processes which are *intended* to have impact on organisational and individual learning. The term assumes that organisations can be constructively conceived of as learning entities, and that the learning process of both organisations and individuals are capable of influence and direction through deliberate and *planned interventions*. Thus, HRD is constituted by planned interventions in organisational and individual *learning processes*.
>
> (Stewart 1999: 17)

Three points arise from the definition. First, the last sentence contains the essence of the definition. Second, the highlighted words are critical. Interventions abound in everyday experience, but only those which are intended, deliberate and planned constitute HRD practice or processes. Third, there are two key components of HRD practice: interventions and learning processes. The resulting model is shown in Figure 6. 2.

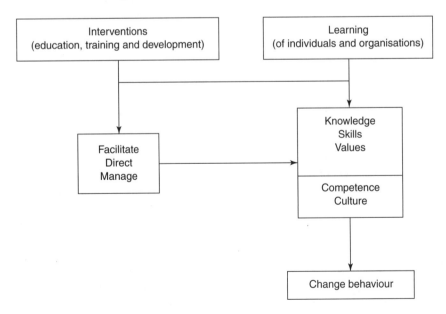

Figure 6.2 A model of HRD.

Some explanation of the model is necessary. There is no direct connection between interventions and learning because there is no necessary and certainly no causal relationship, which a direct connection might suggest. For human beings, learning is a biological imperative and we learn naturally in the same sense as we breathe naturally; we are born to do so. Moving down the right side of the model, both biological and social understandings would support the view that learning is an influencing factor on behaviour. I do not believe, and nor do I wish to claim, that behaviour is linked in a direct causal relationship with learning. But, I do believe and claim that learning is a significant influencing factor.

Turning to the left side of the model, it suggests that interventions constitute HRD practice. Various labels are used to categorise different types of intervention. Here, despite my view that debates on defining different categories are often sterile and of no value, (see Stewart, 1999) three commonly recognised categories of education, training and development are used. I use these simply because the categories *are* commonly used and understood, a point which can be illustrated by two examples of applying the first two categories. First, if I require an operation then I would much prefer a trained surgeon to an educated surgeon. Second, I am very happy for my child to receive sex education in school, but there is no way I am going to approve of sex training! These amusing (hopefully!) illustrations conceal the problem of distinguishing the categories, a point reinforced by the lack of such an illustration for development.

While the focus of interventions is learning processes, they serve three separate but related purposes. First, they serve to facilitate learning. This simply means to make the particular content of learning more likely and easier than it would be otherwise. Second, they serve to direct learning to achieve particular and specified outcomes rather than others. Third, they serve to manage the resources allocated to facilitating and directing to achieve efficient and effective utilisation. It is recognised that these purposes suggest a performative orientation for HRD. However, in my view, this does not necessarily equate with performance objectives in organisations.

What links interventions and learning are the mediating factors specified in the centre of the right side of the model. Within HRD practice, these factors are seen to be the outcomes of learning which, in turn and in part, influence behaviour. At the individual level, these factors are referred to as knowledge, skills and values, or, sometimes, attitudes. At the organisational level, the notion of competence encompasses knowledge and skills while the concept of culture stands for attitudes or values. These distinctions – between knowledge, skills and values, or between competence and culture – are, as we will see later, of the same form as the categories of interventions. That is, they are analytical devices with some useful applications rather than representations of any true or experienced reality. One of the useful applications is to allow me to express another of my opinions.

The traditional focus of learning in higher education has been and remains subject knowledge. That has and does provide the content of learning. Over the last ten years or so, there has been a growing emphasis on skills of various forms, especially those related to what is termed 'employability'. Currently, we who work in higher education are required to specify our intended learning outcomes in terms of both subject knowledge and a range of skills sets. It has always struck me as strange that little attention is either demanded or paid to values. Certainly at the levels of modules, courses and programmes almost no debate occurs on the values that the learning experiences actually develop, or might aim to develop, in students. Unlike knowledge and skills, we are not required to identify or specify attitudinal or value outcomes in our descriptors. I find this situation more than a little worrying.

To return to the model, the box at the very bottom right provides the ultimate rationale for HRD practice. This is simply to change behaviour. The purpose of HRD practice is to take an individual or collection of individuals with an existing set of behaviours through a planned learning experience, so that those behaviours are changed. This is as true of higher education as it is of practice in employing organisations. Changed behaviour is the success criteria of HRD. Or, perhaps more accurately, an increased range of behavioural options and choices.

The previous sentence has, for me, ethical echoes, which I hope are apparent to readers. The echoes also signal that it is now time to turn our attention to the subject of ethics.

The nature of ethics

Bowie and Duska succinctly express the fundamental focus and purpose of ethics. 'Ethics . . . is a study that attempts to shed light on the question "What should one do?".' Bowie and Duska (1990: 3). While these authors provide a useful summary of the focus and purpose of ethics, they go on mistakenly to create a distinction between serious and non-serious questions and issues which have, according to them, serious or non-serious consequences. The notions of 'serious' and 'non-serious' consequences are of course problematic. This can be illustrated by the example given by Bowie and Duska, an example which in my view also illustrates their mistake. '... not putting oil in one's car ... will not have serious consequences.' Ibid. The consequences of not putting oil in a car will include the car itself becoming scrap and therefore a waste of the earth's resources, and the adding to of physical waste which has to be dealt with in ways which add to environmental problems. As with issues in business ethics, I find it difficult to conceive of questions or issues which do not have 'serious con-sequences', and so I would argue that the question, 'What should one do?' does not require any qualification.

Apart from the issue of identifying issues that matter and issues that do not, the most vexed question in ethics is perhaps whether or not there are universal answers, in the form of 'natural law', to the question 'What should one do?' My position is that there are indeed universal answers which are, literally, based on natural law. The form of that natural law is very well expressed by Andrew Brown. 'Humans are naturally idealistic and altruistic among many other, some-times contradictory, things.' Andrew Brown (1999: 79). Brown's use of the word and concept of 'natural' is the same as that used previously by me in relation to learning; behaving in an idealistic and altruistic manner is, for human beings among some other animals, a biological imperative. He reaches his conclusion based on a review of debates in evolutionary biology. This position is also argued very persuasively by the moral philosopher Philippa Foot in her book *Natural Goodness*, and so it has both scientific and philosophical credibility. The implication is that the natural law determining what is ethical, in the sense of being 'right' or 'good', is behaving in an idealistic and altruistic manner. Brown's quote implies, though, that we, as human beings, are also naturally the opposite of idealistic and altruistic; we are also materialistic and selfish. But, without that contradiction and the existence of agency, there would be no possibility of choice, and therefore the question posed by Bowie and Duska as the central focus of ethics would not arise. Nor would there be the need for any natural law to guide answers to the question.

The position suggested by Brown and argued by Foot finds support in the work of the ethicist, Timothy Gorringe. Gorringe relates ethics to the meaning and value of life which, according to Brown and to Foot, must in part have a biological answer. He then goes on to argue the following.

> We, as humans, are fundamentally concerned with what is life conserving. ... what it is that promotes human well being, ... that makes for joy, creativity, security, the flourishing of love and happiness ... Whatever promotes all these things is good; whatever destroys them is bad. Therein lies our ethics, our morality, and the foundations of what we call social justice.
>
> (Gorringe 1999: 9)

It is clear from this quote that Gorringe is arguing universal answers and a natural law. If we accept that by 'fundamentally' Gorringe means 'natural' in the same sense that Brown and Foot use the term, then Gorringe too is making the same case in relation to a biological imperative towards idealistic and altruistic behaviour as the basis of the natural law. Gorringe calls on support from what may seem a strange authority in this context when he cites Hayek. 'Hayek recognises that the altruistic virtues are deeply ingrained, perhaps innate.' Gorringe (1999: 19).

As with Brown and, in particular, Foot, Gorringe relies on the view that human beings are social animals as the basis for arguing the centrality of altruism to ethical questions.

> Sociological and psychological studies, however, seem to confirm Aristotle's view that we are indeed community animals. We are not 'individuals' but persons in relation to each other. The only absolutely 'individual' thing about us is a corpse.
>
> (Gorringe 1999: 31)

Interestingly, what we have in this quote is a philosopher using the social sciences to support a position argued by the natural sciences. We can add the words of another scholar and writer to provide further support to the argument. Umberto Eco (Eco 2001) argues the existence of what he refers to as 'universal semantics'. These might be referred to as 'natural understanding' if not 'natural laws'. However, Eco goes on to argue that these universal semantics provide the basis for a 'natural' ethical system. And, he further argues that the social nature of human beings is at the centre of that ethical system. This is apparent in the following quote.

> ... and the ethical dimension comes into play when the other arrives on the scene. ... Just as we couldn't live without eating or sleeping, we cannot understand who we are without the gaze and reaction of the other.
>
> (Eco and Martini 2000: 93–4)

According to the moral philosopher Mary Midgley, Darwin himself argued a position very similar to that of Gorringe. Midgley's summary of Darwin's argument is presented in Figure 6.3. The word 'natural' is used here as I have used it consistently in this chapter. Darwin argued that the list of characteristics on the left is part of our biological make-up and heritage. These biological characteristics find corresponding cultural expression through the activities and aspects of social life listed on the right. But, as Midgley points out and as Brown implied, Darwin suggested additional biological characteristics, especially in relation to social motives. We are altruistic but we are also selfish. We do cooperate but we also compete. This creates conflicts and the need for choices to be made. As the following quote illustrates, Midgley argues that without those conflicts there is no choice and therefore no need for ethics.

> It is the conflicts which give rise to the need for rules and priorities, and therefore for morality.
>
> (Midgley 1996: 98)

Midgley's analysis and argument supports that of Bateson and Martin; biological imperatives do not deny the existence and role of human agency. For Midgely, agency is the basis of freedom. And it is the freedom to choose that creates both the need for and the focus of ethics. So, what choices are faced in HRD practice and what can guide them?

Natural curiosity	maths and science
Natural wonder and admiration	art
Natural amusability	jokes
Natural social motives (sociability)	morals

Figure 6.3 Darwin's contribution. Based on Mary Midgley (1996) op. cit.

Implications of ethics for HRD

In this final part of the chapter I want to examine the connections between ethics and HRD. I think there are three important implications for HRD that arise out of what I have said about ethics. The first is fairly obvious. If the rationale, purpose and success criteria of HRD is changed behaviour, two sets of questions need answering. What is the desired or required behaviour? How will current behaviour be changed? Application of these questions illustrates their significance and ethical nature. As students, are we content to leave those decisions to others? As parents, are we happy to allow others to decide what and how the behaviour of our children will be changed? As employees, are we willing to follow blindly the paths determined by our employers? I think and hope not. And, if not, why not? I suggest the reason is that we instinctively (a deliberate choice of word) recognise the essentially moral nature of the questions and the moral implications of the answers. Sadly, the questions are not often or readily posed in the form I have framed them here. This can just as often and readily lead to unethical answers. As Timothy Gorringe observes in relation to the final of my three examples – employers and employees – managerialism is the ethic of manipulation.

The second implication arises from the distinctions drawn between knowledge, skills and values. I argued in my first book, published in 1991, that the distinction is a useful analytical device rather than an accurate representation of reality. The concepts themselves can be related to psychological theory which distinguishes three domains of experience, as illustrated in Figure 6.4.

Knowledge	Cognitive domain	'We think'
Values	Affective domain	'We feel'
Skills	Action domain	'We do'

Figure 6.4. Psychological domains of experience. Based on Stewart (1996).

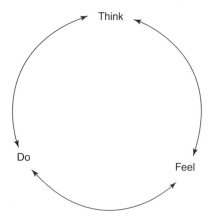

Figure 6.5 Circle of being.

The domains of experience, and the distinctions between knowledge, skills and values, imply that 'we think, feel and do' separately. In my view, this is inaccurate and misleading. We actually experience all three at the same time and do not ourselves, in our lived experience, draw those distinctions. And, not only do we 'think, feel and do' all at the same time, but it follows logically that our thoughts, feelings and actions are mutually immanent. This argument is represented in the model in Figure 6.5.

What follows from Figure 6.5 is that any and all HRD interventions will have an impact on values. It is irrelevant that the intended purpose is merely to pass on knowledge; and a lecture, for example, is a common means for achieving that kind of intended purpose. Since the supposed distinction and separation of knowledge, skills and values do not reflect or represent the reality of lived experience, it is not possible to design or conduct an intervention that is value free or neutral. Therefore, HRD always has impact on values and, consequently, always has an ethical content and dimension. The premise which supports this argument – that knowledge, skills and values are mutually immanent – finds support in the work of two authors I have cited already, as the following quotes illustrate:

> The behaviour of brain-damaged patients reveals how crucial the emotions are in real-life decision-making.
>
> (Bateson and Martin 2000: 243)

> Communication [which] is, among animals as opposed to machines, always an emotional as well as an intellectual business.
>
> (Midgley 1996: 138)

We now turn to the third and final implication. It concerns the nature of interventions. Intervention is an interesting word and concept. It is used, I believe, to hide the real implications of what it means to 'intervene'. *The Oxford English Dictionary* uses the word 'intervene' to define 'interfere', and vice versa, (see Box 6.1).

Box 6.1 Definitions of 'intervention' and 'interfere'

'*Intervention*'
Interference, especially
by a state in another's affairs

'*Interfere*'
Meddle, obstruct a process. Take part
or intervene, especially without
invitation or necessity

Oxford English Dictionary

We might with some confidence conclude from these definitions that the words 'intervene' and 'interfere' are synonyms. But, if I say that I am, as an HRD practitioner interfering with the learning of others, rather than intervening, your response will be quite different. Something seems not quite as it should be. You 'feel' differently about me, about yourselves and about what is happening within my HRD practice. Using the language of Bateson and Martin, non-conscious responses have a greater impact on conscious and rational analysis, and they more quickly enter conscious awareness. Why is that? I would argue it is again an 'instinctive' stirring because of the ethical nature of HRD practice. The simple question, 'By what right does one person interfere with the learning of others?' highlights the ethical dilemma inherent in HRD practice. Generating the question by using the word 'interfere' also, I would argue, supports the view that morality is a central component of the human condition. Your, indeed our, response to the word is, in that sense, entirely 'natural'.

One final observation on the word 'intervention'. It is commonly used in the medical profession. That profession pays significant attention to its ethics. Perhaps they recognise the connection with interfere. HRD practice, though, is still faced with the question 'what should one do?'.

A categorical imperative

I have so far attempted to show how things are in relation to HRD and ethics, and the connections between them. Assuming some success in that task, does describing how things are allow me to argue how things should be? According to enlightenment thinkers such as David Hume, the answer to that question is a straightforward 'no'. We cannot make statements on how things should be based on how things are. This rests on the distinction drawn between empirical and normative statements. What I have argued so far should suggest that I have problems accepting that distinction and, therefore, the logical conclusion that follows from it. In other words, Hume was and is wrong. Mary Midgley agrees with that statement. So too does Timothy Gorringe, who has this to say on the subject:

> This distinction [between positive and normative studies] was specious from the start because the distinction between positive and normative science itself represents a value judgement. (p. 44)

> … fact and value belong together, and not only can we derive an 'ought' from an 'is', but we can also derive a categorical imperative from the way things are.
>
> (Gorringe 1999: 59)

My earlier argument on the immanent nature of knowledge, skills and values supports the position so forcefully argued by Gorringe. Taking support and permission from Gorringe's position, I now want to offer a categorical imperative for HRD practice and practitioners. And, it is important to note that I continue to include academics working in higher education, in any and all subjects and disciplines, in my definition of HRD practitioners.

The categorical imperative follows, I believe, from the arguments I have presented in this chapter. It is, though, also based on an insight from Mary Midgley that I hope many readers will agree with. Midgley writes the following in her book:

> Our unity as individuals is not something given. It is a continuing, lifelong pro-
> ject, an effort constantly undertaken in the face of endless disintegrating forces.
> (Midgley 1996: 23)

Midgley is referring to the sense of self, to personal identity. Supporting the constant struggle to maintain that sense and identity is, I think, promoted by the
values of cooperation and altruism. This is the basis of the categorical imperative
I want to promote for HRD. It is put very well by Bateson and Martin.

> The best gift that can be given to a child is the happiness that comes from
> being able to cope successfully in a complex world. (2000: 254)

If we substitute the word 'child' with the word 'person' we have, nearly, a categorical imperative for HRD. The practice of HRD ought to serve the purpose
suggested in Bateson and Martin's words. It can best achieve that purpose by promoting the qualities listed by Gorringe – joy, creativity, security, etc. – which, in
turn, are more likely if the idealism and altruism identified by Brown are also promoted by and through HRD practice.

There is, though, a limitation to the imperative as it stands. Coping successfully
in a complex world is a valuable and worthwhile aspiration. But, as we have seen,
HRD is about change. And, as we have also seen, humans have the gifts of freedom and agency. As Karl Marx advised, it is not enough to understand the world;
the point is to change it. So, any final categorical imperative for HRD will not
only reflect the sentiments in the quote from Bateson and Martin, it will also
embrace changing as well as coping with the world.

A syllogism and a closing

I want to close the chapter with a final argument in support of my original proposition. The argument is in the form of a syllogism. To be valid, a syllogism has to have
a logical construction. I am confident it has, but readers can also judge. To be true,
a syllogism has to have premises which are true. I rely on the authority of Watson
for the truth of the first premise, and on the work of two major writers on HRD for
the truth of the second premise. The work and status of all three mean that we can
accept the premises as being true with, as they say in Australia and increasingly here
in the UK, 'no worries'. The syllogism is given in Box 6.2 on page 98.

I had the honour of writing the first ever 'Soapbox' article in the first issue of
the journal *Human Resource Development International* (HRD1). That article addressed
the same topic as this chapter and presented different and additional arguments
on the same proposition. My intention in that article was to stimulate and provoke
debate. This chapter has a similar purpose. If I have demonstrated the truth and
validity of the proposition, it does not follow that I believe or claim to have provided the last word on the subject. I do believe that the ethics of HRD contributes
significantly to its complexity, and to the complexity of the world in which HRD
operates. For that reason, much more work is required. Tim Hatcher's book and

his chapter in this volume are welcome, timely and important contributions. My hope is that Tim's work, and this chapter, will be more effective in stimulating and provoking others than was my Soapbox in *HRDI*.

Box 6.2 Syllogism

'Organising and managing are, through and through, ethical and moral endeavours.'
(Tony Watson 1994, 1998)

'Human resource development is an organising and managing function.'
(Rosemary Harrison, 1998, John Walton, 1999)

'HRD is an ethical and moral endeavour'

(QED)

References

Bateson, P. and Martin, P. (2000) *Design for a Life: How behaviour develops*, London: Vintage

Bowie, N. E. and Duska, R. F. (1990) *Business Ethics*, 2nd edition, Englewood Cliffe: Prentice Hall, Inc.

Brown, A. (1999) *The Darwin Wars: The scientific battle for the soul of man*, London: Simon and Schuster

Davies, P. (1997) *Current Issues in Business Ethics*, London: Routledge

Donaldson, J. (1992) *Business Ethics: A European Casebook*, London: Academic Press Limited

Eco, U. (2000) 'Ethics are born in the presence of the other', in Eco, U. and Martini, C. M., *Belief or Non Belief: A confrontation*, New York: Arcade Publishing, Inc.

Eco, U. and Martini, C. (2000) *Belief or Non-Belief: A confrontation*, trans. Proctor, M., New York: Arcadian Publishing

Foot, P. (2001) *Natural Goodness*, Oxford: Oxford University Press

Gorringe, T. (1999) *Fair Shares: Ethics and the global economy*, London: Thames and Hudson

Harrison, R. (1998) *Employee Development*, London: CIPD

Hatcher, T. (2002) *Ethics and HRD: A new approach to leading responsible organisations*, Cambridge, MA: Persens Publishing

McGoldrick, J., Stewart, J. and Watson, S. (2002) 'Researching HRD: Philosophy, process and practice', in McGoldrick, J. *et al.*, *Understanding HRD: A research-based approach*, London: Routledge

Midgley, M. (1996) *The Ethical Primate: Humans, freedom and morality*, London: Routledge

Sorell, T. (1998) 'Beyond the Fringe? The strange state of business ethics', in Parker, M. (Ed.), *Ethics and Organisations*, London: Sage Publications

Stewart, J. (1991) *Managing Change Through Training and Development*, London: Kogan Page

Stewart, J. (1996) *Managing Change Through Training and Development*, 2nd edition, London: Kogan Page

Stewart, J. (1999) *Employee Development Practice*, London: FT Pitman Publishing

Walton, J. (1999) *Strategic Human Resource Development*, Harlow: FT Prentice Hall

Watson, T. (1994) *In Search of Management*, London: Routledge

Watson T. (1998) 'Ethical codes and moral communities: the Gunlaw Temptation, the Simon Solution and the David Dilemma', in Parker, M. (Ed.), *Ethics and Organisations*, London: Sage Publications

Woodall, J. and Douglas, D. (2000) 'Winning hearts and minds: Ethical issues in human resource development', in Winstanley, D. and Woodall, J. (Eds) *Ethical Issues in Contemporary Human Resource Management*, Basingstoke: Macmillan Business

7 Reconciling autonomy and community

The paradoxical role of HRD

Carole Elliott and Sharon Turnbull

Introduction

The stimulus for this chapter arises from a particular set of demands that we see confronting practitioners and theorists of HRD in the late twentieth/early twenty-first century. Our purpose is to examine whether or how these demands might be reconciled, and how we might better understand and practice HRD in the light of these competing realities/claims on the self. The wider notions of individuality and community, and the changes in social and communal relationships that are shaping organisational practices have arguably not been sufficiently addressed within HRD. Our aim is to open a debate that will help us to make sense of these contradictory tensions in HRD. Our secondary purpose is to encourage a more interdisciplinary form of HRD research that extends its exploratory and explanatory reach.

In many ways the tensions faced by those who align themselves to HRD in its Anglo-American manifestation do not differ significantly from those that have faced organisations since the end of World War II. In this chapter we focus particularly on the long-standing lament by communitarians that the modernist obsession with autonomy, freedom and the self has damaged the traditional values of community which, they suggest, once existed in pre-modern and pre-capitalist times. This tension has underpinned much HRD theory and practice since (at least) the appropriation by organisations of the socio-psychological theories of the human relations movement to increase employee motivation, and hence productivity. However, as we will highlight below, it is now becoming exacerbated as it is set against a social backdrop of fragmentation, instability, blurred boundaries and constantly shifting identities that characterises postmodern times.

In order to expose this tension – the struggle between individual and organisational needs – we focus on two more recent bodies of literature that we see as illustrative of this conflict. In presenting and examining these bodies of literature we wish to draw attention to their ontological and epistemological bases, in order to demonstrate the generally unseen dilemmas that face practitioners and theoreticians of HRD. In so doing we are following a sociological tradition that associates the changing nature of work practices with broader movements in social relations.

We will ask how HRD might respond to the growing demands within organisations to strike a balance between a performative orientation (that has arguably been dominant in organisations over the last two decades), and the call of authors such as Chalofsky (2000, 2001) for organisations to take into account individuals' needs to discover potential meaning through work. Is the answer to come from a new wave of gurus (pun intended) that advocate the 'spiritually-based firm' (Wager-Marsh and Conley, 1999), or is it to come from envisioning the organisation as a community in itself where the behaviours of organisational citizens reciprocally advantage fellow citizens and the productivity of the organisation? (Organ, 1988.)

The bodies of literature that we will discuss are placed under the broad banners of 'autonomy' and 'community'. Our interest in these sets of literature arises from concern around the ways in which we see these concepts being inappropriately instrumentalised within organisations. Both the literature on autonomy and community might be seen as characteristic of the contemporary western (or at least Anglo-American) *Zeitgeist*, and so it seems timely to consider the socio-cultural system in which they are located, and the ways in which HRD might respond to them.

Our examination of these literatures (that have grown enormously over recent years) suggests that the twin quests which seem to be struggling for domination are a purported search for meaning through work, alongside the search by organisations for employees who are committed to ensuring the organisation's survival in a free-market economy. And we must not forget the context within which talk of individuals' search for meaning, and envisioning the organisation as community, takes place. New technologies, the demise of large-scale industrial manufacturing, the growth of the service industry and the reshaping of organisations have all led to a blurring of boundaries between and within organisations, and to what we see as unacknowledged ambiguity and confusion in the workplace. No longer, it seems, can employees rely on a clear identity and sense of place in the hierarchy. Anthony has referred to a 'managerial schizophrenia' (1994, p. 79), which, he says, may result when corporate rhetoric directly conflicts with first-hand experience. Heelas and Morris (1992) attribute this phenomenon to the 'enterprise culture', which, they suggest, began to dominate western society in the 1980s.

Employees are constantly bombarded with ambiguous messages. On the one hand they are entreated to maximise their individual performance through life-long learning, be innovative and creative in their roles, and develop their leadership qualities. More recently, on the other hand, they are being encouraged to subscribe to their organisation's values (and hence to subordinate their individuality), to work towards the organisation's vision and mission, and to be good corporate citizens.

There is obvious conflict between these demands that illustrates the struggle to reconcile the needs of the individual with those of the collective.[1]

Martin suggests that the fragmentation of organisations today is often overlooked by organisational practitioners, business school academics and consultants. This perspective focuses on 'ambiguity, complexity of relationships among manifestations, and a multiplicity of interpretations that do not coalesce into a stable consensus' (1992, p.130). Her view supports Watson's view of organisation as 'a temporary and fraught coalition of coalitions which can only ever be held together by constantly negotiated agreements and understandings' (1994, p.111).

The implications this raises for HRD in today's organisations are significant. The connecting theme of the chapter is to expose the ontological assumptions that are influencing an emphasis on either the individual or on the collective, on either performance or on learning. We argue that it is vital that HRD practitioners and theorists are at least cognisant of these ostensibly dialectical forces within late twentieth/early twenty-first century organisational forms. In other words, we are returning to the hoary old issue of the purposes of HRD.

Having now set out our stall, we shall present findings of a literature review that focuses on the discourses contained in the contemporary 'autonomy' and 'community' literature. In the final discussion section we will then examine the potential implications of these discourses for practitioners in today's organisations. Before we do that, however, we will move beyond the confines of work organisations to look more broadly at the roots of the contemporary socio-ideological milieu. This will be our first step on a path that we hope will lead us towards making some sense of the dilemmas faced by HRD in today's organisations.

'Individualisation' and the autonomous self

The tension between the construction of the self as *impulsive* and autonomous and the alternative self as communitarian and *institutional* has been attributed by Turner (1976)[2] to the human reflexive process. He suggests that this sense of self directly reflects the social structure of the time and 'to varying degrees, people accept as evidence of their real selves either feelings and actions with an *institutional* focus or ones they identify strictly as *impulse*' (p. 991). The *institutional* view of the self sees the *real self* being revealed when an individual achieves a high standard in pursuit of institutional goals, and remains in full control of their faculties, behaviours and feelings. The *self* is something to be 'attained, created, achieved' and hypocrisy consists of failing to live up to one's standards. This, he suggests, is evidenced in Shakespeare's plays in which 'the true self is formed in self mastery' (ibid., p. 991). Turner claims that recent decades however, have seen a marked shift in western society away from the previously popular *institutional* self toward the *impulsive self:*

> institutional motivations are external, artificial constraints and superimpositions that bridle manifestations of the real self. One plays the institutional game when he must, but only at the expense of the true self. The true self consists of deep, unsocialised, inner impulses. Mad desire and errant fancy are exquisite expressions of self.
>
> (ibid.: 993)

The distinction between these two interpretations of self is an important one for our debate around autonomy and community in HRD. Whilst today's organisational rhetoric contains much talk of community, the underlying values and beliefs of both managers and employees, as reflected in the theories and practices of HRD, appear to reflect the current leaning towards the view that the self is free and impulsive, as we see in, for example, empowerment, self-directed learning, self-managed teams, and a strong emphasis on individual career management.[3]

Turner posits some explanations for this. He argues that reliance on institutional frameworks for self-identity is more likely when the 'dependability of that framework makes the world predictable' (ibid.: 1,005). Clearly, the institutional frameworks in which individuals find themselves today are not characterised by order and dependability. The sociologist Zygmunt Bauman in his book entitled *Liquid Modernity* makes a compelling case for the disorder of today's society:

> These days patterns and configurations are no longer 'given', let alone 'self-evident'; there are just too many of them clashing with one another and contradicting one another's commandments, so that each one has been stripped of a good deal of compelling, coercively constraining powers ... Ours is as a result, an individualized, privatised version of modernity, with the burden of pattern-weaving and the responsibility for failure falling primarily on the individual's shoulders. It is the patterns of dependency and interaction whose turn to be liquefied has now come.
>
> (Bauman, 2000b: 7–8)

Instability and the fast pace of change, therefore, make it difficult for individuals to define their sense of self as being rooted in their institutional identities, or to find fulfilment in institutional participation.

An alternative view of the self as discursively constituted, is presented by Rose (1989), who takes a Foucauldian perspective to argue that the focus on the autonomous self is constituted in the overriding social discourse of today's society:

> The self is to be a subjective being, it is to aspire to autonomy, it is to strive for personal fulfilment in its earthly life, it is to interpret reality and destiny as a matter of individual responsibility, it is to find meaning in existence by shaping its life through acts of choice.
>
> (Rose, 1989: 151)

The need to find 'meaning in existence' that is characteristic of the late twentieth century self, described by Rose, suggests that each self lacks something, that it is empty. Cushman (1990) proposes a link between this post-War 'empty' self and the wider political economy that perhaps helps to begin to illuminate the struggles and tensions experienced between individuals and organisations. He argues that it is no coincidence that a society that has seen the rise of the empty self has concurrently witnessed a shift from the savings economy of the early part of the century to the post-World War II debtor economy. This shift:

is a consequence of how the modern nation state must currently regulate its economy and control its populace: not through direct physical coercion, but rather through the construction of the empty self and the manipulation of its needs to consume and ingest.

(Cushman, 1990, p. 608)

Empirical studies by Du Gay (1996) and Casey (1995) have demonstrated that within the work organisation this need takes the form of individual consumption of self-improvement strategies, either through shaping one's identity into an entrepreneurial self or as consumers (willingly or otherwise) of the latest management fad.

The implications of this focus on the self (e.g. through strategies of self-development, self-assessment, self-motivation, individual career planning etc.) for HRD are wide ranging, but become more complex when set against an increasingly popular ideology of community. Over the last twenty years the ways in which individuals' everyday working lives are regulated and governed have focussed increasingly on them as individuals. Before even becoming an employee individuals are psychometrically assessed to test their organisational 'fit'. They then face a panoply of schemes, such as personal development plans, appraisals, or 360-degree feedback, to ensure they develop in a way that is beneficial to the organisation. Performance schemes and bonuses are also calculated on individual performance.

Confusingly, running parallel to this has been the focus on teams. These micro-communities, or communities within communities, are a constituting element of the 're-engineered' and 'lean' organisation operating within a 'just-in-time' method of production. The individual employee is therefore both asked to work within a team, but is then treated as an individual when it comes to their recruitment, development and remuneration. Employees are effectively being encouraged to believe in their potential to 'stage manage' (Beck and Beck-Gernsheim, 1996: 27) their lives to ensure their individuality, thus demonstrating how they 'add value', whilst simultaneously being asked to interact with others to create the goods or services that constitute the organisation's products.

These wider notions of community, and the changes in social and communal relationships that are shaping these sorts of organisational practices, have arguably not been sufficiently addressed within HRD, so in the following section we open a debate which will help us to make sense of these contradictory tensions in HRD.

The quest for community and tensions with autonomy

Bauman (2000a) points to a desire for both freedom *and* security as 'indispensable' human needs, which can rarely be fully reconciled without friction. Being in a community, he suggests, inevitably reduces freedom, yet losing community also means losing security.

One of the central features of communalism, says Bauman, is fraternal obligation, making it a 'philosophy of the weak' which appeals to those not able to practice individuality, i.e. those for whom the support of one's neighbours and the immediate collectivity is a prerequisite for survival, since they do not have sufficient independent resources for survival outside of their community. Conversely, he suggests, community is unattractive to those powerful and wealthy enough not to need to sacrifice individuality for communal obligation. This distinction may be seen in organisations where those working at the lower levels of the organisational hierarchy have traditionally organised themselves for purposes of industrial bargaining through trade union membership. Managers, on the other hand, with their greater positional power have traditionally preferred to negotiate individually according to their perceived worth.

Bauman confirms the fragility of the concept of community in today's organisations:

> After the era of great engagement the times of great disengagement have arrived. The times of high speed and acceleration, shrinking terms of commitment, of 'flexibility', 'downsizing' and 'outsourcing'. The times of staying together only 'until further notice' and as long (never longer) as satisfaction lasts.
>
> (Bauman, 2000a: 41)

This fragility is also exemplified, he suggests, by a love of heroes (e.g. sports personalities, models, television personalities, musicians, film stars) in modern society. These heroes provide a sense of belonging, and 'conjure up the experience of community without real community, the joy of belonging without the discomfort of being bound' (Bauman, 2000a: 69). This tendency to hero worship can also be found inside organisations, in which great leaders (past and present) are often felt to bind employees together in a common purpose.

Few commentators on 'community' have specifically related it to HRD. Reynolds (2000) is the exception, as he seeks to incorporate notions of community into pedagogical approaches to management development. Reynolds found, however, that the romantic attraction of community often camouflages a darker side that ignores asymmetries of power (Fielding, 1997) and sometimes even oppresses in exerting 'a compelling pressure towards conformism' (Giddens, 1994: 126). Furthermore, he asserts, one of the major critiques of the concept, particularly highlighted by post-modern analysis is in its denial of difference (Usher, 1992). In considering alternative pedagogies of management education, Reynolds concludes that most of these apparently emancipatory methods 'reflect utopian values based on consensus and an idealized vision of equality which engenders pressures to conform' (Reynolds, 2000: 78).

We believe that the paradox identified by both Reynolds (2000) and Legge (1999) lies at the heart of the wider question of HRD beliefs, values and moral codes, and may contain an explanation for the apparently irreconcilable differences we sometimes find in debating our desire to encourage the development, and to 'maximize the potential' of individuals, at the same time as to consider the health and moral basis of the organisations themselves. (Kuchinke, 2000a and b; Holton, 2000; Torraco and Swanson, 1995, Ruona and Roth, 2000.)

In the next sections we explore two relatively new discourses of citizenship and spirituality which are growing in popularity, and which, we suggest, may offer alternative ways to reconcile the tension between autonomy and community.

Organisational citizenship behaviour – participative democracy in organisations?

Some scholars have suggested that it is the intensification of individualism combined with the rise of the 'enterprise culture' (Du Gay, 1996; Heelas and Morris, 1992; Goss, 1996; Rose, 1989) that has led to a loss of community. Morris (1996), for example, notes that the 'selfishness' of modern capitalism leaves the modern individual 'bereft of personal connections, de-politicised, without clear guidance or certainty, and raises the very question of the possibility of any community at all in today's world.' The only antidote to this, he suggests, is 'to try to overcome this loss of community by striving for a renewed sense of collective purpose, shared values and the common good'. Contradicting the laments of Morris is the largely optimistic view portrayed within the large body of literature on organisational citizenship behaviour (OCB). This has its roots in the belief that individuals' sense of obligation toward colleagues is at the heart of organisational survival, and would appear to demonstrate that the collective purpose sought by Morris does in fact exist within contemporary organisations. Organ (1988) is credited with publishing the first major text on OCB and his definition of it is revealing. He describes it as:

> ... behaviour that is discretionary, not directly or explicitly recognized by the formal reward system, and that in the aggregate promotes the effective functioning of the organization ... the behaviour is not an enforceable requirement of the role or the job description ... the behaviour is a matter of personal choice.
>
> (Organ, 1988: 4)

Given the number of studies devoted to testing the existence of this behaviour (see Elliott, 2001), it would seem that individuals are, consciously or otherwise, engaging in behaviour that is beneficial to themselves, to their colleagues, and to the organisation. However, in stressing that it 'is a matter of personal choice', OCB is at least partially predicated on the belief that it is not a behaviour that can be readily instrumentalised by organisations.[4] As Elliott (2001) has already discussed, the OCB literature is predominantly North American in origin and arises from political conceptions of community based in the civic republican tradition. More relevant for the purposes of this chapter are the implications that arise from the methodological limitations of the studies on OCB. These leave unquestioned the wider socio-economic environment in which the studies take place.[5] By way of example, inherent to many of these studies are the assumptions of social-exchange theory that 'employees engage in OCBs in order to reciprocate the actions of the organisation' (Bolino, 1999, p. 82). However, when these assumptions are put to the test, for example by Van Dyne and Ang (1998) who tested whether contingent workers (whom they define as those without an explicit or implicit employment contract) in Singapore are more or less likely to engage in so-called citizenship behaviours, we see that factors such as the nature of the employment contract impact upon individuals' behaviours. In brief, Van Dyne and Ang found that contingent workers are less likely to engage in citizenship behaviours than colleagues with explicit employment contracts.

Others (e.g. Parker, 1997), have discussed what an employee-led citizenship might look like. Unlike the OCB literature, Parker begins his discussion from the tradition of citizenship as a political institution and speculates how this might look within contemporary work organisations. Organisational citizenship in this sense is concerned with establishing a form of employee rights based on prevailing technologies of organisational governance, such as organisational mission statements. The metaphors contained in mission statements to sell the organisational vision to employees contain, Parker suggests, 'formulations of management, worker, and organisation [that] contain a notion of citizenship that is potentially very interesting' (Parker, 1997: 79). These ideas, he suggests 'might help to construct an idea of participative democracy in organizations' (ibid.).

The quest for the spiritual – the defining moment of the twenty-first century organisation?

Lately there has been a surge of interest in the concept of spirituality in organisations among practitioners, consultants and latterly among academics[6] seeking to explore what the concept might mean for the reshaping of work and organisation. This interest may be interpreted in a number of ways, since it is ambiguous whether this reflects a renewed desire to engender shared meaning in organisations through renewed forms of community, or by contrast a desire to loosen the perceived constraints of the collectivity in favour of the quest for autonomy.

Paradoxically, our analysis of this literature found the simultaneous development of both these discourses. Some commentators focus their work on spirituality on organisational development, for example on creating cultures and climates in organisations that encourage moral behaviour and a focus on the common good and well-being, and others focus on spirituality as an intensely private and personal experience.

Wager-Marsh and Conley's (1999) article 'The fourth wave: the spiritually-based firm' is an attempt to focus on both individual spiritual growth as well as a broader communitarian ethos for the organisation. For them, the measures required to become 'spiritual' are: *honesty with self, articulation of the corporation's spiritually-based philosophy, mutual trust and honesty with others, commitment to quality and service, commitment to employees,* and *selection of personnel to match the corporation's spiritually-based philosophy.* The findings of their research, which is based on a literature review,

professional observations, and 'in-depth personal interviews with leaders of spiritually-based firms' reveal three types of attributes to be important:

- those pertaining to the leader him or herself e.g. honesty with self;
- those relating to the culture and values of the organisation e.g. commitment to quality, service and employees;
- attributes related to organisational processes e.g. selection of appropriate personnel.

Arguably, commitment to quality and service might also be seen in process terms but in the article these are described in cultural terms. The argument of this article seems to be that if all these things can be achieved, then the result will be a 'spiritual' organisation.

Mitroff and Denton's (1999) empirical study found that their respondents viewed spirituality as 'highly individual and highly personal' (p. 87). This conclusion is supported by much of the literature on spirituality. Walsh and Vaughan (1993), for example, cited in Butts (1999), suggest six essential elements 'that constitute the heart and art of transcendence' all of which focus clearly on the individual. These are: 'ethical training; development of concentration; emotional transformation; a redirection of motivation from egocentric, deficiency based needs to higher motives, such as transcendence; refinement of awareness; and the cultivation of wisdom'. Indeed, Cavanagh (1999) criticises this emphasis in the literature which he attributes as much to Evangelical Christianity as to the New Age movement, both of which emphasise the relationship between the self and God (or gods), paying little attention to the importance of organisations and the common good. Freshman (1999) supports his findings. Her own thematic analysis of survey responses found that spirituality is seen as uniquely personal, with the word personal occurring several times in the words of her respondents.

Citizenship and spirituality in the new entrepreneurial organisation – reconciling autonomy and community?

As has been discussed earlier, many commentators have argued that community and autonomy cannot be reconciled, as they are based on entirely different moral propositions. The organisational citizenship literature and the organisational spirituality literature appear to be attempts to overcome this previously irreconcilable dichotomy. Du Gay (2000) warns of the seduction of what he terms 'new wave' organisations that apparently offer both autonomy and community. Following the demise of bureaucracy he identifies the rise of a new entrepreneurial organisation, which contains two key images. The first is the re-imagining of the organisation as something akin to a global village (Du Gay, 2000: 64) in which corporate citizens can find happiness, belonging and wealth. The second is 'the transformation of work into pleasure'. In these two steps, the power of communitarian governance is *apparently* successfully combined with the pleasure of individual autonomy and responsibility (p. 64), thereby *purporting* to overcome the tensions between autonomy and community highlighted by Bauman (2000a), Legge (1999) and others. Furthermore, he suggests that through a variety of techniques, this synthesis ostensibly *appears* to enable corporate citizens to become 'corporate entrepreneurs', each with responsibility for their own business, yet mutually interdependent through the umbrella of the larger organisation: 'This strategy of "autonomization" and 'responsibilization' makes paid work ... an essential element in the path to self-fulfilment'. (Du Gay, 2000). This form of entrepreneurial organisation, which requires the involvement of the whole and not just a part of the person, is not held together by rules or controls imposed from the top. On the contrary, what incites employees to involvement and effort is a shared sense of vision and mission, which is socialised into newcomers through sophisticated forms of organisational induction processes.

It is perhaps unsurprising then that followers of these entrepreneurial visions offering hope of self-fulfilment through autonomy of action and a strong sense of belonging within an organisation are often seduced by 'quasi-religious' excitement. Resistance is all but eradicated through an emotional engagement not found in bureaucratic organisational forms. Furthermore, the need for idols found by Bauman in such fabricated and artificial forms of community is satisfied by the charismatic forms of leadership illustrated in much of the spirituality literature (Konz and Ryan, 1999; Delbecq, 1999).

In an empirical study of one organisation which sought to introduce a new set of corporate values through a major culture change programme, Turnbull (2001) found a strong sense of hope and expectation among the managers at which the programme was aimed, and a frequently expressed desire for a common bond which was represented by the symbolism and values of the programme, and reinforced by the organisation's heroes, the charismatic senior managers who had been designated to 'sell' the new message. Turnbull also found that much of the behaviour, and indeed the language and discourses which the programme embodied, paralleled the behaviour and language of religious groups studied by Durkheim(1912/1995).[7] The desire for a sense of belonging (community) was strong, yet this had not replaced the strong sense of individuality expressed by the managers in their quest for self-development. As Du Gay has suggested, in today's organisations the previously clear distinction between autonomy and community appears to have begun to blur.

In the entrepreneurial organisations identified by Du Gay, for example, there is no longer a clear distinction between employees as purveyors of labour and the organisation as purchasers of their skills. Indeed, the boundaries between employees and the organisation are now less distinct, so that work is represented to employees, and by employees, as a spiritual experience. Not only can individuals undertake to develop themselves to improve their work performance, as they have been encouraged to do since the 1980s, it seems that within the late twentieth/early twenty-first century organisation, the individual can also attain spiritual salvation.

Reconciling autonomy and community – advancing the role of HRD as critical educator and moral conscience raiser

Since much new managerial discourse, as highlighted by Du Gay, now represents the employee as an individual in search of meaning and fulfilment, whose boundaries between work and home identities have become blurred, how should HRD respond? The advocates of this form of life, characterised as 'holistic' by Tom Peters (Peters and Waterman, 1982) and other evangelists of change, argue for blurring the distinctions between work and home, and claim that alienation and anomie were previously the result of the fragmentation of the self into work and home lives, and the requirement of the individual to take up roles which challenged the authenticity of the self. Advocates of this new organisational relationship suggest a romanticised ideal of the person as 'a whole expressed in each of its parts and that all spheres of existence should be united' (Du Gay, 2000: 67). They neglect, however, to deal with the tensions which derive from this evangelical call for bringing the whole self to work, and the implications of this for HRD.

We believe that the HRD function has a number of potential roles in these new organisational forms, not least of which will be to act to prevent the unrealistic sense of hope which employees of these organisations might experience, only to be brutally disappointed when the reality does not meet their aspirations (see Turnbull, 1999 and 2001). A common economic reality, which affects the new entrepreneurial organisations as much as the old bureaucracies, can be seen, for example, when the organisation ultimately decides to 'downsize' and therefore the organisational reality cannot match these fantasies (Casey, 2000).

It is perhaps for this reason that the concept of trust has begun to be discussed by HRD theorists (Grey and Garsten, 2001; Duffey et. al. 2000; Williams, 2000). Trust is seen by Grey and Garsten as a more appropriate mechanism for regulating behaviour in post-bureaucratic organisations than conventional hierarchical forms of control. In conjunction with this they identify the replacement of rules with values. The way that trust and shared values are sought, they suggest, is through the 'enrolment of individuals into these values, rather than selecting individuals who already share these values' (Grey and Garsten, 2001: 5). Yet, as they point out, the very act of downsizing organisations removes the basis for trust, and in turn can lead to it breaking down. Such a movement would of necessity also disturb current methods of governing the employer-employee relationship, such as psychometric testing, performance related pay etc., rooted as they are in dominant positivistic epistemic frameworks that actively discourage the development of trust between and amongst individuals (Porter, 1995). The increasing popularity of 360-degree feedback, in which employees are asked to report on the behaviours and performance not only of their subordinates, but also of their managers and colleagues, is further evidence of this as it can actively set up moral dilemmas for employees asked to choose between self-interest, loyalty to their colleagues and loyalty to the organisation. In introducing 360-degree feedback mechanisms, often as part of HRD initiatives, organisations inadvertently change the nature not only of the employment relationship, but also of the relationships that exist between colleagues at work.

The notion of humans as resources is also less explicit in these entrepreneurial organisations in which each individual takes responsibility for 'running their own show' inside their organisation. The adopted metaphor in such organisations has become that of employees as corporate entrepreneurs and also as consumers, who seek to customise their relationships. Recent research (e.g. Casey, 2000; Bell and Taylor 2001) has also revealed how some organisations are now appropriating metaphors of the sacral to ensure individual compliance to organisational needs. There is no doubt that the appropriation of these new technologies by organisations are inevitably changing employees' relationships with the HRD function.

A further paradox inside these entrepreneurial organisations is that attention to corporate citizenship, individual responsibility and self-management is often manifested by an emphasis on self-advancement, survival, and a quest for personal power. As Du Gay (2000) points out this can give rise to personal patronage, corruption, and deal-making which could not have occurred as readily within bureaucratic organisations with their clearer rules and procedures.

This is a considerable challenge to those thinking about HRD in these organisations, particularly those who may be described as coercive in their desire to invoke moral compliance through value based norms. Du Gay (2000) notes the evangelical language in Peters' work, and the implicitly Christian tones threatening damnation and disaster for those who do not follow his advice and react quickly to the destructive forces of chaos. However, HRD does not as yet appear to have given much attention to its role as critical educator and moral conscience raiser in such organisations.

Ruona's (2000) research into the underlying beliefs and values amongst senior HRD scholars found that the starting points expressed by these scholars tended to focus either on the individual or on the organisation, with the other as a secondary beneficiary of HRD. Russ-Eft (2000) has summed up the debate as being about: 'Developing the human resources of an organisation or the resources of the human' (2000: 50).

Neither perspective, however, questions the assumptions behind the discourse of humans as resources, nor enters into the debate we have opened in this chapter into the nature and forms of today's postmodern, post-bureaucratic organisations. This claim, although potentially contentious, moves us into the realm of political and moral questions and existential assumptions. There are, of course, parallels between the rivalry of the individual and the organisation for HRD's attention identified by Ruona, and the debate we open between autonomy and community in organisations. However, before attempting to confront these paradoxes, we believe that it is vital to ask for what purpose and to what ends we are engaging in HRD, whether it be focussed on individual development, or organisational prosperity. We want to argue in this chapter that an understanding of the dominant organisational discourses of entrepreneurship and consumption in organisations which, we have argued, reflect the social and political trends in the

Western world, is vital for understanding the tensions between autonomy and community, individual and organisation, and the paradoxical role facing HRD in today's organisations.

The debate we raise in this chapter represents just one tension facing HRD practitioners and researchers. The contemporary socio-economic climate, and the organisational forms arising therefrom, places specific demands on HRD that would not have been encountered in earlier decades. HRD is itself a product of nation-states' desire to create and maintain a trained and flexible workforce (Stead and Lee, 1996), which suggests for HRD a predominantly performative function. Whether HRD practitioners and researchers accept such organisational demands as the basis for their role might be framed as being ultimately a matter of personal choice. However, HRD practitioners and researchers are also members of work organisations and are consequently contracted, implicitly or explicitly, to perform their role in a certain way. Defiance of these expectations might therefore come at great personal expense. Through raising awareness of one of the implicit assumptions contained within HRD practice, we acknowledge that we are suggesting HRD practitioners and researchers take on a different, and undoubtedly difficult, role. We accept too that, in highlighting the tension between autonomy and community, we might be perceived as reinforcing these competing claims for the self. We, however, do not perceive HRD's focus on either the individual or the wider collective as inevitable.

Rather, for us, HRD is a constantly evolving field, which must take account of social, moral and existential debates, as well as taking responsibility for raising awareness of these not only within the academic community but also within the wider practitioner network. We therefore favour Lee's (2001) perspective. She has argued against a definition of HRD, instead favouring an 'ontology of becoming', which obstructs the reification of social constructs.

It is clear that the issue of reconciling autonomy and community in organisations posed at the outset of this chapter is inherently one rooted in deep existential, social and philosophical questions. HRD's role in considering this tension will inevitably always be paradoxical, since embedded within this question are a number of moral and political dilemmas for our field. However, it is our view that this challenge can no longer be avoided, and that a deeper understanding of social trends and the ontological assumptions that underpin twenty-first century Anglo-American thinking can help us to make sense of this tension. We must engage with HRD practitioners in the moral choices they inevitably face on a daily basis, many of which reflect this dilemma.

Notes

1   An interesting point, but not one we will discuss in this paper, is the lack of acknowledgement within the performatively oriented HRD literature, and the literature that envisions the organisation as community, that individual employees are members of a host of other organisations and might achieve their 'meaning' beyond the workplace. The refusal to entertain the idea that individuals, as employees, might be motivated to work by money alone seems to have been buried since Maslow and MacGregor's ideas were appropriated by the business world. This is a curious omission though, particularly

in a society such as the US, where money provides the lubricant to assist one's ascent up the social ladder.

2 Turner acknowledges that this bipolarity draws on Freud's distinction between the *id* (the impulsive self) and the *super ego* (the institutional self).

3 However, as we shall discuss later, there remains the contradiction between theories and practices that ostensibly promote individual autonomy whilst looking towards these same theories and practices to enhance and extend organisational aspirations.

4 Based on the belief of the ability of the autonomous individual to control their own identity, this would seem to be a somewhat naïve view in the light of social constructionist and postmodern theories on the shaping of individual identity. It also stands in contrast to much of the organisational culture change literature that suggests individuals' behaviours can be changed.

5 Elliott identifies the development of a contextualisation approach in the OCB literature, but argues that as a body of research it continues to be preoccupied with the display by individuals of a set of behaviours, previously categorised by researchers, within an employment context. Inherent to our argument in this paper is that the misappropriation of socio-cultural concepts by researchers and practitioners leads to knowledge and practice that ultimately only continues to confuse the relationship between the individual and the organisation.

6 Interestingly, research into spirituality has attracted scholars from a wide range of disciplines from religious studies to sociology, psychology and organisation theory.

7 Although Durkheim's modernist orientation led him to seek a grand theoretical explanation for religious behaviour, his observations around the construction of shared meaning and community through religious narratives and semiotics are also illuminating for postmodern scholars of social and organisational discourses.

References

Anthony, P. D. (1994) *Managing Culture*, Buckingham: Open University Press

Bauman Z. (2000a) *Community: Seeking safety in an insecure world*, Cambridge: Polity Press

Bauman Z. (2000b) *Liquid Modernity*, Cambridge: Polity Press

Beck, U. and Beck-Gernsheim, E. (1996) 'Individualization and the "precarious freedoms": perspectives and controversies of a subject-oriented sociology' in Heelas, P., Lash, S. and Morris, P. (Eds) *Detraditionalization*, Oxford: Blackwell

Bell, E. and Taylor, S. (2001) 'The resacralization of work', *Proceedings of Critical Management Studies Conference*, Manchester: Manchester University, July

Bolino, M. (1999) 'Citizenship and impression management: good soldiers and good actors?', *Academy of Management Review*, 24(1): 82–98

Butts, D. (1999) 'Spirituality at work: an overview', *Journal of Organizational Change Management*, 12(4)

Casey C. (1995) *Work, Self, and Society. After Industrialism*, London: Routledge

Casey, C. (2000) 'Spirit at work: incorporating the New Age', presented at Working Knowledge Conference, Sydney, Australia, December

Cavanagh, G. (1999) 'Spirituality for managers: context and critique', *Journal of Organizational Change Management*, 12(3)

Chalofsky, N. (2000) 'The meaning of the meaning of work: a literature review analysis' in Kuchinke, K. P. (Ed.) *Academy of Human Resource Development Conference Proceedings*, AHRD: Raliegh, Durham

Chalofsky, N. (2001) (interviewed by Callahan, J. and Ward, D.) 'A search for meaning: revitalizing the "human" in human resource development', *Human Resource Development International*, 4(2): 235–242

Cushman, P. (1990) 'Why the self is empty. Toward a historically situated psychology', *American Psychologist*, 45 (5): 599–611

Delbecq, A. (1999) 'Christian spirituality and contemporary business leadership', *Journal of Organizational Change Management*, 12 (4)

Duffy, C., Lafferty, C. and Lafferty, B. (2001) 'Organisational trust and attachment to an immediate leader: a pilot study' in Aliaga, O. (Ed.) *Academy of Human Resource Development Conference Proceedings*, AHRD: Tulsa, Oklahoma

Du Gay, P. (1996) *Consumption and Identity at Work*, London: Sage

Du Gay, P. (2000) *In Praise of Bureaucracy*, London: Sage

Durkheim, E. (1912/1995) *The Elementary Forms of Religious Life*, trans. by K. Fields, New York: Free Press

Elliott, C. (2001) 'Organizational citizenship: insights from Bakhtin's philosophy of language', working paper

Fielding, M. (1997) 'Learning organization or learning community?', paper presented at the International Conference on Philosophy, Education and Culture, University of Edinburgh, 11–14 September

Freshman, B. (1999) 'An exploratory analysis of definitions and applications of spirituality in the workplace', *Journal of Organizational Change Management*, 12(4)

Giddens, A. (1994) *Beyond Left and Right: The future of radical politics*, Cambridge: Polity Press

Goss, D. (1996) 'HRM in the era of reflexive modernity' in *HRM: the inside story*, conference proceedings, Milton Keynes: Open University

Grey, C. and Garsten, C. (2001) 'Trust, control and post-bureaucracy', *Organization Studies*, 22 (2): 229–250

Heelas, P. (1996) *The New Age Movement*, Oxford: Blackwell

Heelas, P. and Morris, P. (Eds) (1992) *The Values of the Enterprise Culture: The moral debate*, London: Routledge

Heelas, P., Lash, S. and Morris, P. (Eds) (1996) *Detraditionalization: Critical reflections on authority and identity at a time of uncertainty*, Oxford: Blackwell

Holton, E.F. III (2000) 'Clarifying and defining the performance paradigm of human resource development', in Kuchinke, K. P. (Ed.) *Academy of Human Resource Development Conference Proceedings*, AHRD: Raliegh, Durham

Konz, G. and Ryan, F. (1999) 'Maintaining an organizational spirituality: no easy task', *Journal of Organizational Change Management*, 12(3)

Kuchinke, K. P. (2000a) 'Debates over the nature of HRD: an institutional theory perspective', *Human Resource Development International*, 3(3): 279–283

Kuchinke, K. P. (2000b) 'Development towards what end? An analysis of the notion of development for the field of human resource development' in Kuchinke, K. P. (Ed.) *Academy of Human Resource Development Conference Proceedings*, 32–39, AHRD: Raliegh, Durham

Lee, M. (2001) 'A refusal to define HRD' in Aliaga, O. (Ed.) *Academy of Human Resource Development Conference Proceedings*, 1,072–1,079, AHRD: Tulsa, Oklahoma

Legge, K. (1999) 'Representing people at work', *Organization*, 6(2): 247–264

Martin, J. (1992) *Cultures in Organizations: Three perspectives*, New York: Oxford University Press

Mitroff, I. and Denton, E. (1999) 'A study of spirituality in the workplace', *Sloan Management Review*, Summer

Morris, P. (1996) 'Community beyond traditions', in P. Heelas, S. Lash and P. Morris (1996) *Decentralization: Critical reflections on authority and identity at a time of uncertainty*, London: Blackwell

Organ, D. (1988) *Organizational Citizenship Behaviour. The good soldier syndrome*, Lexington, Mass: Lexington Books

Parker, M. (1997) 'Organizations and citizenship', *Organization*, 4 (1): 75–92

Peters, T. and Waterman, R. (1982) *In Search of Excellence*, London: Harper & Row

Porter, T. (1995) *Trust in Numbers*, Princeton NJ: Princeton University Press

Reynolds, M. (2000) 'Bright lights and pastoral idyll. Ideas of community underlying management education methodologies', *Management Learning*, 31(10): 67–82

Rose, N. (1989) *Governing the Soul: The shaping of the private self*, London: Routledge

Ruona, W. (2000a) 'Should we define the profession of HRD. Views of leading scholars', in Kuchinke, K. P. (Ed.) *Academy of Human Resource Development Conference Proceedings*, AHRD: Tulsa, Oklahoma

Ruona, W. (2000b) 'Core beliefs in human resource development: a journey for the profession and its professionals' in Ruona, W. and Roth, G. (Eds) *Philosophical Foundations of Human Resource Development Practice, Advances in Developing Human Resources*, No. 7, AHRD

Ruona, W. and Roth, G. (Eds) (2000) 'Philosophical foundations of human resource development practice', *Advances in Developing Human Resources*, No. 7

Russ-Eft, D. (2000) 'That old fungible feeling: defining human resource development', in Ruona, W. and Roth, G. (Eds) *Philosophical Foundations of Human Resource Development Practice, Advances in Developing Human Resources*, No. 7, AHRD

Stead, V. and Lee, M. (1996) 'Inter-cultural perspectives on HRD', in Stewart, J. and McGoldrick, J. (Eds) *Human Resource Development. Perspectives, Strategies and Practice*, London: Pitman

Torraco, R. A and Swanson, R. A. (1995) 'The strategic roles of human resource development', *Human Resource Planning*, 18(4): 10–21

Turnbull S. (1999) 'Emotional labour in corporate change programmes – the effects of organizational feeling rules on middle managers', *Human Resource Development International*, 2 (2): 125–146

Turnbull, S. (2001) 'Corporate ideology – meanings and contradictions for middle managers', *British Journal of Management*, 12(3): 231–242

Turner, R. (1976) 'The real self: from institution to impulse', *American Journal of Sociology*, 81 (5): 989–1,016

Usher, R. (1992) 'Experience in adult education: a post-modern critique', *Journal of Philosophy of Education*, 26(2): 201–214

Van Dyne, L. and Ang, S. (1998) 'Organizational citizenship behaviour of contingent workers in Singapore', *Academy of Management Journal*, 41 (6): 692–703

Wager-Marsh, F. and Conley, J. (1999) 'The fourth wave: the spiritually-based firm', *Journal of Organizational Change Management*, 12(4)

Walsh, R. and Vaughan, F. (Eds) (1993) *Paths beyond Ego: The transpersonal vision*, Los Angeles, CA: Tarcher/Pedigree

Watson, T. J. (1994) *In Search of Management*, London: Routledge

Williams, S. (2001) 'A conceptualisation of interpersonal trust in the workplace', in Aliaga, O. (Ed.) *Academy of Human Resource Development Conference Proceedings*, AHRD: Tulsa, Oklahoma

8 The urge to destroy is a creative urge

Kim James

Foreword

The title of this essay is a phrase used by Bukharin, the Russian anarchist. When I first decided to use it we had not seen the massive destruction wrought on the World Trade Centre in New York. My first instinct was to change the title but then I thought of all the creative thinking which is going to be needed to combat a descent by the world into a new barbarism, and I have decided to keep it since what I have to say applies at all levels of human organisation. I have therefore added this one opening paragraph.

Why creativity at this moment in time?

There is a tendency for swings of fashion to happen where particular interventions to improve the success of industry and commerce struggle to achieve market dominance before disappearing in face of new theories and practice. Everything is marketed for profit, and newness is the criterion by which things are judged. The fashion industry is only one area where newness is all – the dominant aesthetic today is the triumph of the 'new'. Just as in the art world, 'new' quantity is preferred to lasting quality. The people who make real money are those who can dream up a new product claiming to be able to reap rich dividends. The fact that five years later the nostrum is forgotten, and has not made any particular difference, should always be borne in mind. Among today's fashions is that of the buzzword 'creativity'. If this quality of being is seen as important today it is because even the gurus who ladle out advice are scared of the changes taking place in the world at present.

Nearly fifteen years ago Tom Peters (1989) offered a scenario of chaos as the way of existence for the future. There was an uneasy feeling that he was correct but the form of this chaos could not be envisaged. It is difficult to realise sometimes that it is only fifteen years since there were two superpowers that dominated world events. The European Union was still just a Common Market, and although changes took place in those far off days, they took place at what now seems a leisurely pace.

The great acceleration in change started truly in early 1989; the Hungarian authorities opened their frontiers and the process of irreversible change was set in motion. Within six months from September 1989 the Berlin Wall fell, President Ceaucescu was deposed and executed in Romania and Nelson Mandela was freed from prison and started negotiations with the South African Government. Since then the Gulf War has been and gone. In less than ten years the socialist governments of East Europe are only a memory and the Soviet Union itself has disappeared. The Yugoslav Federation disintegrated and was replaced by a series of bloody ethnic wars. Terrorism in September 2001 destroyed the wishfulfilment hegemony fantasy of the developed world. The world has become globalised in its economy and fragmented in its structure leaving it more dangerous than at any time in its history, in every aspect of activity. No matter how the current situations are resolved, the effect on the political, financial and business world means that there will be no return to the reasonably predictable stability the world enjoyed over the previous fifty or so years.

> ... There exist innumerable forces, which interlace, an infinite number of parallelograms of forces giving a resultant, the historical happening. This in its turn can be regarded as the outcome of a force acting as a whole, without consciousness or will. For that which each individual wishes separately, is hindered by all the others, and the general upshot is something which no one in particular has willed
>
> (Engels 1941: 55)

Success in the world today depends strictly on the speed with which we can abandon old thought patterns and adopt the ones which necessity imposes. Whilst we cannot easily welcome such events we must learn to use what they bring. Our humanity has to be re-affirmed through our existence in whatever situation we find ourselves. We have to *live* change; we cannot plan for it, only be ready for it in our attitudes and mental set. We need to perform a 'mind-shift' of enormous depth and breadth in order to challenge the future.

In the rest of this chapter I shall first look at the dominant paradigm that rules the lives of those in the West, and then the new paradigm arising through complexity, before exploring some of the implications of the 'mind-shift' from one to the other.

The dominant paradigm

The universal conservative impulse is to maintain the dominant paradigm. The dominant paradigm in the West is sometimes called the Newtonian paradigm, though it is probably more accurate to describe it as the engineering paradigm. At the heart of this paradigm are two essential features. One is that problems are solvable if you divide them into smaller parts: two, that a clear statement of proposals for action and a measurement of the results of carrying out the proposals ensure a transition to a more efficient function of activity. The key elements in the population over the whole of the first industrial revolution (the entrepreneurs and scientists who made the proposals and the technicians and workers who put the proposals into effect and measured their effects) were the heart of economic success. You could measure success. You could lay down rules for achieving future success by repeating faithfully the actions of the past. And for many, many years – over two hundred – this paradigm was immensely effective.

Because the paradigm we live under is so pervasive, we can only interpret problems and information from within it. It is a cage that we are trapped in. In the West we are conditioned from the first months of our lives into linear logic and doing what others require. Linear, logical and sequential words dominate our education. Words are vital, spoken, written or conveyed in various symbolic shorthands. Words dominate our reasoning. The dominant communication process takes place through the spoken word. Words form our world and reinforce the linearity associated with the engineering paradigm.

Problems are solved within the existing paradigm. Paradigms lay out the boundaries, such as what problems are to be tackled. The existence of a particular paradigm can, in fact determine whether a problem is even seen to exist. It certainly determines the way the problems are perceived. The paradigm will decide how a problem is approached once it is perceived as being real and what data are to be properly included or excluded. It will decide the kind of solution, which is sought, and the ways and means by which it is sought. The solution sought will be one that confirms the validity of what is already known, and, most importantly, the paradigm determines the criterion of proof or falsification.

Kuhn (1962) used the concept of paradigm in his study of how scientific ideas develop. According to Kuhn most science takes place in long periods when developments are not world shaking and traditional attitudes meet with little opposition. Gradually ideas are changed as discovery is added to discovery, until at a certain point, paradoxes arise within the body of knowledge and a revolutionary leap is necessary to overcome these contradictions by using a new way of looking at things. The evolutionary leap into a new paradigm which is demanded by today's world is one where an urge to destroy is not too extreme. As William Morris said 'to shatter this sorry scheme of things entire / And mould it nearer to the heart's desire'.

Unfortunately we do not have to look very far before we are confronted with problems which are not capable of being solved by linear logical sequential calculation.

The new paradigm

As our understanding of the world develops it is becoming clear that it functions on discontinuities, and can be better understood through non-linear equations and non-linear thinking. Chaos theory and catastrophe theories show quite clearly that the form of change is best represented in waveform in graphs. They show that change builds up a resistance to itself in the same way the wave changes its form as it hits the beach; except that in the case of living systems the wave builds up its own beach in a counter movement of force. When sufficient build-up is achieved there is sudden change into a new state. In this new state all the old constituents are there but in different relationships. Therefore, the theories which are shaping the science of tomorrow, and which are loosely grouped around the various theories of complexity and chaos and the new forms of 'fuzzy' logic, offer a new way of seeing the world.

The new paradigm is that of complexity and it is essentially a creative paradigm. It is one of quantum leaps and relativity. It is the philosophical underpinning of the various theories loosely grouped under the heading of complexity; from catastrophe theory in the late sixties through chaos theory in the seventies and eighties via René Thom (1972), Ilya Prigogine and I. Stengers (1979), Maturana and Varela (1972) and Gibson (1979) that constitute the new paradigm, which has aesthetic feelings as a key element. It functions through processes instead of plans. Plans are replaced by planning which is continuous. Creativity is the name of the new paradigm and creativity is a process and a way of being.

This new paradigm already 'exists' in so far as it is being researched, theorised and practiced, and many leading thinkers are working within it. It has not, however, fully impacted upon softer sciences such as psychology, as thinking in this area continues to be largely linear with a defence of particulate approaches being dominant. Over the past hundred years psychology has attempted to mirror the so-called hard sciences with a desire to shape the discipline by old-fashioned linear experimental laboratory science. In contrast to developments in biology and physics, psychology has become increasingly reliant on the linear approach and finds its chief support in an alliance with neurophysiology. This has led to the contradiction that the more areas and processes of the neural structure have been clarified, the more interest has centred on the emergent property called consciousness which resolutely refuses to be modelled in any linear programme. The future, however, lies with new approaches, particularly those of James Gibson's (1979) ecological psychology with its emphasis on the observation of the real world outside the laboratory as the foundation.

Gibson made many valuable contributions to applied psychology, in particular his formulation of the senses considered as perceptual systems. He developed an approach, which has found applications in a wide variety of fields ranging from automotive, and aircraft control to the design of control systems for nuclear power stations and computer-aided design in architecture. Gibson's approach is based on the ecological unity of mankind in its environment. From this point of view the environment consists of elements nested one in another. From the physical point of view, reality has structure at all levels from the micro level of atoms to the macro level of galaxies.

> There are forms within forms both up and down the scale of size. Units are nested within larger units. Things are components of other things. They would constitute a hierarchy except that this hierarchy is not categorical but full of transitions and overlaps.
>
> (Gibson 1979)

This is a systems approach, which fits well with the biological approach of Maturana and Varela in that it observes the world as a series of nested systems and not as the end-to-end linear image of traditional behavioural psychology. It enables the conjunction of various disciplines in the service of understanding our world, drawing upon biology, mathematics, art and philosophy.

The difficulty of facing up to necessity

It is all very well to acknowledge the necessity for change in thinking patterns but what Wilfred Trotter (1930) remarked in a paper on Scientific Imagination remains only too true today.

> The mind likes a strange idea as little as the body likes a strange protein and resists it with similar energy. It would not be too fanciful to say that a new idea is the most quickly acting antigen known to science. If we listen to ourselves honestly we shall often find we have begun to argue against a new idea even before it has been completely stated.
>
> (Trotter 1930: 230)

In the management of human society there is a trend to emphasise certain traits, modes of connection, which have proved, in the past, to favour the maintenance of stability. In the course of time these manners of regulating affairs restrict the desires of individuals to function differently. Those whose own position feels threatened by any change resist these desires. As Nissani says,

> Human beings possess a deep-rooted and insistent need for continuity. Once we understand the anxieties associated with the loss of cherished convictions, the tenacity of clinging to old beliefs can be understood. We often argue, for instance, about the need for social change, and we tend to explain conservatism as ignorance, cowardice, or protection of privilege. This is true in some cases, but our resistance to change is often traceable to a universal conservative impulse, which is more pervasive and profound than simple prejudice or class interest.
>
> (Nissani 2001)

Adoption of the new paradigm requires a fundamental shift – away from the linear to the spatial (Lee and Flatau, 1996) and thus demands a re-focus upon spatial activities and thinking.

The substrate of the new paradigm

If the word is the substrate of the linear form of the dominant paradigm, then art, and particularly graphic art, is the substrate of the new paradigm. The appeal of the creative imaginative solution is a very subtle process, taking place below the level of normal conscious life. We are so aware of the difficulty of using words to describe a new idea that we use the words 'imagine', 'visualise' and 'intuition' when we seek to articulate such newness. When we speak of visualising or imagining or using our intuition we are speaking about activities which are not verbal. We talk of 'calling up' images from the depths of our minds. These are forms of knowledge, which are the precursors of verbal knowledge: there is a deep level of cognition where the images, which we call up, are formed in our pre-conscious. They are dependent upon our direct perception of the meaningfulness of our environment, to use Gibson's term (Gibson 1979: 267).

Imagination is the faculty which ensures that our minds are not satisfied with circumscribed activity but ensures that we desire to create and go beyond the given.

> Imagination reveals itself in: the balance or reconcilement of opposite or discordant qualities; of sameness with difference; the individual with the representative; the sense of novelty; freshness with old and familiar objects; a more than usual state of emotion with more than usual order; judgement ever awake; steady self-possession with enthusiasm; feelings profound or vehement.

The above list is the work of the English poet Samuel Taylor Coleridge (in Read 1943). It could not be better put. Attempts to fully comprehend creativity are impossible without these attributes.

Imagination which links the 'more than usual states of emotion with more than usual order', is the establishing of new relations between the elements, which have accumulated in our memory, our past experience. This is the predictive capacity in its human form. It consists in structuring in advance the world of tomorrow, and conforming our behaviour to the bringing about of this new structure. It is this faculty, which enabled Einstein to formulate the theories of relativity.

Imagination is the common factor in all the subjective aspects of art and the factor that reconciles diverse subjective aspects with the invariable laws of beauty, balance, harmony, symmetry and rhythms. Composition is the sum total of all these properties whose purpose is to organise the physical elements which make up a coherent pattern.

The feature which distinguishes imagination is aesthetic consciousness.

Aesthetics is defined in the Larousse dictionary as 'the defining of the beautiful. That which is beautiful is that which most clearly conveys the modes of seeing given by Moral authorities, Science and Government'. It is this sort of aesthetic that dominates our way of thinking, and brings about the survivors of 'Big Brother' and increasingly brutal attitudes toward human life and our very species survival. It is this acceptance of the beautiful as conveying the accepted dominant way of thinking of those who hold power that is often called academic art. For the creativity, which we need today, another aesthetic is needed. A new aesthetic must encourage the change of structures to meet new needs and is the sole guarantee that the change enhances our human condition.

The role of aesthetics as a tool for thought

French polymath Henri Laborit, (ex French naval officer, chemist, biologist and philosopher and discoverer of the range of the first successful tranquillising drugs used to treat mental illness) defined aesthetics as follows:

> One has to admit … that which is beautiful good useful etc., is that which is most ordered and most meaningful. Even if from a dialectical point of view, a period of destruction is sometimes necessary for the progression towards order … Aesthetics [must be] understood as a search for structures, that is to say the set of relations existing between the elements of the whole of our knowledge … the search for, discovery and the use of relations makes action efficient.
>
> (Laborit 1968:12)

If we discard the old description of aesthetics as the standards of accepted established beauty and replace it with Henri Laborit's definition, we have a truly creative tool rather than a cosmetic one. If we can learn to search for new structures as a natural part of our ability to perceive the information that is available to us, it can provide us with a tool for working in conditions where there is a lack of clarity and too much ambiguity. If we can learn to use this collectively, where we build a collective reference, which creates a rational framework with its own checks and balances, our work teams, both formal and informal, will provide a fertile ground for a creative company. If we do this we will not miss the opportunity, but we will see the signal in the noise and create new opportunities for action.

> There is … the peculiar fact that progress in physics is often guided by judgements that can only be called aesthetic. This is very odd. Why should a physicist's sense that one theory is more beautiful than another be a useful guide in scientific research? There are several possible reasons for this, but one of them is special to elementary particle physics: the beauty in our present theories may be 'but a dream' of the kind of beauty that awaits us in the final theory.
>
> (Weinberg 1993: 12)

In linear problem solving particular beliefs and behaviours may play little or no part in the solution of the problem. However, as the problem becomes a question of intuition, gut feeling, then the beliefs and behaviour of the person become increasingly important. Global solutions demand powerful inputs of creativity. Those cultures whose structure and organisation have the capacity to adjust rapidly to information in a pro-active fashion will be those who prosper and survive in the long term

This is why an aesthetic approach and the development of an aesthetic attitude is essential for all genuine understanding. It allows us to be 'tuned in', to be in a state of 'information' where we can pick up what works, what makes sense, what is a 'good' solution, an appropriate intervention. It is perceptual, functioning at the level of Gibson's Direct Perception of Meaning. As Philip Sadler said twenty years ago, the education of managers should be more closely modelled on the arts than the sciences, and of all the arts the fine arts provides more than a model, it provides a method for achieving a new mind-set. We place no real importance on the learning to learn experience activity of the graphic act. Yet in this activity, from its very start, we teach ourselves at first hand. Art activity is the creative arena *par excellence*. The start of creativity is the child's first scribble. (See Carol McKenzie's chapter in this volume for a detailed exploration of this idea.)

> A single drawing … is in effect an operating system regulated by feedback … the clearly sequential and cumulative nature of the traces, and the fact that a terminal product results, set drawing apart as a prime example of a regulated system in operation.
>
> (Beitel)

The graphic act uses error as a self-learning instrument, which simulates all the complex interactions found in social organisations of all types. It can show slow build-up progressions, which suddenly break into new forms. It shows possibilities and probabilities. It demonstrates the build up of aggregations of power and shows how 'mergers' and 'take-overs' happen. Both the necessity to pay attention to the least little detail and the consequence for the original ideal vision is brought into play. Aesthetics, whose subjects are truth, duality values, technique and expression, is a generalising function, which corresponds to the need to work at the same time on the details and on the global plan. Drawing is the *lingua franca* of the new paradigm.

The part of creativity

In our efforts to understand the complexities of a chaotic world we admire intuition and imagination in problem solving. We admire creativity and we strongly desire to be creative ourselves but creativity cannot generally be present outside a relativist culture: one where we can tolerate ambiguity, creativity (both in ourselves and others, since this is the source of much of the ambiguity), and where we can seek out new structures in a continually changing environment. Creativity entails imagination, visioning and symbolising, developing heightened perception and intuition. It demands self-discipline. Mankind is a creative animal but most creative thinking has to be acquired and maintained in spite of and against academic instruction. Creativity is not something which can be taught. Short courses, which propose training in creative thinking, are nonsense.

> The educational processes required to develop managers who are innovative, who can cope with uncertainty, who can manage change, develop visions and provide transformational leadership are, in my view, much closer to those involved in education in the fine arts or in philosophy than in engineering or economics. In my lecture to The Royal Society of Arts in 1984 I said that

'although management involves very high level and complex skills, it is essentially a practical art rather than an intellectual process and that in consequence the more conventional kinds of academic learning have little relevance. Along with this goes the realisation that success in management has much less to do with rationality, logic and quantitative analysis than we previously believed and is much more closely related to non-rational elements such as vision, creativity, leadership and attitude of mind'.

(Philip Sadler CBE. Psi International Breakfast meeting, Paris 1992)

To be creative is to solve a problem in life in a way that is new to the solver, and to most other people around. Creativity is not given out in equal measure. There may be an overwhelming amount or so little that it is hardly noticeable. Someone may be very creative at one moment and then never again in his or her whole life.

Creativity is a point in process, a sort of deformation in an otherwise smooth plane, which alters the course of events significantly. How far this alteration goes determines the level of creativity and its significance. The high point of creativity alters the course of events for humanity in a way that improves the lot of the people it affects, though evidence suggests that life for highly creative people may not be a bed of roses. Creativity usually means seriously disturbing some people (both the creative person herself and those who are affected by the creativity) and when they are in positions of power then the urge to destroy in order to create is significant.

It is not surprising that we have such a fear of doing what might liberate us from our own fear for, as the artist Paul Klee noted in 1924,

It is not easy to arrive at a conception of a whole which is constructed from parts belonging to different dimensions ... This is due to the consecutive nature of the only methods available to us for conveying a clear three-dimensional concept (of the world) and results from the deficiencies of a temporal nature in the spoken word. For we lack the means of discussing, in its constituent parts, an image which possesses simultaneously a number of dimensions.

(Klee 1924: 17)

Those rules and practices, which have proved effective in application to particular problems, will continue to be used, but from within the new paradigm. In this way a new vision of reality will develop, in the same way that Newton's laws work in a world which increasingly functions on principles formulated in the last years of the nineteenth and continually through the twentieth century. This process will not be smooth. It is not possible to put on a new way of seeing the world like a new overcoat. Adoption of the new paradigm, means thinking (or being) a different way. It means breaking through the bars of the cage and renewing ourselves. The urge to destroy old patterns of thinking and being will be everywhere as creativity comes to the fore.

A sure sign of a breakdown in a system is when it becomes rigidly formalised. A strange situation has arisen since Philip Sadler made his plea for an education of managers modelled more on the arts than a pseudo-science. In 1982, when Philip Sadler first wrote, the education of artists was based loosely on a master-apprentice studio practice, which allowed each individual to develop in their own way. Over the past few years an obsession with measurement has been allowed to develop within the general education system from the first nursery pre-school through to post-graduate level in universities. It is no longer a question of looking at the art school as a model for creative thinking and activity. There are still a very few private schools where this obtains but in the major schools, after the brief faint flicker of originality seen in pickled cows and unmade beds, the studio practice has been eliminated in favour of computer-based projects with quality control built in by external quangos. Eliminated also is the use of error and ambiguity as raw material for progress. The destruction of the controlled processing of thought is now a vital necessity.

This arises from a phenomenon, which has a strong historic antecedent. In the tenth century St Bernard undertook the re-organisation of the Benedictine order, which he felt had departed from the original intentions of the founding fathers. In the beginning organisations grow and develop more or less by chance, with few explicit rules since the numbers of participants tends to render lists of rules unnecessary. More common at the beginning are lists of aims to be achieved. Over time a consensus of opinion grows up, based on the success of the organisation's activities and habits, and customs are acquired which may or may not be written down as rules. Gradually, changes in the environment of the organisation take place without corresponding changes within. Past a certain point the inside structure no longer corresponds to that which would ensure a continuous exchange of energy between the outside and the inside. With further development, practices are seen as no longer in the spirit of the origins. At this point the organisation may be felt to be in decay, corrupt or whatever. At this point the re-organisation, usually at the instigation of a single leader, takes on the character of a new institution.

It is, frequently, more in the re-organisation of an institution than in the recorded intention of the founders that we tend to find explicit descriptions of what the development should be. The model chosen tends to be much more prescriptive than the original foundation since it attempts to avoid the errors which have crept in to the organisation.

Since the remodelling of the education system fits into the historic description of change, we can see quite easily that the rigorous prescriptions of quality control and measurement of outcomes are merely the logical outcome of attempts to re-vitalise a decaying system and avoid the apparent failures of what has gone before. We have witnessed over the past few years throughout Europe what a colleague called the Sovietisation of Western thought where academic excellence is thought to be capable of being measured by ticks in boxes, and where academic processes are to be controlled by external bodies. This is in fact a symptom of a system in rapid decay.

The management of human society tends, in the presence of selective pressures, to optimise some aspects of behaviour or modes of connection, but it is necessary to be wary of imposing too rigid constraints on the optimisation of what may locally be considered desirable traits to optimise. Models of development which lay down too strict guidelines for the optimisation of particular desirable traits change the definition of the problem and thus the kind of solution sought in the wider context. The very act of establishing too formal constraints eventually forces the system into a disastrous way of functioning. This is particularly so in definitions of progress which are laid down in terms of maximisation or minimisation criteria, and which appear to present reassuring representations of reality as an all-powerful and rational calculator, and history as coherent and characterised by global progress.

Conclusion

There are signs that the decay of society is leading to a genuine realisation of the need for new ways of thinking. There is a desperate need for a new education where a referential methodology would aim at the introduction and use of aesthetics as a predictive and investigative capacity. This will allow a new effective thought process in management, which can liberate and use imagination, intuition and the power which arises from emotion. In a supportive framework, where all the elements of day-to-day reality can be simulated, such a new model will allow the use of elements previously considered as negative, such as confrontation, conflict, ambiguity, indecision and error, to be used as dynamic values. These values then become the creative potential for a new paradigm where the complexities of situations and chaos become opportunities to obtain a higher perceptual ability in decision-making. These values cannot however, be engendered without first destroying the old.

References

Beitel, F. (1970) *Concepts in Art and Education*, Toronto: Ed Pappas, p106

Engels, F. (1941) *Fundamental Problems of Marxism*, Plekhanov G. V., London: Lawrence and Wishart

Gibson J. J. (1979) *The Ecological Approach to Visual Perception*, Boston: Houghton Mifflin

Klee, Paul (1964) *Théorie de l'Art Moderne*, Bale: Editions Gonthier

Kuhn, T. (1966) *The Structure of Scientific Revolutions*, 3rd edition, Chicago: Chicago University Press

Laborit, Henri (1968) *Biologie et Structure*, Paris: Gallimard

Lee, M. and Flatau, M. (1996) 'Seriova Logika v paralelnom svete' (Serial logic in a parallel world) in *Predpoklady Zavadzania ISO 9000 Na Slovensku*, Mitzla, M. (Ed.) Kosiche: IBIS Publishing, 11–13

Lissack, Michael (1977) *Chaos and Complexity – What does that have to do with knowledge management.* Published on the web at www.Lissack.com

Maturana, H. and Varala, F. J. (1972) *Autopoieses and Cognition*, Boston: D. Reidel

Nissani, Mati (1995) *Social Studies of Science*, 25: 165–183

Peters, Tom (1989) *Thriving on Chaos*, London: Pan Books

Prigogine, I. and Stengers, I. (1979) *La Nouvelle Alliance*, Paris: Gallimard

Royal Society of Arts Journal, May 1984

Read, Sir Herbert (1943) *Education through Art*, London: Faber

Sadler, Philip (1984) 'Educating managers for the 21st century', *The Royal Society of Arts Journal*, May

Thom, R. (1972) *Stabilité Structurelle et Morphogénèse*, Reading Massachusetts, USA: WA Benjamin Inc: Advanced Book Programme

Trotter, Wilfred Batten Lewis (1930) 'Observation and Experiment and their Use in the Medical Sciences', *British Medical Journal*, 2: 129–134

Weinberg, Steven (1991) *Dreams of a Final Theory*, London: Hutchinson

Part III

Realising HR
Applying the theories

The four chapters in this section of the book each examine the practical implementation of theory. Jamie Callahan and Denis Gračanin start the section, with their chapter which proposes a theoretical framework for capturing information about emotion as it relates to the organisational context and demonstrates how visualisation technology can be used within this framework. Maurice Yolles and Paul Iles build on the theoretical framework they present in the first section in order to introduce a tool by which the way that organisations can be diagnosed in complex change situations can be improved. Carole McKenzie picks up from Kim James's chapter to lay the foundations for, and illustrate the use of, graphics in developing the aesthetic and creative aspects of management. Finally, Lloyd Davies and Paul Kraus focus on learning from exceptional events and describe an iterative model of experiential learning and use this to illustrate how a senior manager in the water industry learned from a disaster.

In each case the authors are exploring the use of a particular tool, however, as is emphasised in this section, theory and practice cannot be taken apart, and the theoretical and empirical context within which these (very different) tools are located generates strong links to and tensions with the other chapters in this volume. The structured nature of the tools presented by Maurice Yolles and Paul Iles and Jamie Callahan and Denis Gračanin in this section resonates well with the chapters by Paul Iles and Maurice Yolles, and to a certain extent with that of Monica Lee, both in the first section of this book. In contrast, the tools presented in the last two chapters of this section (Carole McKenzie, and Lloyd Davies and Paul Kraus) adopt a more individualistic approach, with a focus on the exceptional that resonates with chapters by Kim James and Heather Höpfl. The dilemmas associated with use of tools for intervention and analysis can be scrutinised through the critique of intervention presented by Rosemary Hill, and the chapters by Tim Hatcher, Jim Stewart, and Carole Elliott and Sharon Turnbull.

9   Clarifying the complexity of emotion in HRD

The use of visualisation technology

Jamie L. Callahan and Denis Gračanin

> The only way of expressing emotion in the form of art is by finding an 'objective cor-relative'; in other words, a set of objects, a situation, a chain of events which shall be the formula of that *particular* emotion; such that when the external facts, which must terminate in sensory experience, are given, the emotion is immediately evoked.
>
> (Eliot, 1921: 95–103)

Introduction

The essence of chaos and complexity theories is that 'simple processes in nature [can] produce magnificent edifices of complexity *without* randomness. In nonlinearity and feedback lay all the necessary tools for encoding and then unfolding structures as rich as the human brain' (Gleick, 1987, p. 306–307). Faith in the tools we use, whether they are accurate or not, has brought extraordinary insights and results. For example, Weick (1995) relates the story of the soldiers who used a map of the Pyrenees to find their way successfully in the Swiss Alps. For centuries we used Newtonian laws to solve quite adequately complex problems in the physical world until the general theory of relativity provided a better understanding of what occurs in time and space. Our attempts to find tools that will better clarify the complexity that confronts us may not give us an accurate picture of 'reality'. Nevertheless, our attempts very often yield tools that reveal extraordinary insights that are 'real' for those seeking answers to practical issues. Thus, in the spirit of chaos and complexity, this chapter offers a tool that represents our attempt to begin unfolding the 'objective correlatives' of emotion structures in the workplace that influence the practice of HRD.

We first explore the nature of HRD and the role that emotion plays in the practice of HRD. We then offer a theoretical framework for capturing information about both emotion and its relationship to the organisation. In other words, we create a guide for finding the objective correlatives that will allow us to visualise the pattern of emotions related to HRD activities in an organisation. We then demonstrate how visualisation technology provides a vehicle for understanding and acting upon the patterns of emotion that emerge in an organisation by offering a series of simplified visual models. We conclude the chapter with some applications and implications of this technology for HRD professionals.

Human resource development and emotion

Human resource development is an interdisciplinary field of research and practice. In its most essential form, HRD involves theories and practices about people, learning, and organisations. The name of the field itself suggests this tri-partite nature of HRD – *humans* are, or have, *resources* that can be *developed*. A resource is an asset, a means to reach an end, something that can be developed or transformed to better achieve the goals of the system. Resources, both human and otherwise, are fundamental components of goal-oriented social systems, such as organisations (Parsons and Shils, 1962/1951). Historically, HRD has employed learning theory to accomplish the development of resources for organisations (Callahan, in press).

As distasteful as this may be to many, the applied field of HRD must serve the interests of organisations because it would not otherwise exist as a field of practice. However, it cannot be understated that HRD also must serve the interests of the humans within organisations. Professionals within the field of HRD walk a fine line between serving two masters – the organisation and the people. We believe the challenge for the field of HRD is how to effectively balance our service to these often-competing interests to optimise benefit to both.

One area of human interest that can either support or conflict with organisational interest is emotion. Emotion is relevant to HRD professionals in at least three fundamental ways – through people, organisations and learning. Each of these three interconnected components of HRD can be connected to emotion. Although many disciplines inform each of these components of HRD, for the sake of brevity we will use exemplars to describe each connection. The component of people can be represented by the discipline of psychology, which includes the study of people as individuals. The component of organisations can be represented by the discipline of sociology because it includes the study of goal-oriented social systems (i.e. organisations). The component of learning can be represented by the literature from education.

Emotion has long been connected to the human condition. Ever since William James pondered, 'What is emotion?' in the late nineteenth century, the discipline of psychology has explored the construct of emotion. In fact, much of the contemporary exploration of emotion is found in the literature associated with psychology (Domagalski, 1999). Decision-making, satisfaction, motivation, creativity and leadership are all examples of constructs central to psychology that have been linked to emotion research.

Sociology is another core disciplinary area that includes emotion-related research to inform the organisation component of HRD. In fact, contemporary interest in emotion in organisations was spurred by Hochschild's (1983) work on the sociology of emotion. While many of the topics associated with psychology are certainly found in organisational contexts, sociology tends to focus on the collective issues of emotion. Topics such as organisational culture, individual and collective interaction, social identity, and structuration are sociological constructs that have been linked to emotion research.

Finally, the education literature is filled with research and theory regarding learning. Dewey (1894, 1895) was one of the first education scholars to explore the nature of emotion. In a wide variety of forms, emotion can be associated with learning. For example, anxiety and fear can both inhibit (Short and Yorks, 2002) and enhance (Reio and Callahan, 2000) learning. Educational researchers have explored such varied topics as the role of emotion in learning processes, emotion in multiple levels of learning (individual, group, and organisational), and emotional outcomes of learning.

Clearly, emotion can be linked to people, organisations, and learning – the three core components of HRD. As we seek to understand better how, why, and in what way emotion is associated with HRD and HRD practices, we need to develop more efficient ways of representing our data about emotion in organisations. The visualisation tool presented here is a first step in accomplishing this goal.

Theoretical framework

Byrne (1998) points out that complexity research in the social sciences 'must turn to explicit theories as the basis of the construction of models of how the world is working' (p. 66). Two explicit theories form the basis of our quest to visualise emotion in an organisational context - Talcott Parsons' general theory of action and Arlie Russell Hochschild's emotion systems theory. Emotion systems theory is, in turn, supplemented by emotion structuration theory (Callahan, 2002).

The role of complexity and chaos

The general theory of action (GTA) (Parsons, 1951) has a long and distinguished, although controversial, history. Despite the controversy, Parsons' emphasis on culture is still seen as 'strikingly contemporary' (Turner, 1999: 17) and highly relevant to the study of social systems today. For example, Parsons' treatment of culture has recently been used as a means to understand complex social systems (e.g. Frank and Fahrbach, 1999; Harvey and Reed, 1998). Although generally critical of Parsons' work, Byrne (1998) highlights that Parsons used the concepts and language of complexity long before the scientific community accepted those concepts.

Many argue that Parsons' work is too homeostatic and does not provide a vehicle to understand the essence of change. However, a closer reading of Parsons reveals a clear interest in capturing and understanding the nature of change (e.g. Parsons and Shils, 1962/1951; Parsons, 1951; Parsons, 1964). Parsons argues that 'society is meant to be a developing, evolving entity' (Parsons, 1964/1999: 274). Much like the conceptions of complexity theory, Parsons suggested that, at a very broad level, relatively stable general patterns could be found in social systems. Change is initiated at the micro level of social systems, through interactions of individuals.

Thus, despite the negative claims, we find that many aspects of GTA offer a valuable framework for understanding organisations as dynamic, complex social systems. A number of characteristics that are fundamental to GTA can also be found in complex systems theory (CST), including self-organising and self-similarity (Mainzer, 1994; Cilliers, 1998; Morel and Ramanujam, 1999), adaptation (Holland, 1995), and structural equilibrium (Prigogine and Stengers, 1984; Frank and Fahrbach, 1999). Because we sought to incorporate the concepts of CST in our work, GTA was a key choice as part of the theoretical framework for the study.

General theory of action

We use Talcott Parsons' GTA as the sensitising framework to view emotion-based actions within an organisation. This complex theory of action centres on four 'functions' that Parsons (1961) considered to be the most critical processes of all systems. In the language of chaos and complexity theory, these functions may be seen as the attractors around which the complex social system revolves in a non-linear, interactive pattern. The four functions represent the four primary goals of the many actions taken within and by a system (Wallace and Wolf, 1995). This theory of social systems incorporates both internal and external orientations of the system and the means and ends by which the system operates.

The external orientation of the system is represented by two functions of the GTA – adaptation and goal attainment. The actions of the first system function, adaptation (A), are those that obtain 'disposable facilities' (Parsons, 1961) for the system from the environment. In other words, this function describes the means by which the system interacts with its environment to get needed resources such as information, customers, new employees and the like. The next externally oriented system function is goal attainment (G). The actions associated with goal attainment serve to mobilise those resources that were obtained for the system. Actions associated with this function are those that use these resources to achieve organisational goals; they are the end result of obtaining resources from the environment.

The internal orientation is also represented by two functions – integration and latent pattern maintenance. Integration (I) pulls together (or 'integrates') the various parts of the system so that it forms a recognisable whole. This function includes actions that help link individuals and groups together, for example, information distribution, informal communications, and networking. They are the end result of having an integrated pattern of organisation. The final function is latent pattern maintenance (L); this subsystem is often referred to as the culture function because the actions associated with this function serve to maintain the stability of values, beliefs and interactions. This function is the means by which a social system maintains its unique identity.

These four functions – adaptation, goal attainment, integration and latent pattern maintenance – do not operate as distinct clusters. Instead, these four functions are interrelated; a change in one function will result in a change in the other functions. The connections between the functions are called interchange media. The framework of functions and interchange media is depicted in Figure 9.1.

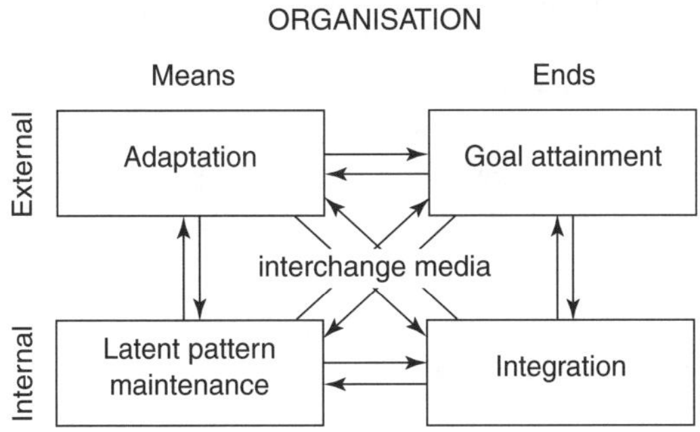

ORGANISATION

Figure 9.1 Key components of the general theory of action.

Emotion systems and structuration

The second component of the theoretical framework is Hochschild's emotion systems theory. We used this theory to begin our exploration of emotional behaviour in the system (or organisation). Hochschild's emotion systems theory includes actions to manage emotions, cultural guidelines for those actions, and interactions between individual actors that create the context for emotion management (Hochschild, 1983). Hochschild proposes two categories of managing emotions, emotion work and emotional labour (for a detailed discussion of the differences between the two see Callahan and McCollum, 2002). For the purpose of this chapter, the overarching term of 'emotion management' will be used as the convention to identify actions associated with either emotion work or emotional labour. Emotion management is the active attempt to change, in either quality or degree, an emotion held by an individual (Hochschild, 1983).

The patterns of emotion management and expression are part of the emotion structuration that occurs in an organisation (Callahan, 2002). Emotion structuration is a more conscious consideration of the role that emotions play in systems, structures and the structuration process. Both the expression and management of emotion follow rules and guidelines embedded in organisational structures. As we follow, or deviate from, these rules in the course of our daily routines, we re-create or change the structures that generate those rules (Callahan, 2002; Tracy, 2000). Following Giddens' (1979) general structuration theory, emotion structuration theory consists of rules, resources, systems, and the interaction of these components.

Because our attempt to visualise emotion in organisations incorporates elements of emotion structuration, a brief description of the theory is warranted. *Rules* include both display and feeling rules; in other words, social guidelines for how an individual should express and experience emotion. *Resources* describe how emotions are controlled as resources. As an authoritative resource, emotion is controlled by external forces, such as the organisation; as an allocative resource, emotion is controlled by the individual. The *systems* component includes sanctions, power and communication. Sanctions are the outcome of individual emotion expression or management – harmony with the social system, deviation from social guidelines, or dissonance with the social system. Power is the application of emotion as a resource; communication is the emotional transaction itself or the feedback loop of emotion. The interconnection of these components is the final element of emotion structuration theory. Our attempts at visualisation of emotion patterns in an organisation will hopefully result in a visual representation of this interaction.

Linking the theoretical framework

Affective connections among group members tend to drive part of the structure found in complex nonlinear social systems (Mainzer, 1994). Thus, emotions may be seen as an important element in understanding complex systems. Emotion management actions theoretically constitute a critical element found in the Parsonian general theory of action. Hochschild (1979, 1983) was interested in how society drives an individual to shape and control *feelings cognitively* in order to fit within that society, in order to achieve *goals* within that society. The cognitive manipulation of feelings in the pursuit of a goal is analogous to the cornerstone of GTA – instrumental action (Ritzer, 1992; Parsons, 1951). It follows then that emotion management can be considered one type of instrumental action. This connection is important for uncovering the 'objective correlates' of emotion in complex systems. The GTA provides a lens to the structure of actions within a complex organisational system. Emotion systems theory offers emotion management as a type of action that is consistent with the GTA framework. Further, the 'affective connections' between individuals so fundamental to the development of system structure in complex systems theory can be seen through emotion systems theory. The result is a picture of a complex system that uses emotion management actions as the means to provide a broad, yet detailed, distributed view of the organisation.

Creating the model

Our initial idea to visualise emotion patterns emerged from a qualitative exploration of an organisation (Callahan, 2000, Callahan, 2002). The primary data collection method from that study was semi-structured in-depth interviews that focused on incidents associated with the organisation in which the individual acted to suppress or evoke emotions. Data collection methods also included traditional and participant observations, and document analysis. The interviews, observation notes and archival material were analysed using a coding system grounded in the theoretical framework presented in this chapter. The four characteristics of systems described earlier, as defined by Parsons (1951), were used as the primary codes. Following Parsons' (1937/1949) conception of analysing action, the unit of analysis was the *action* that occurred. All actions discussed by participants were coded based on the *primary* system characteristic associated with the act. Those actions were also coded based on the emotion associated with the action and the management of that emotion, or lack thereof. The actions were then quantified and subjected to a chi-square analysis to present the differences in emotion structuration in the organisation.

This approach, while useful, was rather antiseptic. To help begin to make the emotion patterns in this organisation more robust, we turned to visualisation technology to create a different type of presentation of our data. Like the iconological modelling discussed by Harvey and Reed (1998), the 'novelty ... resides in the priority it gives to the visual over the analytic' (p. 310). This visual approach is inherently interpretive and is especially suited to understanding nuances of intra-organisational social phenomena. To create a 'picture' of emotion management patterns that makes these patterns more accessible to organisational decision-makers, we propose using visualisation technology to *show* how emotion management and expression are associated with organisational actions in a given context.

Visualisation

Social interactions among members of an organisation may be compared to a very intricate and complex web of connections that is dynamic in nature. An analogy from the area of information technology is the Internet, the World Wide Web and its collection of interconnected documents. There has been a significant amount of work in visualising the World Wide Web, including some work in displaying social interactions when using collaborative software tools. Based on techniques already developed and used for the World Wide Web visualisation (Gračanin and Wright, 1999), we are developing an approach to visualise (based on GTA) organisational structure with a focus on emotion management. Different levels of details associated with emotion management and organisational functions may be selected to cope with the complexity of the presented information.

As discussed earlier, the four main functions of the GTA's conceptual framework are adaptation, goal attainment, integration and latent pattern maintenance (see Figure 9.1). Data sets organised within such a framework include hierarchies and graphs and are similar to data sets related to, for example, telephone calls or World Wide Web sites (Keim, 2001, p. 41). Visualisation techniques used for this type of data involve mapping a two-dimensional graph layout to a three-dimensional structure(s) in order to reduce or even eliminate clutter.

The main challenge is to develop a model that can be used to represent both organisational action and human behaviour as they relate to emotion management and expression. We propose continuing the journey from qualitative explorations of individual perceptions of their emotion management and expression to categorising those perceptions based on a theory of social systems. We then suggest using a visual model of those perceptions both to begin a search for further meaning and to make decisions for larger strategic actions in the organisation.

By utilising a Parameterised Petri net as an underlying model, visualisation can be used to provide a tool for researchers to explore different patterns and structures embedded in qualitative data. Figure 9.2 shows the overall visualisation

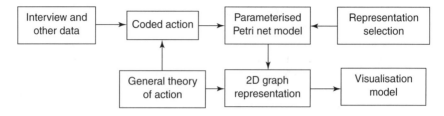

Figure 9.2 Visualisation framework.

framework. Data from interviews, observations, and archives are analysed based on the guiding theoretical framework – GTA, emotion systems, and emotion structuration – to produce coded actions. The coding is then mapped to parameter values in the corresponding Parameterised Petri net model. A two-dimensional graph representation is created and the resulting two-dimensional graph representation is then visualised and mapped to a three-dimensional environment.

Petri nets

In this chapter, we present simplified visual models of how technology can inform our understanding of emotion patterns in organisations. Taking sample components of the underlying theories guiding the visualisation, we demonstrate how Petri nets and Parameterised Petri nets can be used to depict graphically the interactive patterns of emotion in organisations.

Analysed qualitative data can be viewed as multidimensional data where the dimensions correspond to the coding of individual actions. Selecting 'interesting' dimensions and 'collapsing' all other dimensions is used as a mechanism that facilitates exploration of various visual representations at different layers. Previous work on Parameterised Petri nets (Gračanin *et al.*, 1994) provides a mechanism for multidimensional, hierarchical two-dimensional graphical representation that is mapped to a three-dimensional structure. A Petri net is a directed bi-partite graph in which there are two groups of nodes representing transitions and places.

A transition is the link between two different codes while a place is a code itself; for example, in an organisation, inconsistent communication from management may lead to frustration that is not readily expressed to management. Inconsistent communication would be coded under integration in our model; managed frustration would be coded as an emotion management action. Each of these would be a 'place' in the Petri net. The transition from emotion trigger (inconsistent communication) to emotion outcome (managed frustration) would be a 'transition' in the Petri net. Transitions and places in a Petri net model correspond to coded actions and behaviour (emotions) where coding determines the dimensionality of the model. Additional constraints on actions and behaviour are imposed by tokens assigned to places. Dynamic properties are modelled as changes in the token distribution over places.

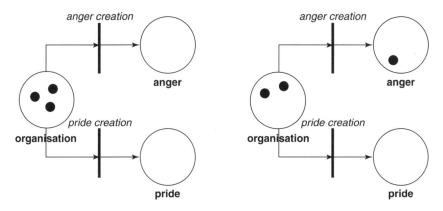

Figure 9.3 Ordinary Petri net example.

Figure 9.3 shows a simple example of an ordinary Petri net where a collection of various 'situations' occurring in an organisation is presented as a place labelled 'organisation'. Each token, represented as a smaller black filled circle, represents one such situation. A transition labelled '*anger creation*' indicates that a situation represented as a token in the 'organisation' place produces anger. The Petri net on the left represents the state before anger occurs. When the transition '*anger creation*' 'fires', a token is consumed from the 'organisation' place and produced in the 'anger' place, as represented by the Petri net on the right. Each arrow going from a place to a transition consumes one token and each arrow going from a transition to a place produces one token. Similarly, if the 'pride creation' transition 'fires', a token is consumed from the 'organisation' place and produced in the 'pride' place.

Unlike an ordinary Petri net, a Parameterised Petri net includes some information in a token. That information (often depicted by colour) can be represented as a set of values. One set of values (or a dimension) can be associated with emotion. In that case the Parameterised Petri net may look as shown in Figure 9.4.

Different shades of tokens indicate different information associated with individual tokens. In other words, while the tokens belonging to the same place in an ordinary Petri net are not distinguishable, the tokens belonging to the same place in a Parameterised Petri net are (that holds for all coloured Petri net models).

In the Parameterised Petri net, the number of places is not fixed. The number of places depends on the dimensions of the underlying theory that describes the properties of the system. These dimensions can be referred to as parameterisation

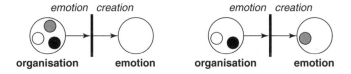

Figure 9.4 Parameterised Petri net example.

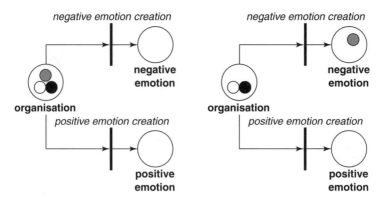

Figure 9.5 Parameterisation using emotion values.

descriptors. A new value of the parameterisation descriptor gives a set of new parameterised places. Given the parameterisation descriptor, one can accordingly group the pattern transitions (i.e. connections betweens codes) to correspond to transitions in a standard Petri net. Using parameterisation it is possible to group patterns in several sets and represent each set with a new place. Pattern transitions are accordingly grouped and each group is represented with a parameterised transition. The example from Figures 9.4 and 9.5 illustrates that concept. Assuming that emotions include anger, happiness, pride and fear, then the Parameterised Petri net in Figure 9.4 can be parameterised by dividing emotions into positive (happiness, pride) and negative emotions (anger, fear), as shown in Figure 9.5.

An example

A hypothetical example has been created to illustrate the proposed approach to visualise the patterns of emotion. The example is based on selected elements of emotion structuration that might occur around activities associated with adaptation (such as interactions with a customer). In the present example, we have incorporated the felt emotion, the organisational display rules for the emotion, the type of resource and the sanction element of the emotion system.

Table 9.1 provides an example for adaptation and relationships among emotion (anger, happiness, pride and fear), display rule (display or don't display emotion), resources (authorative and allocative) and system (dissonance, deviance and harmony). There are forty-eight possible combinations of emotions, display rules, resources and system (four emotion types, two display rules types, two resource types and three sanction types). Not all combinations are feasible.

The simplest Parameterised Petri net representation of the data in Table 9.1 is shown in Figure 9.6 ('10x' indicates ten tokens in the organisation place).

The pattern that can be extracted from this Petri net indicates the relationship between anger (emotion) and deviance/dissonance (system) through display rule

Table 9.1 Adaptation example: serving customers (10 incidents)

Emotion	Display rule	Resources	Sanction
Anger (4)	Don't	Authorative (3) Allocative (1)	Dissonance Deviance
Happiness (4)	Do	Authorative (2) Allocative (2)	Harmony
Pride (1)	Do	Allocative (1)	Harmony
Fear (1)	Don't	Authorative (1)	Dissonance

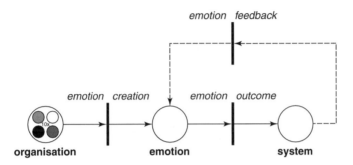

Figure 9.6 Simple Parameterised Petri net.

and resources. The same pattern can be constructed for other emotions from Table 9.1. In a real system, for example, the generation of deviance and disso-nance creates tension and instability in the system, i.e. there is an increase in anger. As a consequence, the Petri net in Figure 9.6 includes 'feedback' transi-tions. Through such increase in emotion, a feedback between the four blocks of the GTA framework (Figure 9.1) can be established that enables construction of more complex Petri nets.

Figure 9.7 shows how the simple Parameterised Petri net can be expanded by focusing on possible system outcomes (dissonance, deviance, and harmony). By further refining the Parameterised Petri net, a more detailed model can be devel-oped. In such a model, Petri net properties can be determined and used to draw conclusions about the corresponding organisation. For example, it is possible that based on the structure of the Petri net and the initial distribution of tokens, the number of tokens in the dissonance place may grow without limits. That indicates instability and potential problem in the organisation. Similarly, if Petri net analy-sis determines that all places are bounded, i.e. the number of tokens in them cannot grow over some limit, the organisation may be considered stable. It is important to note that the Petri net is based on assumptions made about the col-lected data and coded actions. Therefore, the conclusions made based on the properties of the Petri net should be put in proper context. As the Petri net becomes more refined and with more details, a more advanced visualisation is needed. In that case, a three-dimensional representation derived from the two-

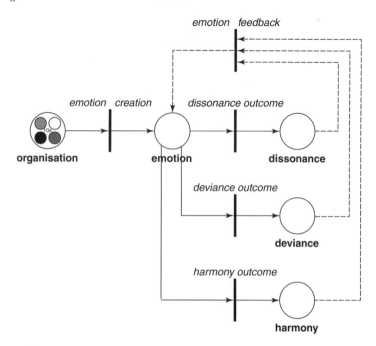

Figure 9.7 Outcome based parameterisation.

dimensional Petri net graph helps to present structure and patterns in a more manageable way.

Applications

Much like current qualitative analysis software packages, such as NVivo™ (Fraser, 2000), Petri nets create graphic representations of coded qualitative data. These representations summarise complex patterns found in social systems. Parameterised Petri nets take this representation further, however. First, this type of visualisation offers a dynamic representation of the data. We can follow simultaneous transitions of data through a theoretical framework. This provides real-time perspectives of what appears to be happening in the social system. Second, and perhaps more importantly, Parameterised Petri nets offer the opportunity to simulate possible futures. At what point does anger management cause instability in the organisation? When does exuberance interfere with performance? Parameterised Petri nets can shed light on these questions.

By creating a means to visualise the emotion management patterns in an organisation, we offer organisational leaders a tool to aid in activities such as decision-making and strategic planning. This type of visualisation may also provide a means to track the impact of decisions in the organisation. For example, if we are able to track systemic changes and compare the timing of those changes to shifts in the emotional web of the organisation, we may make some inferences about the impact of the decisions on the emotional state of the organisation. This visualisation may also offer a vehicle for more in-depth pursuits of the implications of emotion in organisations. If we can *see* how emotion management and emotion expression actions are associated with what is occurring at the organisational level, we might be able to better formulate questions about the emotion patterns of the organisation and determine if the pattern is functional or dysfunctional for both individuals and the social system.

In addition to shedding light on practical matters within organisations, Parameterised Petri nets also have the capacity to further theory building and theory testing efforts. Parameterised Petri nets can help researchers clarify the boundaries of a given theory (Lynham, 2002) by offering flexibility in exploration of the components in the theory. The greatest promise, however, is the manner in which Parameterised Petri nets can help specify the system states of the theory (Lynham, 2002). Because the dynamic properties of Parameterised Petri nets can identify the point at which a system becomes stable or unstable, this tool helps us understand the conditions under which the theory operates most effectively. Finally, in terms of testing theory, Parameterised Petri nets can simulate real-world conditions in order to test whether hypothetical or real data can effectively explain a phenomenon. The unique contribution of this technology is that both qualitative and quantitative data can be used as the foundation for building and testing theory.

Conclusion

Our attempt to visualise the patterns of emotion is not without recognition of both positive and negative implications. By creating an application that enables us to visualise these patterns, we introduce a new symbol to the organisation. Because symbols are the means by which we represent culture, we must consider how such a symbol would influence both the system itself and the emotional behaviour within the system. We also must concern ourselves with how such a visual representation might be used by organisational leaders. The literature on emotion management has increasingly focused on the exploitative and oppressive nature of organisational control of emotion (e.g. Fineman and Sturdy, 1999, Turnbull, 1999). To what extent might we be providing a tool to exploit employees further?

Transferring qualitative accounts of emotional behaviour to computer applications requires a simplification of the rich narrative. However, the depth of meaning and sense of accuracy may be compromised in favour of greater generalisability and simplicity. We must question, then, where and how do we balance the need for depth of meaning and the need for clarity of complex issues? Can we have both?

Harvey and Reed (1998) claim that we must have both and that the revolutionary concepts introduced by chaos and complexity theory allow us to incorporate both meaning and clarity. The advances made in visualisation technology offer us a vehicle to do just that. In their comparison of visualisation tools for Web information retrieval, Heo and Hirtle (2001) stress the importance of creating visualisation applications that both reduce complexity for the user while, at the same time, providing the context necessary for understanding. Our continued quest for visualisation of emotion structuration will attempt to bring both clarity and context.

References

Benford, S., Taylor, L., Brailsford, D., Koleva, B., Craven, M., Fraser, M., Reynard, G. and Greenhalgh, C. (1999) 'Three dimensional visualization of the World Wide Web', *ACM Computing Surveys* 31(4es): 1–16

Byrne, D. (1998) *Complexity Theory and the Social Sciences: An introduction*, New York: Routledge

Callahan, J. L. (2000) 'Emotional management and organizational functions: A case study of patterns in a not-for-profit organization', *Human Resource Development Quarterly* 11(3): 245–268

Callahan, J. L. (2002) 'Masking the need for organizational change: Emotion structuration in a non-profit organization', *Organization Studies* 23(2): 281–297

Callahan, J. L. (in press) 'Organizational learning: A reflective and representative critical issue for HRD', in A. G. Maycunich, J. L. Callahan and L. A. Bierema (Eds) *Critical Issues in Human Resource Development*, Cambridge: Perseus Books

Callahan, J. L. and McCollum, E. E. (2002) 'Obscured variability: The distinction between emotion work and emotional labor' in N. M. Ashkanasy, W. J. Zerbe and C. E. J. Hartel (Eds) *Managing Emotions in the Workplace*, Armonk, NY: M.E. Sharpe, pp. 219–231

Cilliers, P. (1998) *Complexity and postmodernism: Understanding complex systems*, New York: Routledge

Darwin, C. (1872/1955) *The Expression of the Emotions in Man and Animals*, New York: Philosophical Library

Dewey, J. (1894) 'The theory of emotion: Emotional attitudes', *The Psychological Review* 1(6): 553–569

Dewey, J. (1895) 'The theory of emotion: The significance of emotions', *The Psychological Review* 2(1): 13–32

Domagalski, T. A. (1999) 'Emotion in organizations: Main currents', *Human Relations* 52(6): 833–853

Eliot, T. S. (1921) 'Hamlet and his problems', in T. S. Eliot (Ed.) *The Sacred Wood: Essays on poetry and criticism*, London: Methuen, pp. 95–103

Fineman, S. and Sturdy, A. (1999) 'The emotions of control: A qualitative exploration of environmental regulation', *Human Relations* 52(5): 631–663

Frank, K. A. and Fahrbach, K. (1999) 'Organization culture as a complex system: Balance and information in models of influence and selection', *Organization Science* 10(3): 253–277.

Fraser, D. (2000) *QSR NVivo Reference Guide*, Melbourne, Australia: WSR International Pty. Ltd

Giddens, A. (1979) *Central Problems in Social Theory: Action, structure and contradiction in social analysis*, Los Angeles: University of California Press

Gleick, J. (1987) *Chaos: Making a new science*, New York: Penguin Books

Gračanin, D., Srinivasan, P. and Valavanis, K. P. (1994) 'Parameterized Petri nets and their application to planning and coordination in intelligent systems', *IEEE Transactions on Systems, Man and Cybernetics* 24(10): 1,483–1,497

Gračanin, D. and Wright, K. E. (1999) 'Virtual reality interface for the World Wide Web', in *15th Twente Workshop on Language Technology: Interactions in virtual worlds*, Enschede, The Netherlands: University of Twente, pp. 59–68

Harvey, D. L. and Reed, M. (1998) 'Social science as the study of complex systems', in L. D. Kiel and E. Elliott (Eds) *Chaos Theory in the Social Sciences: Foundations and applications*, Ann Arbor, MI: University of Michigan Press

Heo, M. and Hirtle, S. C. (2001) 'An empirical comparison of visualization tools to assist information retrieval on the Web', *Journal of the American Society for Information Science and Technology* 52(8): 666–675

Hochschild, A. R. (1979) 'Emotion work, feeling rules, and social structure', *American Journal of Sociology* 85(3): 551–575

Hochschild, A. R. (1983) *The Managed Heart: Commercialization of human feeling*, Los Angeles: University of California Press

Holland, J. H. (1995) *Adaptation in Natural and Artificial Systems*, Cambridge, MA: MIT Press.

Keim, D. A. (2001) 'Visual exploration of large data sets', *Communications of the ACM* 44(8): 39–44

Lynham, S. A. (2002) 'Quantitative research and theory building: Dubin's method', *Advances in Developing Human Resources* 4(3): 242–276

Mainzer, K. (1994) *Thinking in Complexity: The complex dynamics of matter, mind, and mankind*, Heidelberg, Germany: Springer-Verlag

Morel, B. and Ramanujam, R. (1999) 'Through the looking glass of complexity: The dynamics of organizations as adaptive and evolving systems', *Organization Science* 10(3): 278–293

Parsons, T. (1937/1949) *The Structure of Social Action*, New York: The Free Press

Parsons, T. (1951) *The Social System*, Glencoe, IL: The Free Press

Parsons, T. (1961) *Theories of Society: Foundations of modern sociological theory*, New York: The Free Press

Parsons, T. (1964) *Social Structure and Personality*, New York: The Free Press

Parsons, T. (1964/1999) 'Youth in the context of American society', in B. S. Turner (Ed.) *The Talcott Parsons Reader*, Oxford: Blackwell Publishers, pp. 271–291

Parsons, T. and Shils, E. A. (Eds) (1962/1951) *Toward a General Theory of Action: Theoretical foundations for the social sciences*, New York: Harper Torchbooks

Prigogine, I. and Stengers, I. (1984) *Order Out of Chaos*, New York: Bantam Books

Reio, T. and Callahan, J. L. (2000) 'Affect, curiosity, and socialization-related learning: A path analysis of antecedents to job performance', paper presented at American Education Research Association, New Orleans, LA

Ritzer, G. (1992) *Classical Sociological Theory*, New York: McGraw-Hill

Short, D. C. and Yorks, L. (2002) 'Analyzing training from an emotions perspective', *Advances in Human Resource Development* 4(1): 80–96

Tracy, S. J. (2000) 'Becoming a character for commerce: Emotion labor, self-subordination, and discursive construction of identity in a total institution', *Management Communication Quarterly* 14(1): 90–128

Turnbull, S. (1999) 'Emotional labour in corporate change programmes: The effects of organizational feeling rules on middle managers', *Human Resource Development International* 2(2): 125–146

Turner, B. S. (1999) *The Talcott Parsons Reader*, Oxford: Blackwell Publishers

Wallace, R. A. and Wolf, A. (1995) *Contemporary Sociological Theory: Continuing the classical tradition*, Englewood Cliffe, NJ: Prentice Hall

Weick, K. (1995) *Sensemaking in Organizations*, Thousand Oaks, CA: Sage.

Weick, K. (1979) *The Social Psychology of Organizing* (2nd edn) New York: McGraw-Hill, Inc.

10 Complexifying organisational development and HRD

Maurice Yolles and Paul Iles

HRD can be seen to derive much of its theoretical basis from OD (e.g. Iles and Yolles, 2002; Swanson, 1999; McLean, 1999), and indeed Grieves and Redman (1999, p. 82) contend that HRD is ' living in the shadow of OD'. We contend that any analysis of the response of HRD to complexity involves an analysis of the theoretical roots of OD, especially in systems theory (e.g. Iles and Yolles, 2002).

OD developed from the work of Lewin (1947), and integrates Nadler's idea that an open system is a transformer of inputs to outputs. Such systems need to have 'favourable transactions of input and output with the environment in order to survive over time' (Nadler, 1993, p. 86). OD offers an approach to organisational inquiry that seeks to find a balance of forces with its environment (Pugh, 1993) by instituting appropriate change in an organisation's system. It was originally conceived as a strategy for large-scale cultural and/or systemic change that depends on many people accepting the need for change, and until recently was based on diagnosing gaps between what is and what ought to be (Weisbord and Janoff, 1996).

OD maintains a paradigm that is consultant orientated and people centred. It is a soft system methodology developed prior to that of Checkland (1981). It is concerned with intervention into problem situations to achieve change management through individuals and their relationships. OD's intended use was 'to articulate a mode of organisational consultancy that paralleled the client-centred approach in counselling and contrasted with consultancy models that were centred on expertise' (Coghlan, 1993, p. 117). However, at its broadest, OD is concerned with 'boundaries and relationships at a number of different levels between enterprises, their stakeholders and society, and the way in which these relationships could change over time' (Pritchard, 1993, p. 132).

Harrison explains that consultants who use traditional OD tend to assume that organisations are most effective when they 'reduce power differences, foster open communication, encourage cooperation and solidarity, and adopt policies that enhance the potential of employees' (Harrison, 1994, p. 8). To help assist organisational forms and cultures towards this ideal, consultants use small group training, feedback on interpersonal processes, participative decision-making, and build on strong cohesive organisational culture.

Traditional OD has been described as being based on a narrow view of organisational effectiveness. It 'does not seem to work well in organisations that emphasise status and authority differences or in nations that do not share the values underlying development. Even where they are appropriate, traditional organisational development interventions usually yield minor, incremental improvements in organisational functioning, as opposed to the radical transformations needed for recovery from crises and decline' (Ibid., p. 8–9). The needs of fast change in complex situations should be added in here. Given HRD's roots in OD, we argue that these criticisms apply to HRD also (Iles and Yolles, 2002; Grieves and Redman. 1999).

To make OD more flexible and broaden its ability to deal with complex organisational situations, it must be able to deal with changes in organisational form, strategy, and culture; power alignments, political bargaining, cultural diversity (at different levels of the organisation), stability and instability. Harrison (1994) therefore proposed some changes to diagnosis in OD. However, it still has a limited capacity to guide inquiry through a variety of political and cybernetic attributes of organisations that are pertinent to change. It would be ideal if a map could be found that enhances the capacity of OD, and by implication HRD, to do this. To satisfy this, more theory needs to be embedded into the theoretical bases of OD and HRD. In due course we will show that this theory can be derived from viable systems theory or VST (e.g. Yolles, 1999; Iles and Yolles, 2002).

In order to develop the capacity of OD (and therefore HRD) to deal better with greater complexity in organisations, it will be useful to develop its paradigm. As we shall show, this can be done by embedding it in managerial cybernetics and illustrating that one of its developments, VST, is an evolutionary paradigmatic development of OD with significant implications for HRD.

Paradigmatic metamorphosis

It has only been within the last 30 years or so, largely since the work of Kuhn (1970), that we have considered how paradigms change their form. Incremental change involves the development of concepts and their structural relationships, creating new knowledge. Paradigms also change dramatically as new fundamental concepts arise that alter their frames of reference, i.e. as new conceptual extensions enter their frames of reference (Yolles, 1998). In so doing, paradigm holders expand their capacity to explain and therefore diagnose the phenomena that they perceive. Such dramatic change has also been referred to as paradigmatic revolution or metamorphosis. It occurs because of a perceived need by paradigm holders to respond to inherent inadequacies, anomalies or paradoxes. Such metamorphosis can be part of an evolutionary process within which a new species of paradigm arises that has its basis in an existing paradigm. Metamorphosis is not spontaneous, and paradigms first pass though a 'virtual' stage (Yolles, 1996; Midgley, 2000). VST is an example of this; its original development occurring because of a perceived need to respond to the problem of paradigm incommensurability (Burrell and Morgan, 1979; Yolles, 1996) when other approaches seemed unable to respond adequately to it. VST can be historically related to both OD and managerial cybernetics as encapsulated by the viable systems model (VSM) e.g. Beer (1979).

In socially complex situations it is useful to have a theory of the organisation that can help structure problems and manage change where requirements for change in the open system result in interventions. However, there are three traditional barriers to systemic change: (a) resistance to change by members of the organisation, (b) control and (c) power (Iles and Yolles, 2002).

The managerial cybernetics paradigm that underpins VSM can be argued to be a metamorphosis of that underpinning OD. It maintained the OD paradigmatic extensions of the open system, but included the concept of a metasystem. Decisions that arose in the metasystem were transformed in some way to become manifested in the system. VST makes explicit this implicit transformation, and indeed introduced its own metamorphosis by identifying it as a domain in its own right. Linking and developing VST with the ideas of Habermas (1987) and Schwarz (1997) has enhanced its paradigm significantly, and provided a broad potential for inquiry into complex situations. Unlike OD and VSM, VST does not attempt to offer particular interventions, but rather provides a conceptual framework of analysis, for considering appropriate existing models, and for creating new ones. Hence, both OD and VSM (and we contend HRD) can sit comfortably within VST. One problem is that OD and HRD are not currently part of the managerial cybernetic paradigm, despite the urgings of Swanson (2001), and so to relate them better to VST requires a linguistic shift. This can occur without altering its underlying paradigm, and can result in an enhanced and more effective way of dealing with complex change situations.

HRD, OD and the organisation as a transforming system

Nadler's model underpinning much OD, and to an extent HRD (Swanson, 2001) is referred to as the congruence model of organisational behaviour (Nadler and Tushman, 1977; 1979) because it supports the notion that organisations need to have congruency between four subsystems: tasks, individuals, formal organisation and informal organisation. Thus, for instance, there needs to be congruency between tasks and individuals, or between the formal organisation, its control structures and processes, and the informal power structures and processes that exist within the organisation. The basic hypothesis of the model is that an organisation will be most effective when all the four components of the system are congruent with each other. Nadler's four subsystems have been subsumed into a *system definition*, part of the *systems as a transformer*, in Table 10.1, which also incorporates Harrison's (1994) distinctions of organisational focus.

Table 10.1 A focussed view of the organisation through organisational development

System focus	Inputs	System as a transformer		Outputs
		System	Focus environment	
Organisational	Resources facilitate the establishment and maintenance of structures, and activities of the organisation. Strategy: a set of key decisions about the match of the organisation's resources to environmental imperative	Goals, culture, technology, process, behaviour, formal and informal organisation. History provides a background that validates the organisation, its structures, and activities	Provides constraints, demands and opportunities for the organisation	Products and services. Performance indicates the ability of the organisation to achieve its desires
Group	Resources facilitate the maintenance of structures and activities of the group	Group composition, structure, technology; group behaviour process, culture. Effectiveness in a group's performance is determined by strategic goals	Organisation provides task definition and redefinition, control of change, resistance to change, power to shape organisational dynamics	Products, services. Performance indicates the ability of the group to satisfy its intended function
Individual	Human resources	Individual jobs/tasks; individual behaviour, attitudes, orientations	Group/organisation provides quality of work life, well-being	Products, services, ideas. Performance indicates the ability of individuals to operate

Generic problems, needs and actions for organisational change

In the underlying theory of OD coherent organisations have political systems composed of individuals, groups and coalitions, all of which may be competing for power (Tushman, 1977). New ideologies can also influence power positions. Balances of power exist within organisations, and changes can upset these, generating new political activity that forges stable power relationships. In order to facilitate change, it is necessary to shape the political dynamics of an organisation, enabling change to be accepted rather than rejected.

Nadler (1993) argued that change situations have three generic problems, all of which pose challenges also to HRD. Change might upset existing power relationships, and a political dynamic for change is needed. Change may also make people feel that their existing power positions are threatened. Nadler has also identified resistance to change as a generic problem. This may occur (Watson, 1969; Zaltman and Duncan, 1977) when individuals are faced with change situations that they feel may affect their security or stability. Not only can it generate anxiety and affect a sense of autonomy, but it can also alter the patterns of behaviour that have enabled people to cope with management structures and processes. Finally, Nadler has also identified control as a factor necessary to manage change processes. Table 10.2 is indicative of Nadler's view that each of these three factors are generic problems that have associated with them organisational needs, and prescribes HRD actions for intervention that can be used to improve problem situations.

We have said that it will be of use to take OD and HRD through a linguistic shift, thereby explaining Nadler's generic problems in terms of VST for later use. Resistance to change is expressed in terms of four actions that are intended to motivate the organisation to adopt a re-orientation that can deal with change and development. Thus, action steps (1) and (2) develop the fundamental support that is able to motivate a new orientation for the organisation, and in step (3) the use of social symbols can be used to share meanings through which explicit and implicit patterns of behaviour are acquired and transmitted. In step (4) the creation of stability can concretise the orientation that has been created. Hence, Nadler's idea of the problem of resistance to change can also be expressed in terms of providing a re-orientation in the change for the organisation as a whole. The idea of an organisational re-orientation will subsume within it the need to reduce resistance to change. Table 10.2 builds on the perspective of HRD as methodological inquiry presented in Iles and Yolles (2002, Tables 2.5 and 2.6) to indicate some action steps that may be useful for HRD practitioners in dealing with change, learning and development situations.

Table 10.2 Actions relating to problems and needs for change, learning and development

Generic problem		Need		HRD action steps
Nadler	*Yolles and Iles*	*Nadler*	*Iles and Yolles*	
Resistance	Changing orientation	Motivate change	Support the change Underpin the change	1 Assure support of key power groups 2 Use leader behaviour to generate energy in support of change and development 3 Use symbols and language 4 Build in stability
Control	Manifesting possibilities	Manage the transition	Manifest perturbing unrest Manifest support and variety generation Introduce new variety dynamically	5 Surface dissatisfaction with present state 6 Participation in change and development 7 Rewards for behaviour in support of change and development 8 Time and opportunity to disengage from the present state
Power	Energising kinematic processes	Shape political dynamics	Cybernetics Polity Semantic communication	9 Develop and communicate a clear image of the future 10 Build in feedback mechanisms 11 Develop organisational arrangements for the transition 12 Facilitate support for change and development

Control is normally cybernetic, but this is not consistent with the notion of managing the transition. Rather, managing the transition might be better expressed in terms of the actions that relate to an organisation's *possibilities of development*. The action step (5) of surfacing dissatisfaction is a pre-requirement that will in part also seek the views of the membership of the organisation, thereby identifying the unrest that perturbs the organisation and enables the possibility of creating variety. Action step (6) is directed at the manifestation of variety, as is action step (7). Action step (8) provides for the possibilities thrown up with the variety generation to be selected and instituted, and is therefore part of the dynamics of the change, learning and development process.

In Nadler's problem area designated by power, action steps (9) and (12) are cybernetic processes that may be considered to be independent of power. Further, step (11) relates to an organising process rather than to power, and thus is a function of polity that enables the creation of order. All three points therefore are an energising process as opposed to a powering one, and perhaps are better described as kinematic – an energetic movement that can be considered abstractly without reference to the source of that motion. Action step (10) identifies leverage points to facilitate learning, development and change. While leverage is consistent with the creation of force and the use of power, other approaches are possible, as much HRD theory acknowledges.

While these proposed modifications may seem trivial, they will in due course assist in facilitating entry for OD and HRD into the VST frame of reference.

The viable system model

Beer (1979), in his development of managerial cybernetics, explored the nature of viable systems as he created his viable systems model (VSM). Viable systems participate in the autonomous development of their own futures. A viable organisation participates in automorphosis, when it is responsible for and participates in changing its own form, enabling it to maintain appropriate operational behaviour under a changing environment and survive. The form is determined by its structure (Yolles, 1999) that both facilitates and constrains that behaviour. A refinement over OD is that strategic decisions are not simply seen as an input to the system. Rather, they derive from its metasystem (the metaphorical 'cognitive consciousness' of the systems) that is responsible for manifesting and maintaining its structure. While OD sees the system itself as the transformation, the management cybernetics that underpins VSM invents a metasystem, and it implicitly supposes a transformation between the system and the metasystem. Thus, for instance, in OD strategy decisions are often seen as inputs to the system, while in VSM they derive from the metasystem. In this way the metasystem formally becomes one aspect of a structured inquiry (e.g. Iles and Yolles, 2002).

When decision-making is part of a formalised determinable process in an organisation, so the metasystem is also formalised, and decisions are made within it with respect to the perceived needs of the organisation at the level of focus concerned. This does not mean, however, that there may be another informal metasystem from which informal decisions derive. The metasystem ultimately operates through and is defined by the worldviews that determine the nature of the organisation. When a worldview exists formally it may be called its paradigm (Yolles, 1999).

VSM is a generic model of the organisation that promotes principles of communication and control that help it to maintain its viability (Schwaninger, 2001). It is axiomatic in VSM that any organisation that can be modelled as a viable system can also be modelled as a set of five subsystems. They each represent an interactive function that acts with the others as a filter between the environment and the organisation's management hierarchy, and connect management processes and their communications channels. The filter is sophisticated because it attenuates (reduces the importance of) some data while simultaneously amplifying other data. The filtered data is converted into information that is relevant to different levels of management within the organisation. A final control element addressed in the model offers auditing tools to make sure that the correct data is being collated. The audit channel mops up variety by sporadic or periodic checks. However, making sure that the appropriate data is assembled is only one of its functions.

The five subsystems of VSM (e.g.. Beer, 1979) are referred to as S1–S5, and their direct relationship is shown in Figure 10.1. Some of the subsystems are assigned to the metasystem (S3, S4, S5). The system (S1) itself, S2 and S3* do not

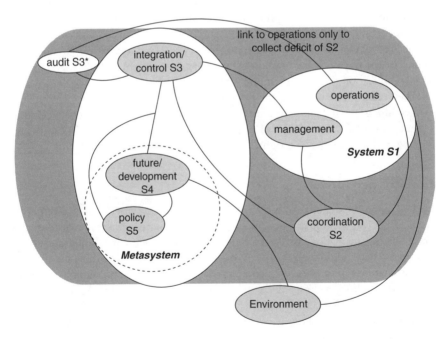

Figure 10.1 Relationship diagram showing the outline concept of the viable system model. (The subsystem entities in S1 (management and operations) are implicitly interconnected).

have assignment, one supposes because together they define a general system. However, for us it would be more sensible to define a system related to OD and HRD in terms of its technology, structures (including jobs/tasks), process, and activities/behaviour (including jobs and operational activities). OD and HRD also include culture and its associated belief system, but this is not part of the VSM model, and it is better distinguished from the system.

VSM has an anomaly. While it properly defines the S1–S5 subsystems, it does not actually clearly define what it means by a 'system' in such a way that it is differentiated from the metasystem. Thus, when it looks for 'structural faults' to correct (Yolles, 1999), it seeks to structure problems that relate to the S1–S5. However, if we adopt the definition of the word system given above (that it is composed of the structural components that are connected with operational behaviour), then S2 and S3* cannot join S1 to be part of the system because their functions are beyond that of the system. This anomaly leads to the notion that VSM should actually be talking about seeking 'metastructural faults' in the organisation.

The basis for viable systems theory

Viable systems theory was stimulated through some of the managerial cybernetic theory that grounds VSM. Like soft systems methodology (Checkland, 1981) and critical systems theory (Midgley, 2000), it adopts a subjectivist epistemology (as embedded in critical theory). In VSM, decisions that derive from the metasystem are transformed so that they can become manifested in the system. This has been expressed explicitly in Figure 10.1 (based on Yolles, 1999) using a dotted line to define a new version of the metasystem (S4 and S5), and leaving S2, S3 and S3* as part of the transforming domain between the metasystem with the system (S1). This modification does not affect the working of VSM in any substantive way.

The relationship between the system and the metasystem has been made explicit in Figure 10.2 (deriving from Yolles, 1996). Though the space between the system and metasystem is one of transformation, it is also susceptible to being defined as domain in its own right, resulting in a three domains model.

Domain properties

Each of the three domains of VST can be associated with a set of cognitive properties. They are cognitive because they relate to human orientations that are manifested from worldview. We identify three classes of such orientation: interests, properties and influences. Taken together, it is possible to formulate a picture of the cognitive properties of any purposeful activity system, as illustrated in Table 10.3. This develops on the cognitive properties table of Yolles (2000a), including some of Vicker's (1965) ideas on the notion of the appreciative system, and a development of the organisational surfing table of Yolles (2000b) that we shall discuss further in due course.

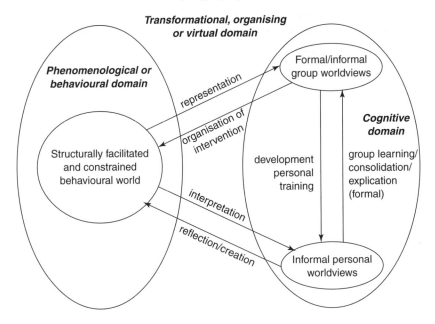

Figure 10.2 Relationship between the behavioural and cognitive domains in the three domains model.

Cognitive interests

Developing on Habermas's (1970) theory of human constitutive knowledge interests (KCI), Yolles (1999, 2001) differentiates three primary generic cognitive areas in which human interest generates knowledge. They can be termed '*knowledge constitutive*' because they determine the mode of discovering knowledge and whether knowledge claims may be warranted. The three generic cognitive areas concern work, interaction and power. Empirical-analytic sciences incorporate a '*technical cognitive interest*' that connects with knowledge about work, and is associated with the instrumental control of the environment that identifies what is appropriate action. The historical-hermeneutic sciences provide access to facts through the understanding of meaning rather than by observation, which involves the interpretation of texts. Their validity is dependent on a mutual understanding derived from traditions, which actors in a situation aim to attain. It is this level of inquiry that Habermas claims is driven by the *practical* knowledge interest. Finally, *emancipatory* knowledge enables us to become self-aware of both the internal and external forces that distort our communications.

It should be said that Habermas's KCI was directed at the individual within a social environment. By adopting his concepts as properties of the organisation KCI plays a slightly different role. This is illustrated by the distinctive use of emancipation. Habermas uses it in a way that is directed towards the self-development, self-knowledge or self-reflection of the individual, and beyond the

Table 10.3 The three domains, their cognitive properties, and organisational patterning

Organisational pattern			
Cognitive properties	*Kinematics (through energetic motion)*	*Orientation (determining trajectory)*	*Possibilities (through potential development)*
	Technical	*Practical*	*Critical deconstraining*
Cognitive interests Phenomenological or behavioural domain	*Work.* This enables people to achieve goals and generate material well-being. It involves technical ability to undertake action in the environment, and the ability to make prediction and establish control	*Interaction.* This requires that people as individuals and groups in a social system gain and develop the possibilities of an understanding of each other's subjective views. It is consistent with a practical interest in mutual understanding that can address disagreements, which can be a threat to the social form of life	*Degree of emancipation.* For organisational viability, the realising of individual potential is most effective when people: (i) liberate themselves from the constraints imposed by power structures (ii) learn through precipitation in social and political processes to control their own destinies
	Cybernetical	*Rational/appreciative*	*Ideological/moral*
Cognitive purposes Virtual or organising domain	*Intention.* This is through the creation and strategic pursuit of goals and aims that may change over time, enables people through control and communications processes to redirect their futures	*Formative organising.* Enables missions, goals, and aims to be defined and approached through planning. It may involve logical, and/or relational abilities to organise thought and action and thus to define sets of possible systematic, systemic and behavioural possibilities. It can also involve the use of tacit standards by which experience can be ordered and valued, and may involve reflection	*Manner of thinking.* An intellectual framework through which policy makers observe and interpret reality. This has an aesthetic or politically correct ethical orientation. It provides an image of the future that enables action through politically correct strategic policy. It gives a politically correct view of stages of historical development, in respect of interaction with the external environment
	Social	*Cultural*	*Political*
Cognitive influences Cognitive domain	Formation. Enables individuals/groups to be influenced by knowledge that relates to our social environment. This has a consequence for our social structures and processes that define our social forms that are related to our intentions and behaviours	Belief. Influences occur from knowledge that derives from the cognitive organisation (the set of beliefs, attitudes, values) of other worldviews. It ultimately determines how we interact and influences our understanding of formative organising	Freedom. Influences occur from knowledge that affect our polity determined, in part, by how we think about the constraints on group and individual freedoms, and in connection with this to organise and behave. It ultimately has impact on our ideology and morality, and our degree of organisational emancipation

limitations of one's roles and social expectations. Self-emancipation gains knowledge through reflection leading to a transformed consciousness. However, our reference to 'degrees of emancipation' in Table 10.3 is intended to describe the condition of an organisation in respect of the emancipation that it provides for the individuals within it. This of course notes that the emancipatory condition will vary between different classes of individuals in an organisation (e.g. director, manager and subordinate). Most organisations involve structural violence (Yolles, 1999) that is directed differently towards different classes, and it limits the potential for 'improvement' of both the individual and ultimately the organisation, at least in respect of variety generation and thus viability. This does not limit the capacity for any individual to seek his or her own emancipation.

The other cognitive properties

Organisations adopt the *purposeful* behaviour associated with the individuals that compose them (Espejo *et al.*, 1996). The concept of purposefulness comes from the idea that human beings attribute meaning to their experienced world, and take responsive action that has purpose. Bertalanffy (1968) attributed the idea of *purposefulness* to Aristotle. Purposefulness (Ackoff, 1981, p. 34) enables the selection of goals and aims and the means for pursuing them. Checkland and Scholes (1990, p. 2) tell us that human beings, whether as individuals or as groups, cannot help but attribute meaning to their experienced world, from which purposeful action follows. They, like Flood and Jackson (1991), also note that purposeful action is knowledge based. One would therefore expect that different knowledge is responsible for the creation of different purposeful behaviours. Consider now that purposeful behaviour is a property of an organisation that can be associated with its paradigms (and thus knowledge) and their linked cognitive models, processes and intentions. It is thinking as part of this that enables the creation of the goals and the taking of actions to achieve them. Goals provide a target towards which purposeful behaviour can be directed.

Cognitive purpose is a property of the organising or virtual domain. In Table 10.4 (see p.162) three cognitive purposes are assigned to the organising domain: cybernetic, rational/appreciative and ideological/moral. Cybernetic cognitive purpose is connected with intention. This occurs through the creation and strategic pursuit of goals and aims that may change over time. It enables people through control and communications processes to redirect their futures. The rational cognitive purpose is connected to formative organising that has logical and/or relational connections. It enables missions, goals and aims to be defined and approached through planning, all of which derive from worldview. It may involve rational aspects that refer to logical and relational abilities to organise thought and action, and thus to define sets of possible systemic and behaviour possibilities. We have in addition included Vicker's (1965) concept of the 'appreciative system', where appreciation provides a reflective view of a situation that entertains both cognitive and evaluative aspects, and it may involve tacit standards by which one can order and value experience. Appreciation might also be related to attitudes with reflection.

Ideological/moral cognitive purpose is concerned with the manner of thinking. It provides an intellectual framework through which policy makers observe and interpret reality. It may be defined as a collection of rationalised and systemised beliefs that coalesce into an image that establishes a phenomenological potential or experience. Political ideology can be instrumental in defining (Holsti, 1967, p. 163):

- an intellectual framework through which policy makers observe and interpret reality;
- a politically correct ethical orientation;
- an image of the future that enables action through strategic policy;
- stages of historical development in respect of interaction with the external environment.

Ideology/morality has an ethical orientation. Ethics is a term that Midgley (2000) refers to as 'values in purposeful action'. However, for us it is the harnessing of ethical and aesthetic values to form a virtual image that an autonomous system will try to manifest phenomenologically. It can provide an image of the future that enables politically correct action through appropriate strategic policy. It also gives a politically correct view of stages of historical development, in respect of inter-action with the external environment, and occurs through values that distinguish between right and wrong. While aesthetics is related to ethics (Mackie, 1977), it does not have associated with it social objectification that is normally associated with ethics, that is, it is not supposed to be taken as socially normative or common.

We have been referring to cognitive purposes, but cognitive influences are also said to exist. This occurs because every coherent organisation can be defined in terms of differentiable cultural, political and social belief systems. The three cog-nitive influences then, are (a) social relating to the formation of groups, (b) political relating to individual and group freedom, and (c) cultural relating to knowledge and meaning about self and others. Further exploration of cognitive influence can be found, for instance, in Yolles (2000b; 2000c).

Organisational patterning

The origin of the idea of organisational patterning derives from Yolles (2000b). It is represented in Table 10.3 as column headers that indicate horizontal interactiv-ity between the row attributes. The proposition is that just as the rows each have empirical and analytical independence so do the columns. Thus, both horizontal and vertical interactivity can occur between cells through their ontological inter-connections.

The first column involves: (a) technical cognitive interests connected to work that may be associated with some form of creation; (b) cybernetical cognitive pur-poses connected to intention, implicitly involving time through feedback if nothing else; and (c) social properties connected to the formation of something, suggesting an idea of something in motion, for which we adopt the term *kinematic*. We recall that the motion being considered is abstract, without reference to a source.

Since the kinematic classification relates to work, intention and formation, it may be seen as being representative of 'viability in action'. Work knowledge con-ditions knowledgeable action, and may be explored by examining how work processes change with the introduction of new knowledge through HRD. Measurements for this control process are qualitative, requiring an inquirer such as an HRD practitioner or researcher (Iles and Yolles, 2002) to search the local environment for ways in which knowledge has been applied by a learner (directly or indirectly) to varied situations. Social influences represent knowledge about the way in which social processes operate. This dimension can perhaps be measured not in terms of social meaning, but in terms of the reticence that actors have to the introduction of new social meaning in a learning process.

Consider the second column now. The first cell relates to practical cognitive interest that is a function of interaction, and enables people in the organisation to work together in a particular way. This can be taken with logical and relational aspects of the rational cognitive purposes that orient the organisation through its rational base and nature of the interactions that can occur. Also the orientating cultural belief system of cognitive influence can be added in, all contributing to an organisational *orientation* that determines its present and future trajectories. One metaphor for organisational orientation leads us to the notion of the study of an organisation's formative orientation within the complex that it creates for itself, and that determines its present and future trajectory.

We have said that orientation is a classification concerned with interaction, logical and relational attributes, and beliefs. These are all connected with what we may call relevant others, that is those other actors who are relevant to a situation from the perspective of an inquirer, such as an HRD researcher or practitioner. Interaction knowledge conditions knowledgeable action (action that results from knowledge), and might possibly be explored by examining how interaction processes change with the introduction of new knowledge through HRD interventions. Cultural cognitive influences can be evaluated by examining beliefs, values and attitudes (cognitive organisation). One way of doing this may be to examine individual and group resistance to new classifiable patterns of cognitive organisation within a compound actor introduced through HRD. The classifications should be indicative of beliefs that limit the possibility of variation and variety in the organisation.

Finally, in the third column, we have emancipation, manner of thinking, and freedom, suggesting that by releasing greater potential to individuals or groups in learning and development situations, the *possibility* of greater organisational viability is ultimately enabled. This can liberate more possibilities for the organisation. Let us consider these three classifications a little more fully.

The possibilities classification relates to emancipation, manner of thinking and freedom, and is concerned with the liberty that is essential for the creation of variety. As such, variety generation may be one way of evaluating the *possibilities* dimension of an organisation, and as a criterion to assess HRD interventions. We can now attempt to propose specific approaches to measurements about an organisation's possibilities, which function as attributes of variety generation. Knowledge about emancipation may be determinable through in-depth questioning of relevant others involved in HRD interventions. It may relate to the structural violence that may be believed to exist within an organisation. This is reflected, for example, through the rules that staff within an organisation may need to follow. It may be possible to measure this qualitatively by obtaining perceptions of the equity among different sets of rules that relate to specific groups or stakeholders (e.g. Storey and Winstanley, 2001; Iles and Yolles, 2002). Manner of thinking relates to the ideological and ethical attributes of actors, and can be explored through in-depth questioning of participants in HRD research and practice. It filters and restricts the way that information is considered.

These ideas have meaning that is able to describe aspects of the viability of organisations in a holistic rather than piecemeal way. Further, it seems that there are measurable qualities and quantities that may be able to produce a complete profile of an organisation and its capabilities within a given environment. This could tell us more about an organisation than a set of different individual explorations intended to address a particular problem through the application of a particular methodology, as is often the case in much HRD practice.

It is now possible to generate a new framework appropriate to OD and HRD that relates to organisation patterning. It provides the possibility of extending the conceptual brief of OD and HRD by taking into account the properties associated with VST, such as ideology, ethics and the development of potential. This provides a new and powerful option for OD and HRD that is more appropriate to complex situations than the previous more simplistic approach. A practical orientation to this is initially suggested in Table 10.4.

Noting that cognitive influence is linked to the creation of knowledge enables us to explain Table 10.4. Social kinematics is related to providing people with an image of the future that will act as a basis for change motivation and can help facilitate learning and development. Cognitive purposes linked to information are local, and involve politics that enables polity. In kinematic cybernetics, communication must be logically enabled through social design; that is formal accessible channels of communication should be created through which common meanings can be accessed. As part of this, feedback must also be seen as an essential component of the logical design. Transition processes must also be rationally or appreciatively designed so that new structures can materialise within which people can work. This is the same for organisational arrangements for the transition. Facilitating support is also a political process that links to control and logical communication. Cognitive interest is linked to data and data collection. OD and HRD tie into technical cognitive interest kinematics as far as they require that people actually use communication as a part of their designated learning and performance improvement agenda. The potential for communication may not be adequate. Motivating routines must be established in which people take communication to be an important part of their performance improvement and learning agendas. This row has been enhanced with the knowledge constitutive counterparts of Habermas's cognitive interests that refer to the use of causal and empirical-analytical methods, descriptions and practical understanding, and the use of critical approaches (Habermas, 1987; MacIsaac, 1996). Knowledge management processes might well further develop from this (e.g., Iles *et al.*, 2000; Yolles, 2000c).

Orientation is affected by cultural purposes in that the nature of the language used will provide something of an image and meaning to participants in change, learning and development situations. For cognitive purposes, the rational and appreciative aspects of orientation formulate key power group support by the political creation of that support (with the help of the appropriate language). Stabilising this support is an important feature of change management and learning and development. The practical interest aspect of orientation involves the adoption of symbols that people can apply in the technological communications that they establish. Practical interests are facilitated by the provision of, say, the use of technology in creating networks of communication, or more simply just schedules for regular meetings or workshops. These clearly link to technical interests, so that, for instance, people may be stimulated to attend a scheduled workshop. Leaders should have energy that can be put at the disposal of change and development, and their political behaviour should also be coincident with the perceived needs of the change, learning and development process.

No cognitive influences in the area of possibility for change are indicated within OD, or within much HRD theory. They could involve awareness that an existing despotic political culture does not provide sufficient empowerment for participants in a change or learning and development situation to help carry it through, and that a new more open political structure is required. The ideological attributes of organisational potential for change and development occur through ensuring that people become dissatisfied with the logical or political basis of the organisation, and their beliefs can be developed or harnessed to encourage them to want to participate in change, learning and development. Ethical considerations that are part of ideology also do not form a significant part of the traditional OD paradigm, and have only recently become part of the HRD agenda. Within critical deconstraining, people are provided with rewards for their behaviour in participating in change, learning and development. These rewards may or may not take the form of exchange media like money or power (Habermas, 1987); but they should contribute to an increase in their liberation, thus enabling them to see that they should disengage from the present state of the organisation. Part of this process could also involve the ability of people to decide their own constraints about their behaviour, learning and development. However, at best this must be a lifeworld process that enables semantic communication.

Conclusion

In this paper we have developed a cybernetic theory of organisational patterning that can enrich and complexify OD and HRD, enabling them to be more effective in creating intervention strategies for organisations in need of change, learning, development and performance enhancement. This development has arisen because we have argued that OD and HRD, the theory that underpins VSM, and VST are supported by paradigms that represent distinct species of managerial cybernetics as it has passed through paradigmatic metamorphoses, with all these lying on the same evolutionary pathway. This is illustrated by the creation of a

Table 10.4 Extending organisational patterning of HRD

Organisational pattern and HRD implications			
Cognitive properties	Kinematics and HRD (through energetic motion)	Orientation and HRD (determining trajectory)	Possibilities and HRD (through potential development)
Interest	*Technical* Routines for communication. Causal explanations. Use empirical-analytic methods	*Practical* Symbols; energy of leader; encourage appropriate behaviour. Seek descriptions of perceived situation and practical understanding	*Critical deconstraining* Rewards for behaviour; disengage from present state. Use critical approaches
Purposes	*Cybernetical* Logical processes of communication and feedback; design of transition processes; organisational arrange ments for transition; facilitate support	*Rational/appreciative* Key power group support. Build in stability processes. Encourage reflection	*Ideological/moral* See dissatisfaction in ideological terms. Mobilise change, learning and development through participation. Evaluate ethical or aesthetic political attributes
Influence	*Social* Images of the future in the management of social processes are important. An under-standing of the cybernetic purposes is also important to enable technical aspects of the organisation to materialise. Objectives play an important part here, and must be understood	*Cultural* Use of language and related concepts that can give meaning to knowledge (metaknow-ledge). It supports myths that can misdirect the organisation. The propositions of the organisation are defined here, those that give meaning to its existence. Organisational mission and objectives derive from this	*Political* Creates a culture's normative boundaries through its beliefs, values, symbols, stories and public rituals that bind people together and direct them in common action. These deter-mine the creation of ideologi-cal/ethical and power constraints. They connect to the structure of an organisa-tion and the way that power is distributed and used

frame of reference in which transformation is seen as a conceptual device. In each case the number of fundamental dimensions of the frame of reference has increased as a new way of defining transformation has been adopted. The notion that the boundary of each of the domains of VST is also a transformational device has been mentioned but not explored here, and provides entry into another new and potentially exciting paradigmatic metamorphosis open to a new process of research.

OD and much of HRD see the open system as a space that transforms inputs into outputs (e.g. Swanson, 2001). To enable the organisation to become more operationally effective, and thus to create improvement in its outputs (for given inputs) that it perceives to be more appropriate to its environment, the system and the cultural base that defines it must be modified. To enhance its capacity to map aspects of the organisation, we have modified OD and HRD to adopt a terminol-ogy that is consistent with that of viable systems. Doing this it becomes clear that traditional OD and HRD theory do not explore many of the facets of an organisation that can be pertinent to change, learning and development.

VSM operates through a system and a metasystem, with an implicit transformation that couples the two. In this sense it can be seen as an evolutionary development of OD and HRD. It can also be thought of as a model that sits within VST, where the implicit transformational processes of VSM are attributed to an independent domain. Here, transformational processes become assigned to the boundaries of the domains.

Since VST admits more fundamental conceptual extensions than does VSM or traditional OD and HRD, it would be expected to encompass more capacity to model complex situations. This has occurred because of the relationship that has been developed between VST, Schwarz's (1997) cybernetic theory of viable systems, and Habermas's theory of communicative action. Schwarz's theory provides a grounded theory of the complex cybernetic mechanics of autonomy. The cognitive properties of VST domains were inspired by Habermas's KCI theory. This provides a conceptual map through which cultural, virtual, and behavioural attributes of an organisation can be considered. The cognitive properties of the conceptual map are row attributes, but column attributes also exist, and these can be used to pattern an organisation in such a way that its viability could be more clearly assessed. These column attributes are capable of patterning an organisation. They do this by identifying its overall kinematic processes that energise its movements in its environment, its orientations that determine an intended trajectory for action, and its possibilities through potential development.

This conceptual development can enable HRD inquiry into coherent organisation, its groups, or its individual participants, thereby exploring its viability within more complex situations than normally occurs within traditional OD and HRD. This is because it extends the brief of OD and HRD through its organisational patterning map significantly beyond that proposed by Nadler (1993), Harrison (1994), Swanson (2001, 1999) and McClean (1999). Having claimed this, the suitability of this platform for OD and HRD will need to be evaluated (Iles and Yolles 2002, Yolles and Guo, 2002).

References

Ackoff, R. L. (1981) *Creating the Corporate Future*, New York: Wiley

Beer, S. (1979) *The Heart of the Enterprise*, New York: Wiley

Bertalanffy, L. von (1968) *General Systems Theory*, Harmondsworth: Penguin

Burrell, G. and Morgan, G. (1979) *Sociological Paradigms and Organisational Analysis*, London: Heinemann

Checkland, P. B. (1981) *Systems Thinking, Systems Practice*, Chichester: Wiley

Checkland, P. and Scholes (1990) *Soft Systems Methodology in Action*, New York: Wiley

Coghlan, D. (1993) 'In Defence of Process Consultation', Mabey C. and Mayon-White B. (Eds) *Managing Change*, London: Paul Chapman Publishing Ltd.

Espejo, R., Schuhmann, W., Schaniger, M. and Bielello, U. (1996) *Organisational Transformation and Learning*, Chelmsford: Wiley

Flood, R. L. and Jackson, M.C. (1991) *Creative Problem Solving: Total systems intervention*, Chichester: Wiley

Grieves, J. and Redman, T. (1999) 'Living in the shadow of OD: HRD and the search for identity, *Human Resource Development International* 2(2): 81–102

Habermas, J. (1970) 'Knowledge and interest' in Emmet, D. and MacIntyre, Al, (Eds) *Sociological Theory and Philosophical Analysis*, pp. 36–54, London: Macmillan

Habermas, J. (1987) *The Theory of Communicative Action*, Vol. 2, Cambridge: Polity Press

Harrison, I. H. (1994) *Diagnosing Organizations: Methods, models and processes*, Thousand Oaks, Cal: Sage

Holsti, K. J, (1967) *International Politics, a Framework for Analysis*, London: Prentice Hall

Iles, P. A., Yolles, M. and Altman, Y, (2000) 'HRM and knowledge management: Responding to the challenge', *Journal of Research and Practice in HRM*, 8(2): 1–31, pp 3–33

Iles, P. A. and Yolles, M. (2002) 'Complexity, HRD and organisation development: Towards a viable systems approach to learning, development and change' in Lee, M. (Ed.) *HRD in a Complex World*, London: Routledge

Kuhn, S. T, (1970) *The Structure of Scientific Revolutions*, Chicago: University of Chicago Press

Lewin, K. (1947) 'Frontiers of group dynamics', *Human Relations*, 1: 5–41

MacIsaac, D. (1996) 'The critical theory of Jurgen Habermas', http://www.physics.nau.edu/~danmac

Mackie, J. L. (1977) *Ethics: Inventing right and wrong*, London: Penguin Books

McClean G. N. (1999) 'Get out the drill, glue and more legs', *Human Resource Development International*, 2(1): 6–7

Midgley, G. (2000) *Systemic Intervention: Philosophy, methodology, and practice*, New York: Kluwer Academic/Plenum Publishers

Nadler, D. A. (1993) 'Concepts for the management of organisational change' contained in Mayon-White, B. (Ed.), *Planning and Managing Change*, London: Harper & Row

Nadler, D. A. and Tushman (1977) *Feedback and Organisations Development: Using data based on methods*, Reading: Addison-Wesley

Nadler, D. A. and Tushman (1979) 'A Congruence model for diagnosing organisational behaviour' in Kolb, D., Rubin, I. and McIntyre, J. (Eds) *Organisational Psychology: A book of Readings*, (3rd edn), Englewood Cliffs, NJ: Prentice Hall

Pugh, D. (1993) in Mabey, C. and Mayon-White, B. (Eds) *Managing Change*, pp. 109–112, London: Paul Chapman Publishing Co. Originally in *London Business School Journal*, 1978, 3(2): 29–34

Schwaninger, M. (2001) 'Intelligent organisations: An integrative framework', *Systems Research and Behavioural Science*, 18: 37–158

Schwarz, E. (1997) 'Towards a holistic cybernetics: From science through epistemology to being', *Cybernetics and Human Knowing*, 4(1): 17–50

Storey, C. and Winstanley, D. (2001) 'Stakeholding: Confusion or Utopia? Mapping the conceptual terrain', *Journal of Management Studies*, 38, 5 July, 603–626

Swanson, R. A. (1999) 'HRD theory: real or imagined?' *Human Resource Development International* 2(1): 2–5

Swanson, R. A. (2001) 'Human resource development and its underlying theory', *Human Resource Development International*, 4(3): 299–312

Tushman, M. (1977) 'A political approach to organisations; a review and rationale', *Academy of Management Review*, 2: 206–216

Vickers, G. (1965) *The Art of Judgement*, London: Chapman and Hall (reprinted 1983, Harper & Row: London)

Watson, G. (1969) 'Resistance to change' in Bennis, W. G., Benne, K. F. and Chin, R. (Eds) *The Planning of Change*, New York: Holt Reinhart and Winston

Weisbord, M. R. and Janoff, S. (1996) 'Future search: Finding common ground in organisations and communities', *Systems Practice*, 9(1): 71–84

Yolles, M.I. (1996) (Oct) 'Critical systems theory, paradigms, and the modelling space', *Systems Practice*, 9(6): 549–570

Yolles, M. I. (1998) 'Changing paradigms in operational research', *Cybernetics and Systems*, 29(2): 91–112

Yolles, M. I. (1999) *Managment Systems: A viable approach*, London: Financial Times Pitman

Yolles, M. I. (2000a) 'The theory of viable joint ventures', *Cybernetics and Systems*, 31(4): 371–396

Yolles, M. I. (2000b) 'From viable systems to surfing the organisation', *Journal of Applied Systems*, 1(1): 127–142

Yolles, M. I. (2000c) 'Organisations, complexity, and viable knowledge management', *Kybernetes*, 29(9/10)

Yolles, M. I. (2001) 'Viable boundary critique', *Journal of Operational Research Society*, January, 51: 0–12

Yolles, M. I. and Guo, K. (2002) 'Organization development in Chinese state-owned commercial banks: A developing organizational development perspective', *Conference of International Society for Systems Science*, Shanghai, China, August 2–5

Zaltman, G. and Duncan, R. (1977) *Strategies for Planned Change*, New York: Wiley

11 A new perception for a new millennium

Carole McKenzie

The world that we have made as a result of the level of thinking we have done this far, creates problems we cannot solve at the same level at which we created them.

(Attributed variously to C. G. Jung and A. Einstein)

It is not easy to arrive at a conception of a whole which is constructed from parts belonging to different dimension s ...This is due to the consecutive nature of the only methods available to us for conveying a clear three-dimensional concept of an image in space, and results from deficiencies of a temporal nature in the spoken word. For we lack the means of discussing in its constituent parts an image which possesses simultaneously a number of dimensions.

(Paul Klee 1924)

Introduction

The words of Carl Jung and Paul Klee articulate a dilemma. It is immensely difficult to capture the complexity of living and to communicate the meaning of that lived experience. When we form an idea or develop a description of a problem, which is of significance, we are pitched head-long into yet another set of 'things to be solved'. The resolution of a problem is never really a closure or finite resolution. By solving it we set ourselves new problems.

Emotional life, for instance, is integral to fully conscious thought. Emotion is not a sometimes-unwelcome distraction. In its proper use emotion is the wellspring of knowledge, not its inhibitor. A kind of guidance system that shows us what is significant, dangerous, worthy of attachment, to be feared or to be repulsed, and at a complex conscious level, what has meaning for us. In the same way imagination is also integral to thought, not a distraction from the 'real world'. Imagination is necessary for the making of any decision which is not simply a calculation.

Learning defines life. That is to say that the process of cognition from the 'simple' biological level to the more complex social level of learning mediated by 'bodies of knowledge' is essentially the same process that defines what it is to 'live' (Maturana, 1972).

Living people create value; the energy and commitment of individuals and teams of people ultimately determine the value that we enjoy from our products and services. Any increase in the potential of these individuals and teams will result in greater value production. HRD should be central to value production and enhancement and therefore be at the forefront of any changes that challenge traditional approaches. Sadly, it is constrained by policy and law and often becomes the internal policing process of an organisation, which inevitably moves it away from its more innovative role in organisational development where it can actively challenge 'what is'. If we do not challenge traditional attitudes and methods we will be lost and unsustainable. Since so much of human activity is absorbed in the pursuit of value creation, HRD is a pivotal activity at this point in our time.

Turning points

Humanity reaches turning points every so often; the making of stone tools, the use of fire, the start of farming practices, the smelting of ores, the making of machines and now the information age. The new technologies that we have created have changed our social organisation and vice versa. Very gradually we are changing the way we think about our world, how we make descriptions of that world and all the relationships within it, but these attitudes and thinking patterns lag far behind our actual knowledge and questioning of the world we live in.

Written language is both a fundamental facilitator of human progress and learning, and an inhibitor. Its very sequential nature constrains meaning in a useful and more distinct way but, by necessity, it eliminates much of the complexity of life in performing this refinement. Images are, on the contrary, over-determined and many layered and therefore more able to describe what it is to be 'in the world'. (Nothing puts you in the picture as much as a picture.)

Now, more than ever before, we need to adopt new approaches, new ways of perceiving the complexity of our world so that we can sustain our environment and ourselves. The rapid movement of information, the subsequent events that follow from the speed of information flows, and growing globalisation demand the evolution of a new approach to help us comprehend what is of value, what is significant enough for us to make a 'good enough' decision. 'Good enough' decision making is not only a mental calculation but a perceptual function, for it is the proposition here that we perceive meaning directly and need to harness our senses more fully in order to gain knowledge of our complex world.

Change is speeding up!

My grandmother was born in 1872 in rural Argyllshire and died in London in 1968. Her life spanned a vast array of technological and social developments: the steam age, the full development of flight, wireless, telecommunications, the atom bomb, vaccines, TV, the beginning of 'the information age', women's suffrage, and the relative acceptability of divorce, to name but a few.

My great-great-grandmother, born in an isolated pocket of the Western Isles of Scotland, would have seen very little technological and social change.

Communication was dominated by the time it took a boat to travel to the mainland in varying weather conditions (if at all) and the speed of walking. News may have seeped in gradually from the mainland and from Europe but it must have taken time to arrive and have been processed in some way.

The relative poverty of my great-great-grandmother's life is still apparent in many parts of the world but the quality of isolation has been affected by communication patterns and flows that have changed radically. People can live in abject poverty but still be aware of what is occurring in the wider world, or at least have some picture of the difference between their existence and that of others. To some extent, it may be a kind of fiction, a distorted picture, but nevertheless it is just as compelling and increases the level of discontent and anger at the apparent inequalities between populations. A connected world does not necessarily make it a more peaceful or truly integrated one. Nor does it mean that increased information flows give rise to good communication. On the contrary, information may be increasing but good communication seems more difficult to achieve.

The increase in the speed of information flows and the general pace of technology has also created a degree of volatility through the glut of available information. This increase in available information not only affects financial markets but is apparent in the wide range of choices that we in the 'developed world' are able to make about what we buy, how we spend our time, and what we have access to in terms of knowledge and knowledge bases. These potential choices are often bewildering and mask the emerging dynamics of what is significant. It really is getting more difficult to see the wood from the trees.

In such an environment of rapid information flows and consequential ambiguity there is a huge competitive advantage for those able to see the apparent emerging dynamics, that which is significant and meaningful for them, which enable them to make good choices. Not only is this new perception essential in terms of competitive advantage, but it is also an imperative in terms of sustainability. The complexity that presently engulfs us will continue to do so. The information age has only just started and we cannot yet imagine where it will take us. In order to manage with confidence the myriad possibilities that arise for us we need a new way of engaging, of perceiving the value to us of what is occurring. In a sense these are not new skills but old animal sensibilities that have served us well before. Now it is time to re-hone them.

Dislocation – the emergence of the control 'paradigm'

The origin of the modern human social organisation lies with the hunter gatherers perceiving what the land afforded us in terms of roots, berries, fish and game. In this way of surviving there is no 'plan' but openness to the emergent dynamics of the environmental niche. The unexpected, unplanned opportunity is what it's all about. In this niche there is no need to rely on memory in the same way as in the later organised societies, for game is constantly on the move and plants and roots are to be found in different territories. There may be choice places where game comes to take water or to graze, but there is no need to enter into a predictive relationship that measures time and action in the way that farming does (or to consider land as 'owned', as with an object). In fact, it would be counter-productive to plan in this way, as it would inhibit the finely tuned perception needed to notice the subtle changes, the opportunities, in an evolving situation. Access to animals and vegetation changes, depending on circumstances that cannot be planned for or be affected by the hunter gatherer.

Hunter gatherers still exist in parts of our 'globalised' world and what we can surmise about our hunter gatherer ancestors is largely extrapolated from these contemporary people. The mind-set of a hunter gatherer is necessarily different to that of a farmer. Tracking game and gathering seasonal roots and berries demands an acute sensitivity to the changing flux of their habitat. It also involves taking 'time out' to get involved in some activities that might appear, at first sight, to be a waste of time, that is, not directed to any specific outcome. Why, for instance, do modern hunter gatherers trance dance when they need to find new tracks? What possible use can there be in dancing for twenty-four hours when you may go hungry if you don't catch your dinner? It may be that taking time when the trail is lost and there is a desperate need to find sustenance can give the opportunity to see all those missed possibilities, to sense the minute signs of future gainful paths.

The trance dance of the hunter gatherer creates a kind of 'tolerance space' where redundant knowledge can be re-embedded, and where perception can be refined to enable a more critical awareness. This allows the participant to re-engage with the complexity of the environment that will enable sustainability in a complex world. A focus on 'the goal' to the exclusion of all else would be counter-productive and would not enable the hunter to be acutely aware of what the environment offered in terms of possibilities. If anything, humanity in its origins exists because it has been opportunistic rather than goal-driven. The hunter-gatherer society was immensely stable, lasting thousands of years longer than any subsequent form. Its stability lay in large measure in the fact that the hunter gatherer passed on no inheritance or ownership of land but only, perhaps, ownership of artefacts, tools, skills and a tradition of oral history that links the individual, family and tribe with the environment of animals and territory, and the past.

Unfortunately, our present Western culture reinforces the notion of the value of goal through all kinds of subtle messages, including those concerning what it is to be 'masculine' and 'successful'.

When we became farmers we changed how we considered ourselves, how we described our relationship to nature, to our environment. We changed from one of 'integrated within', a part of something that we had little control over so had to keep some kind of balance with, to one of control where we were 'separate from' and could impose some kind of authority over.

Farming brings the beginning of a kind of dislocation of humanity from its niche, an idea that there is a significant separation between man and nature that in turn gives rise to a notion of measurement and 'control over'. In contrast to the hunter gatherer, the farmer is forced to plan. Time becomes a significant factor; where knowledge of the passage of the seasons is used in the cycle of planning. Sequences must be memorised and the farmer has to rely on predictability that things are indeed cyclical and repeatable as the days and months for a successful harvest are measured, fields are measured and seed apportioned according to these measurements. The pattern of unfolding events must be largely predictable to achieve success. One step must follow another in a set sequence and the achievement of success depends on the manner in which these pre-determined steps are performed.

If all goes well, cause and effect follow in an orderly way as you reap a good harvest and congratulate yourself on a well-organised job. The pattern of events that led to a successful harvest was pre-planned with no interest in any potential that might lead to a different future than the one specified. The weather and potential pests are the 'wild-cards', the uncontrollable aspects that have to be watched out for, the 'obstacles' that might destroy the predictability of the activities. Control over that which can be predicted is reinforced by the existence of potential threat from the uncontrollable.

The notion of land ownership, and all the kinship ties that reinforce it, also arises. The wealth from the harvest is related to the quality of the land but, just as fundamentally, to the amount of land. This relationship of humanity to the land affects the social structures and relationships between people, particularly between men and women. Land owned in some finite measured sense can be inherited through bloodlines, thus affecting the social relationships between men and women and the value of gender. Social control becomes a necessity in view of the unpredictable element of human response in the artificial division of humanity and nature.

Other themes

The notion of 'control' runs through the development of mankind. The idea of the 'absolute perfect' has been interwoven within the Christian Church and tradition and further embedded itself into our psyche together with the split of 'good' and 'bad', 'perfect' and 'imperfect', that exists particularly in Western philosophy. This philosophy, deriving from the Greeks, has a long history of creating such distinctions.

The earliest Greek work, shown above all in Heraclitus, had expressed the wholeness, impermanence, and interdependence of all apparent singular elements or parts.

> 0. 'All things flow; nothing abides'
> 30. 'This universe, the same for all, no one, either god or man, has made; but it always was, and is, and ever shall be ever-living fire, fixed measures kindling and fixed measures dying out.'

(Heraclitus)

The focus of Greek philosophy, which follows Heraclitus, is one of the notion of permanence: *how can nature change in detail and still possess an essential permanence?* This topic of 'permanence' gives rise to many new distinctions too rich to be discussed in this chapter alone. The relevant point to make here is that it is the search for resolution of this paradox of change and permanence that gives rise to a body of knowledge that creates distinctions between kinds of matter, from Socrates' 'reality of purpose', to Aristotle's notion of the different substances of heaven and earth, and to the later Cartesian split of 'mind' and 'matter'.

We are left with a 'purposeful' universe with a God that is omnipresent, transcendent, making it impossible for us to achieve such perfection because, paradoxically, we are created from dust. This is probably what gives Western humankind its impetus to strive and to value goal-driven behaviours.

By contrast, the traditions of Chinese thought are more concerned with order and pattern that is not determined by prior actions, but by the position they hold in the 'ever moving cyclical universe'. Everything in existence is therefore a part in relation to a whole world-organism. 'Events and phenomena unfold through a kind of spontaneous cooperation, an inner dynamic in the nature of things.' (Kaptchuk, 2000.) The idea of cause and effect in time still exists in Chinese thought but it is overlaid by the strong notion of 'immanence', whereas, in the West, the prevailing worldview is, or has been, that of 'transcendence'. Farming was also developed in China but was not accompanied by a notion of an ultimate and divine being, which probably, in part, accounts for the different development of its philosophy and world outlook. Kaptchuk (2000) describes this 'immanence' in the following way.

> The Western mind seeks to discover and encounter what is beyond, behind, or the cause of phenomena. In the Chinese view, the truth of things is imminent; in the Western, truth is transcendent. Knowledge, within the Chinese framework, consists in the accurate perception of the inner movement of the web of phenomena. The desire for knowledge is the desire to understand the interrelationships or patterns within that web, and to become attuned to the unfolding dynamic.

Although today much of our thinking is dominated by the notion of substance, of separate objects and forces, we are moving to a more systemic idea of reality where it is the *relationships* between things that are the defining elements and where purpose is not a necessary attribute of the universe. However, the drama still goes on between immanence and transcendence and purpose, and the notion of perfection as opposed to the relationship of opposites, which creates constant movement. One of the consequences of transcendence and perfection concerns how we regard error and this is a limiting factor for us.

The importance of error

> Give me a fruitful error any time, full of seeds, bursting with its own corrections. You can keep your sterile truth for yourself.
>
> (The economist Vilfredo Pareto)

The notion of error is an essential counter-point to perfection. If we strive to create perfection, to 'get it absolutely right' we cannot tolerate error. If we cannot tolerate error we are in danger of creating a world where there is no space for risk or for the seemingly random experience that eventually turns into new and valuable potentials. (Remember the bones of the ear from redundant fish gill cells.) It is not surprising that the machine metaphors of the industrial age still to some extent hold sway in our minds and permeate management thinking. They are very difficult to get rid of, rather like racism, as we are often unaware of how deeply they have affected our unconscious attitudes.

Error, as the quotation tells us, is full of fruitful possibilities, without which many important discoveries would not have been made. Error is a natural part of creativity and 'a by-product of daring'. Without it we cannot make new discoveries. We live in a world that is, especially now, frightened of risk and error. No one sensibly puts themselves or others at risk and yet we have to find a way of tolerating some degree of error. Most of our systems, including our educational systems, militate against daring, risk and error, leaving us with a degree of tunnel vision and limited in how we are going to face and find solutions to our present dilemmas. At the beginning I started with a quotation from Jung which said clearly that our thinking is never evolved enough to cope with the problems and challenges that our development as a species inevitably brings us to. Its a fact of life that we simply cannot catch up with ourselves, cannot achieve finite closure. Our very solutions create new problems and questions. Life is very much a process of, and indistinguishable from, 'learning'. To be cognate in Humberto Maturana's theory of autopoiesis, is to live. So how do we achieve a mind-set that practises the use of 'fruitful error' and operates a continual process of learning to learn? A particular focussed activity with the graphic trace is one way in which we can affect our thinking and perceptual practices. Unfortunately, such practices have long-since been incorporated into the search for profit and the accumulation of objects of value to be bought and sold. This has undermined what I believe to be the intrinsic and original use and value of art or depiction. Art, as Max Beckmann pointed out, is not for amusement but for realisation and transfiguration. Our early ancestors were involved in this process of realisation and it has been almost totally overlooked in terms of how it both formed and articulated our modern psyche.

The graphic trace as a thinking process

Our hunter-gatherer forebears started the process and people have been creating images, using graphic traces, incising in rock, making three-dimensional images for at least 55,000 years. There are many theories about why people have engaged in these activities. We cannot know exactly why early people engaged in activities that frequently took them kilometres deep into the belly of the earth, through narrow channels that widened out into vaulted caverns. It is impossible for us not to be affected by our own 'perspective' drawn from our twenty-first century lives. We can, however, understand something of how these images were made and this gives us some knowledge of why they were important and how they have influenced our thought and communication processes.

Opportunism and learning

I suggest that rather than expression, drawing is a process of exploration and discovery; rather than magical, it is a kind of observation of what chance has brought to the attention of the depicter. I contend that it also affected our language and the development of conceptual repertoire. Our language is scattered with visual references. I have used a few here, 'let's look at it', 'our own perspective', 'let me put you in the picture', for example. There are many references to the visual and graphic act, as it is so fundamental to our conceptual evolution.

We are amazed some 25,000 years after the caves at Lascaux were first painted to see the strength and beauty of the depictions of living animals on the walls. It must have been equally amazing to see the shape of galloping horses take form on the cave wall. The running horse, that in reality would never have been stilled at this moment in time, was now held in mid leap to be viewed as a single silhouette. The artist would have seen, possibly for the first time, the line of the back as a separate aspect; similarly, the trace of its muzzle and the shape of its leg as it moved through the air, frozen in time and space, to be considered as separate aspects of reality. The undifferentiated nature of lived experience was irrevocably changed and with it came a new mastery of thought, a new ability to create distinctions, to conceptualise and to fragment. The distinction could be made between figure and ground, between side view and the totality of the animal. The distinction called *aspect* came into being.

We are used to seeing visual images everyday in all kinds of situations. We are habituated to them and it is difficult for us to take in the impact of the visual opportunistic activities of our ancestors. It is difficult to realise that there was a time when there were no images at all. We are used to picking out figures from ground, seeing things in terms of paintings, of perspective, and of distinguishing a contour or aspect of an object. In a similar way we are used to seeing reflections of ourselves in mirrors, CCTV and in all kinds of reflective surfaces. Imagine a life before the invention of metal or glass. The experience of seeing ourselves in the way that we do now would have been extraordinary.

The new quality of distinctions that the activity of image making in caves gave us allowed us to identify our world as particulate. It encouraged the paying of attention in a special way. It was not an imposition of an idea but the discovery of an aspect or limited particular moment through the peculiarities of texture and form dictated by the available surface of the cave's wall. The discovery of the drawing was not imposed but achieved by a collaboration of artist and surface. This is clearly shown where areas of natural rock have been used to form part of a horse's head, for example. The new way of thinking was derived and achieved from close collaboration between the mark maker and the surface on which the mark was made.

The discrete moment in the 360-degree experience of being in the world is encapsulated within a set of invariant visual indicators that specify an object or space, or both. Not as totalities as in the original lived experience but as aspects which convey the totality. These particulate 'discoveries' must have created a fundamental shift in how we paid attention to our environment, allowing us to build new 'mental muscles' by making new distinctions through which to articulate and communicate our experience. As they communicated these new ways of defining and therefore of experiencing the world they lived in, our ancestors must have formed new domains of discourse that would have, in turn, bound their social groups in more complex ways.

New knowledge and description creates new relationships as it embeds this knowledge within the social group. Notice that it is an open future of potential, not a pre-determined depiction of existing knowledge that made possible the emergence of this particulate knowledge. Similarly, today, finite 'fitness for purpose' blocks the emergence of the 'new' through discovery. There has to be a certain redundancy for these potentials to emerge and therefore what we call 'error' is a necessary part of the ability to evolve and also to discover. The discovery of penicillin and post-its are both non-trivial cases of the use of error. They were both the product of an attempt to do one thing that accidentally formed another product. In the case of penicillin, a contaminated Petri dish was left out and gave rise to one of the most significant medical discoveries of the twentieth century. In the case of the post-it, a search for a new fast-drying glue had a totally reverse effect.

In the case of our early ancestors we have evidence that they did indeed use the redundancy of potential imagery to define their experience anew. They were opportunistic explorers; a characteristic that we now need more than ever. In order to be opportunistic we must learn to tolerate error and redundancy, to use it confidently and happily. This is still a terrible heresy in the world of business where extracting more from less is an increasing preoccupation. Ironically, it is possible to get more from less, but not always by imposing exactitude on every process and function.

The way to get more from less is by harnessing the redundancy hidden in people who simply do not bring their true qualities and potential into the work place. Learning is a huge motivator for most people but it can only occur where the ability to make mistakes is tolerated and not punished. It is often difficult for those of us who have been steeped in the precision of the machine theory of organisations to unleash this ability to learn and discover. We have to develop confidence to use these under-developed muscles.

The new way of thinking

In this new world of global commerce and swiftly changing circumstances how do we achieve a way of thinking and coping which will be in accord with our time? Control seems to be a very temporary condition and plans are swiftly rendered useless. In such times perhaps it is time to look at the sort of 'opportunistic' activity, which brought such long-lasting stability to our hunter-gatherer ancestors. Above all to look at the period of change which seems to have reached a high point in the caves of Altamira and the Dordogne.

The activity of mark making, painting or drawing has been distorted in its value as a tool for thought. Art is a commodity, an object to be bought or sold. Judgements about our ability to 'do art' are coloured by accepted standards of worth. Most of us will have had, at some time in our school life, the experience of either having our picture put on the wall for all to see, or had it rejected. This acceptance or rejection is guided by a view of art as a desirable object rather than seen as an attempt to convey the particular individual view of the artist. Fortunately, to look at graphic activity as a way of making sense and of educating to achieve flexible creative thinking, we do not have to indulge in speculation as to the meaning or worth of past works of graphic art but merely to look at the cybernetic processes which underlie all such activity in all times and places (Beitel, 1970).

All human infants from whatever culture they come, naturally and without any external encouragement, draw on any surface that leaves a trace. It seems that we have a natural urge to engage in this dialogue of trace making where the feedback mechanism from the activity has an intrinsic value to us. Children make these traces spontaneously, from the movement of food on their plates to the drawings in the sand and the marks on the wall or paper. Gradually these trace making activities become more complex where recognisable images start to evolve. The opportunities that exist for the child in the activity of drawing also exist for the adult. How do lines become information or represent the lived experience of the child or adult? And what are the consequences?

New vision – a lost abililty

'It's the difference that makes the difference.' Gregory Bateson (1972) used this phrase to define the notion of information. Information only exists where there is a difference, hence the phrase that the creation of a difference creates a higher level of meaning,

A line, especially when it encloses on itself or bisects another line, creates the very same leap to a higher level of meaning. The 'trace', the precursor of the line, can be experienced at many moments in life. The trace signifies something more complex than itself. A trace is a record of an action which has gone and is the same whether the snail leaves a trace on the pavement, the aircraft leaves a trail across the sky, we leave our footprints in the sand, the child pushes its porridge across its plate or the artist draws a portrait.

When we, or our young children, use line we are engaging in a more complex activity than the noticing of traces. A line creates a distinction between 'nothing' and 'something'. It also embodies the energy that was used to make it and therefore very sparse or limited traces have a value. The random use of line in the simple kinaesthetic actions of a small child inevitably and accidentally intersects those lines. A simple upright line on a flattish surface is limited in the amount of information it conveys. (Collectively, a number of these lines may stand as the depiction of a group of people as they correspond to or mirror our body stance of 'upright'.) But a single line curved in on itself contains more information, is incrementally more complex, because it has 'closure'; it is invariant information for a three-dimensional body, a face, a bottle etc. Likewise bisecting lines signify the invariant quality of corner or space, or the occlusion of one object by another.

The achievement of this ability to define an external object outside the child is also the achievement of the objectification of the child's own 'self'. As we learn to depict our experience through this feedback mechanism of mark making, we also, and at a pre-linguistic level, distinguish our own selves. This early pre-verbal distinction of 'self', results in the development of us as observers of ourselves. The architecture of our nervous system means that we are able to interact with our own descriptions; that is, we are conscious. Consciousness, or observer status as I will call it here, is increased through such an activity as mark making. The achievement of observer status is a pre-verbal acquisition and rather than being created by language, consciousness is enriched by it. In the feedback process involved in the child's early scribble where the energy of the child's body forms the mark, a curious paradox arises in much the same way as it did in those ancestral caves mentioned earlier. The 'me' embodied in the child's action curiously also stands for 'other', 'outside of me' (James, 1974). Thus, the product of the activity defines both the doer and the object depicted. Just as we described the astonishment of the early cave 'artists' seeing for the first time the three-quarter aspect of the horse or bison, so the young child experiences the paradox of an action which is the extension of the self, and yet the 'not me' of an external object. The pre-verbal perceptual self, described by James Gibson (Gibson,1979) is further differentiated through the feedback mechanism of mark making. In the development of this function of the drawing system, the essential organisation of the living system, which defines 'a point of view', is made an object of perception.

> In this perception the picture surface is now dominated by the arrangement of the traces made upon it in such a way that: I notice the surfaces that face me, and what I face, and thus where I am. The attitude might be called introspective or subjective, but it is actually a reciprocal, two-way attitude, not a looking inward.
>
> (Gibson, 1979)

The progression to engaging in more complex feedback activity is a natural one. The child makes increasingly diverse distinctions, differentiating more and more complex levels of experience, which include the perception of its 'self'. Our investigations over some twenty years also go to confirm that this is equally true of the adult in properly structured conditions.

In the drawing process of the child marks are nested one with another. This 'nestedness' offers multiple possibilities of meaning, for they mirror the nested invariants in the perception of our world. Such images are 'over-determined' in that they contain many levels of meaning that can be sampled, returned to and noticed afresh, again and again.

The richness of such discriminatory activity that is able to realise and convey multiple meanings is complex in the most profound sense of the word. Paul Klee's words at the beginning of this chapter aptly described the limitations of verbal description. The consecutive and temporal nature of language, especially written language, is inadequate to describe the conception of the 'whole', in its many-layered complexity.

At the start of our investigations into possible new ways of obtaining a way of thinking which would enable more efficient ways of working we were fortunate enough to be given a large contract with the senior engineers at British Airways shortly after the privatisation of the company.

As adults, the group who joined us from British Airways were as much steeped in the current control cultural value-set as any. As highly responsible managers in an industry where error is anathema and punished severely both in social and legal terms, they were highly risk averse. Initially, they found it difficult and con-fusing to be doing something, where the process was self-organising and where the rules evolved with their capacity to 'learn-to-learn'. There was also a large degree of ambiguity in the process. But this very ambiguity was the key to generating novel solutions and different ways of approaching issues. It is this ability to toler-ate and use ambiguity that gives rise to new knowledge and understanding.

Very quickly the process took over and became a way of accessing the more intuitive but deeper knowledge that each of them had. The 'nested', over-deter-mined quality of picture making makes accessible multiple meanings and the multiple perceptions that make up our complex lived experience. The description in graphic terms of a problem or an issue offered up many dimensions from which to pick the latent aspects of a solution. This made their decision making more adequate for they were able to understand the variety of elements inherent in the actual situation they were facing. This included the emotional aspects implicit, but not always recognised, in the issue. Decision making is not simply a deductive, logical process, but something that requires all the abilities of the indi-vidual and group. It often requires a risky choice between seemingly equal offerings and the imagination to envisage alternatives.

Our British Airways group was able to learn to use their latent knowledge through the process that taught them to be happy with a large degree of ambigu-ity. This confidence with ambiguity allowed them to devote most of their resources to identify more features of any situation that they were facing. The feedback loop that is involved in this process necessarily creates changes in the individual engaging in the activity. I have already described how the 'me' but 'not me' paradox that occurs in this activity gives rise to a richer and more differenti-ated 'self' where unarticulated experience, felt at an intuitive and emotional level, can be brought to the surface and seen as external to that person. This generates a new level of observer status where what has been felt as a frustration, or an unmanageable and sometimes uncomfortable sensation, can be used as a source of knowledge and therefore 'power to act', 'power to choose'.

For the British Airways team the use of such a tool over the period of nine days ensured the growth of greater perceptual acuity and the ability to see the dynamics of the evolving situation. Such new 'mental muscles' remain, just as the muscles of an archer develop in a certain way, so the practice of paying attention to the subtle invariances creates a new ability to see high-level relationships. This ability to perceive and to pay attention to emerging meaning informs and makes possible decision making in what to others may appear very indistinct circumstances.

A shared aesthetic

The graphic tool functions as a self-organising process towards a shared meaning. This achievement of meaning, or the group aesthetic, is not predictable but emerges from the interactions of the group members, enmeshing them in a deep level of understanding.

The development of a shared aesthetic, a kind of unwritten sense of meaning, makes for a shared vision. The deeply shared vision of a team acts as a reference that is present whenever they work together in whatever constellation is required. Individuals are able to trust and rely on each other despite their often-valuable differences. This more profound level of communication makes it possible for them to come together successfully in sub-groups to trouble-shoot or to solve difficult but more long-term problems.

The tool also provides a simulation technique, which allows the group to work through relational issues in a safe controlled space. The collective use of this kind of graphic activity allows for the underlying dynamics to be laid bare so that they can be dealt with without recourse to highly personal attacks and slights. Working it out 'out there' provides a safe arena in which to come to understanding that transcends the usual frames of references and behaviours.

If we are to work happily together in the complex world we now live in we need such safe tools desperately. Such ways of working will increase our perception, our understanding and our attentional capacities, and will re-define how we think.

References

Bateson, G. (1972) *Steps to an Ecology of Mind*, London: Granada Publishing Ltd

Beckmann, M. (1964) 'On my painting', in R.L. Herbert (Ed.) *Modern Artists on Art*, Englewood Cliffs: Prentice-Hall

Beitel, F. (1970) 'Sketches toward a psychology in art', in G. Pappas (Ed.) *Concepts in Art and Education*, London: MacMillan Company, Collier-MacMillan

Gibson, J.J. (1979) *The Ecological Approach to Visual Perception*, Boston: Houghton Mifflin

Heraclitus in Stallknecht, N.P. and Brumbaugh, R.S (1950) *The Spirit of Western Philosophy*, p.6, London: Longmans, Green and Co

James, A. K. (1983) *The Human Knowing System*, unpublished doctoral thesis, Brunel University, Department of Cybernetics

Kaptchuk, Ted J. (2000) *The Web that has no Weaver*, pp. 295–296, London: Random House

Klee, P. (1924) *Pedagogical Sketchbook*, pp. 256–7, London: Faber and Faber

Maturana, H. (1972) *The Neurophysiology of Cognition*, p. 4, Illinois: The Biological Computer Laboratories, University of Illinois

Pareto, V. (1993) 'More light on leaves', in S.J. Gould, *Eight Little Piggies*, London: Johnathan Cape.

12 Individual learning from exceptional events

Lloyd Davies and Paul Kraus

Introduction

Managers face multiple challenges in a complex world: the changes in needs of customers, suppliers, targets, employees, legislators and communities, to name but a few. The one common feature is that each challenge *changes over time*, and when it does, so must we. But to change effectively means *learning* effectively.

Schön (1983) wrote 'In general, the more an organisation depends for its survival on innovation and adaptation to a changing environment, the more essential its interest in organisational learning' (p. 327). He coined the term 'reflection-in-action' to denote the way professionals actually work. One of its products is learning. Elsewhere, Schön singles out managers for particular comment. 'Managers do reflect-in-action, but they seldom reflect on their reflection-in-action. Hence this crucially important dimension of their art tends to remain private and inaccessible to others. Moreover, because awareness of one's intuitive thinking usually grows out of practice in articulating it to others, managers often have little access to their own reflection-in-action' (p. 243).

When we ask managers how they learn from what they do, we are almost always met with blank looks. Prompted, some are able to say *what* they have learned, especially what not to do, but *how* they learn is a mystery. *Learning*, for most, is a formal function when they strive to understand and assimilate what others are teaching them, whether in books, lectures, courses, or presentations. But if we focus on discovery, exploration or experimentation, which are all normal activities in our working lives, then we can account for the fact that almost everyone we ask says that the vast majority of what they need to be able do their normal work, is learned or acquired from experience rather than from books, lectures, etc. Learning, in this sense, is virtually equivalent to discovery, exploration or experimentation.

So here is a paradox. To survive in a complex world we have to change; to change we have to learn; and yet we lack explicit awareness of how we do this crucial activity through experience.

Learning theories

The subject of learning from experience has interested scholars at least since Locke in the seventeenth century. The American educationalist and philosopher Dewey, in 1938, appears to have been the first to put forward a learning theory in which a progressive 'cycle' of impulse, observation, knowledge and judgement led to further sequences of the same components (Kolb, 1984, p. 23). The best known theory of learning, probably because of its categorisation into 'learning types', is that of Kolb (1984), who proposed a sequence:

Concrete ➤ Reflective ➤ Abstract ➤ Active ➤ *et seq.*
experience   observation   conceptualisation   experimentation

Starting with this cycle, Kolb identified four learning types in his 'learning styles inventory', and Honey and Mumford (1992) developed four, slightly different learning types in their 'learning styles questionnaire'.

Boud, Keogh and Walker (1985), and Jarvis (1994) took a significant step forward when they explicitly acknowledged in their models that learning was not a uni-directional process. They incorporate two-way arrows to denote the possibility that, say, reflection on an experience could (for Boud *et al.*) lead back to paying further attention to feelings, or (Jarvis) to further evaluation and possibly experimentation.

None of these theories, however, seemed sufficiently comprehensive to capture the many and varied aspects of experiential learning. Questions they left unanswered include: why could two managers living through the same experience derive very different 'lessons'? Why could a given manager apparently learn extensively on one occasion and hardly at all on another? How does the learning actually take place; what mental processes, or any other bodily processes, are involved? Questions of these kinds led the first author to carry out some research into learning from experience.

Research project (described by Lloyd)

It has been my experience that managers can readily talk about unusual events in their past from which they have learned. So the focus of my research was into the learning that came from these 'exceptional events'. These can be 'good' or 'bad', welcomed or unwelcome, planned and intended, or the product of misfortune. The 'negative' events are the sorts of experience after which people say 'It was awful at the time, but I certainly learned a lot'.

I used two principal and two secondary research methods. The principal methods were, first, to carry out in-depth, largely unstructured interviews with nineteen managers to explore their chosen exceptional events; and at the end of the research, to prepare a case study, a story, which illustrated the model of learning which I had developed, and which I then invited a second group of thirteen experienced managers, consultants and academics to critique. I also carried out a short longitudinal study with a finance manager who was visiting a newly acquired company in the USA for the first time, and I kept a diary of an exceptional event of my own.

The model, shown below as Figure 12.1 gradually grew and changed shape as my thinking progressed. It should be regarded as open to further refinement and development. A fuller account of this research can be seen in Davies (2002).

Two general introductory points should be made. First, the elements displayed in an irregular, cloud-shaped form convey the notion that they are difficult to delineate and cannot be absolutely defined. The one exception is *reflection* [K]

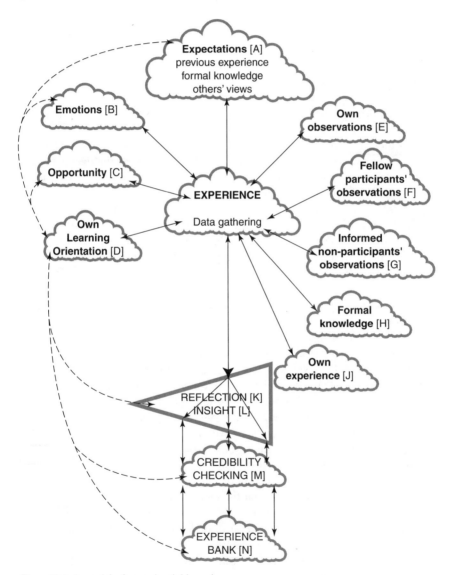

Figure 12.1 A model of experiential learning.

and *insight* [L] where the triangular shape is intended to convey the idea of a prism which opens up strands of thinking in the same way as an optical prism splits white light into its component rainbow colours.

The second general point is that every arrow is two-way to emphasise our observation that learning and sense making is not necessarily a tidy, linear process, in which the learning manager progresses from 1 to 2 to 3, etc. Whilst this might be the case when learning from a simple, straightforward experience, in a world of complexity, with its associated multi-layered data, ambiguities and paradoxes, learning is an iterative process. As more data from one source becomes available, insights change, require more checking with other sources, so that the lessons of learning are never completed, and any 'lesson from experience' is open to reconsideration.

The model can be seen as comprising the following main components. Central to the whole process is the *experience* itself. This may be very short or it may be long, sometimes very long. Of course, the 'lessons' the experience has to offer may range from the obvious and 'surface', such as the acquisition of facts, through to the profound, such as deep insights into people, events or ideas.

How the experience is worked on to yield its lessons appears to depend on clusters of elements; the learner's personal mental infrastructure, the data gathering processes, the sense-making processes, the testing or validating processes, and, as already noted, the iterations between any or all of these elements. An outline of each of these follows, and will be illustrated in the example in the next section.

The *personal infrastructure* elements are those which are deeply embedded in the nature of the learning manager, in her or his histories of experience and learning, and the ways in which the experiences impact on him or her. As two authors we are aware that we see experiences in different ways, which reflect the differences in our backgrounds, abilities and overall life experiences. These personal infrastructure elements go a long way to explaining why different managers derive different lessons from a shared experience.

So, *expectations* are particular to the learning manager. They exist before the experience occurs, even if the expectation is that 'nothing will happen', and colour the reaction to it. Very often, expectations are fully met and the event goes by unnoticed, but when expectations are not met this is likely to be noticed and the question 'Why?' posed. Louis and Sutton (1991) wrote of three causes for engaging in sense making, namely novelty, discrepancy and deliberate initiative.

Emotions are almost always associated with learning experiences. They may be of anger, pleasure, satisfaction, annoyance, curiosity, astonishment, frustration – the list is extensive (Storm and Storm, 1987, listed 525 in their taxonomy). Clore (1994) argues that 'a primary function of emotion is to provide information' (p. 103), and Bower (1994) observed that the inertial persistence of emotion, and its slow decay, ensured that attention to this information would be maintained. Emotions thus play a significant role in drawing attention to important experiences, and in encouraging us to work on them. Initially, they may be so strong as to cause a block, but with their slow diminution the block usually disappears. (Occasionally, however, the block may not diminish; the response then may be to bypass the event as though it is not occurring, or, if past, to rationalise it, making this tactic undiscussable, and to make the undiscussibility undiscussable.)

The *opportunity* to work on, and learn from, an experience is associated with its emotions, perhaps in a direct relationship in which the stronger the emotion the greater is the likelihood of the learner making an opportunity. Thus some experiences which have actual, or potential, disastrous consequences, like the example described below, are of such importance that those involved are compelled to review the events and circumstances leading up to it, to learn its lessons, and to act upon them. Other experiences are less compelling; Jarvis (1994, pp. 35–37) identifies three 'non-learning' responses to experiences: where people discard experiences through presumption, believing that the experience has nothing to teach them; non-consideration, when they are too busy or too fearful of the outcome; or rejection, where they decide to reject the opportunity to learn. Busy managers sometimes argue that they have no time, or opportunity, to work on an experience in order to learn from it, but it is notable that senior managers often make opportunities for reflection. Csikszentmihalyi and Sawyer (1995) report that the creative people they studied, including CEOs and Nobel Prize-winners, usually planned into their working lives some space in which they could ponder on the work they were doing. Professor Norman Amundsen likens 'reflective space' to the cartilage between the bones of the spine; 'without it, the spine would be inflexible, wear away quickly, and be inefficient' (Clutterbuck, 2001, p. 63).

Perhaps the most influential of the personal infrastructure elements is one's *own learning orientation*. In the model it is connected by double arrows with every other element either directly or via data gathering to signify our view that it both influences that element and may, in turn, be influenced by it. For example, one of the *data gathering* elements is *fellow participants' observations* – accounts and thoughts on an experience which a colleague, who shared the experience, might offer. These are potentially valuable because someone else's perspective usually adds to the information on the experience. A manager's learning orientation, in encouraging or discouraging a colleague to contribute or comment, will enlarge or reduce the opportunity to learn from a different perspective.

We see learning orientation as consisting of three separate, inter-linked, components, namely the manager's personal characteristics – certain *personality traits*; their *ability*, which we see as a function of intelligence(s) and their development; and *learned behaviours*. Current thinking amongst psychologists on personality (see Hampson, 1999) favours the big five taxonomy of personality traits, one of which is openness; McCrae and Costa (1997) say:

> Open people are not only *able* to grasp new ideas, they *enjoy* doing so. The merely intelligent people tend to have highly developed interests in specialised fields in which they excel; open people have a wide and ever-increasing range of interest ... Need for variety, tolerance of ambiguity, preference for complexity all represent motivational aspects of Openness.
>
> (p. 832)

They refer to openness as a broad constellation of traits with cognitive, affective (emotion) and behavioural manifestations, and the overall impression of this cluster of traits is that it is receptive to new ideas, though not uncritically so, prepared to have the mind stretched, and to contemplate what has hitherto never been experienced. Other, more specific traits, seem likely to contribute to one's learning orientation. Several managers interviewed mentioned the importance of resilience, determination and self-confidence in pursuing new experiences in order to derive meaning from them.

Ability we view as the combination of intelligences and training and usage. 'Intelligences' are not confined to verbal, numerical and spatial reasoning. We prefer Gardner's (1993) concept of multiple intelligences.[1] The possession of these intelligences is not enough, however. To contribute to learning orientation they need to be developed, whether by formal education or by usage.

Finally, *learned behaviours* also add to learning orientation. These include techniques such as post-project appraisals and other review methods, the checking of assumptions, questioning techniques and effective meeting procedures. All these, and many others, provide the manager with tools for digging into experiences with a view to maximising the data that can be derived from them. They tend to be acquired by mixing with other people who use them, and appropriating and personalising those which serve best. The effect of this process is that two managers may have very similar personalities and abilities but have different learning orientations because their life and work experiences have furnished them with different tools or techniques with which to work through their experiences. Thus the *personal infrastructure* elements are brought to bear on most, if not all, the experiences a manager encounters. Figure 12.1 shows that learning orientation influences the other Elements A, B, C, K, L, M and N, in addition to the data-gathering elements E–J which relate directly to the experience in question.

The *data gathering* processes tend to be more experience-specific. The manager's *own observations* are what he or she sees, hears, or otherwise senses. Sometimes it is all the manager has to rely on, but in many experiences colleagues may have been involved, and in these the manager can have the advantage of *fellow participants' observations*. Weick (1993) said that for there to be a full exchange of observations there should be a state of 'respectful interaction' between the two, or more, people involved; this means that both A and B should be prepared to contribute and receive with equal willingness. If one person feels inhibited for any reason, or tends to discount the other's observations, the exchange is less productive. Weick's respectful interaction thus amounts to more than a double monologue, but a true dialogue where the issue at hand is reasoned through with openness, without the underlying motivation of maintaining one's own point of view (van Deurzen, 1998).[2]

Another form of data gathering, more catalytic than actually contributory, is sometimes available from *informed non-participants' observations*. Such a person would be someone who, although not a party to the experience itself, had had extensive experience of similar situations. Their role would be to help the manager probe overlooked aspects, and also to offer alternative interpretations and different perspectives. These are some of the roles of a mentor.

Formal knowledge is material that is in the public domain, in books, articles, lecture notes, records, archives, drawings and so on. For some experiences, this type of knowledge can be helpful, even essential. The manager might need to access such data to provide background or material against which to view the detail of the current experience. *Formal knowledge* can also be built up through experiment to help explain an experience.

The final source of data is the manager's *own experience*. When expectations are disturbed by a discrepant event, it is natural to look back at similar events to check the nature of any pre-conceptions, to look for differences which could explain the current experience. This process is greatly helped when records have been kept, for example when scientists and medical researchers keep records of their actions and their results.

Each of these sources is distinctive, and it is unlikely that all five will be relevant for every experience. However, it is worthwhile exploring the possibilities of all five, because multiple sources of information greatly improve the chance of deriving sense, and learning, from an experience.

The sense-making processes, *reflection/insight*, are difficult to describe because of the huge variety of experience under discussion. Some are quite simple, such as learning a fact, whereas some alter a belief, which in turn requires us to look afresh at other experiences. Some, more rarely, are of such importance as to construct a new belief system. Several writers put forward a progressive sequence of knowledge acquisition and usage of increasing profundity. Moon (1999), for example, talks about (i) 'noticing' an experience, (ii) 'making sense', that is becoming aware of a sense of order in things, (iii) 'making meaning', that is understanding implications, (iv) 'working with meaning', that is using the learned lessons, personalising and integrating them, and (v) 'transformative learning' where the outcomes of an experience change one's view of the world in a significant respect. Most managerial learning experiences would come within the (i) to (iii) categories, with the most profound learning probably occurring less frequently.

One of the processes of sense making is reconciling discrepancies. Festinger (1957) put forward his theory of 'cognitive dissonance reduction', which says that we are not mentally comfortable when we encounter two (dissonant) facts, statements or beliefs which oppose each other. We therefore work to reduce the discomfort either completely or to levels which are tolerable. Of course, a risk is that to become mentally comfortable we shut out the dissonant experience – the 'ostrich head in sand' syndrome.

Credibility checking is the final element before the lessons learned are incorporated into the manager's *experience bank*. It entails the testing of the sense, or the lessons, that have emerged from the previous processes. Watson (2001a) puts forward three ways of deciding the 'truth' of an item of knowledge. 'Correspondence theories' judge knowledge by how accurately it describes what has actually happened. 'Coherence/plausibility' theories judge according to the extent of how well the new knowledge fits with other, previously learned information. 'Pragmatists' theories' judge knowledge by considering how effective or useful the knowledge is when applied in a certain situation.

Making sense of a disaster

Having summarised the elements of our model in relatively abstract terms, this section illustrates how it could be used by a practising manager to make sense of a complex disaster – a burst water main. Although the event took place many years ago, it was of such significance to those involved, and so memorable, that it was chosen by Ian for discussion with us. Ian was deputy to the general manager (GM) and responsible for all operational matters. During the six days of the crisis, staff in the division worked round the clock tackling repairs and ensuring emergency water supplies were available. The GM led these activities during the days and Ian took the lead during the nights. There were extensive briefing sessions during the hand-over periods in morning and evenings.

Ian's early experiences in the Scouts, CCF and national service, had given him his first understanding of the responsibilities, obligations and techniques of leadership. These early influences bear out Watson's (2001b) point that managers 'emerge' and carry with them their other experiences gained in non-work spheres.

Box 12.1 Water Main Bursts – 140,000 people affected!

In December 1985, one of Leeds' major raw water mains burst. It took six days to repair and reactivate the affected treatment works. Towards the end of this period up to 140,000 people were without piped water, including hospitals and nursing homes. In the proximity of the burst extensive local flooding occurred.

The water treatment works was supplied by three low pressure, large diameter (42ins and 40ins) mains dating from 1866, 1897 and 1921, each being about five miles long. Valves were in place to make it possible to shut off any one of these mains whilst retaining supply via the other two. However, faulty and unmarked valves, human error and inadequate records created extreme difficulties with the repair and these, together with safety reasons, necessitated stopping all supply to the works for three days.

Over the first three days attempts to isolate the burst main by closing the appropriate valves, while retaining supply via the other two mains, were fruitless, because of a series of operator errors and faulty valves. Eventually, the decision to close all the three mains allowed progress on the repair, but even then the work was threatened by a minor, but continuous flow along the burst main. This meant that the final stages of sealing a joint around the main with molten lead was particularly hazardous due to the risk of explosion.

Ian stressed that the focus on his personal learning, for the purposes of this analysis, should in no way imply that others played any lesser role. Just the opposite, he regarded their efforts as superlative, and believed that they, too, learned much from the experience.

How the lessons were learned

The content of this section is based on our conversations with Ian and a formal report of the incident (identified later). After the burst had been repaired, the treatment works returned to normal running. The water supply restored, the management team addressed many questions in order that this type of experience could be avoided in future and major emergencies could be managed better. In addressing three of these questions as a way of illustrating how learning occurs, we will have recourse to the model shown above in Figure 12.1 together with the amplification of its various elements.

Why had the main burst? Why had there been so many problems in isolating the affected main?

These are two separate questions. Taking the *bursting of the main*, management's *expectations* before the event had been that the three mains would continue to run as before. The mains had run for up to 119 years without incident, so the burst was a major 'discrepant event'. Their *emotions* were naturally of dismay, but also, once the crisis was over, of professional curiosity.

Own observations suggested no obvious reasons for the burst. A later report by the British Cast Iron Research Association suggested that the burst section of pipe had a flaw, possibly caused at the time the main was laid in 1897, and that there had probably been corrosion from that time onwards. Nothing else had happened which could suggest a trigger for the timing of December 1985, so to that extent the reason was un-knowable. Thus in terms of the model, the only helpful data source was *formal knowledge*. The *reflection/insight* processes, therefore, stored the incident in the *experience bank* as a puzzle.

More light, however, could be shed on the problems in isolating the main. On day three it was found that the most relevant valve, V13, had *not* been fully closed. The operator had given it two turns, encountered resistance, and concluded that it was fully shut. In practice, forty or fifty turns would have been needed for full closure. This fact emerged when managers, going through the logic processes of their information, saw that there was an anomaly, and went back to check their sources. From Ian's perspective, *fellow participants'* observations took the form of managers being prompted to re-check their data by the failure of *reflection/insight* and *credibility checking* to produce a cogent reason for the continued water flow in the burst main. The managers then returned to the data and found an error – which enabled *reflection/insight* to produce a theory which *credibility checking* this time found acceptable.

But this raised the second question: why did the operator make such a mistake? Collectively, managers could bring together a range of disparate data through most of the *data gathering* sources. Several managers' *own experience* told them that the operation of old valves, the same age as the mains, could cause problems – of sticking, or even of breaking – and the tendency had been, over the years, to follow conventional wisdom and 'leave well alone', and only operate the valves when necessary. *Formal knowledge* from another domain (water treatment, as opposed to water supply) supported by *own experience* authenticated problems in water treatment works when accumulated silt is carried into the treatment work and clogs up filters. A particularly bad case of this had occurred nine years earlier and this had reinforced an established rule of only operating valves at the express instruction of a senior manager. Therefore the poor condition of the valves caused valve V13 to stick, and lack of regular maintenance deprived the operators of first-hand knowledge and experience. The overall consequence, the likelihood of which emerged as the *reflection/insight* processes put together different source data, was that the system was left undisturbed; a record of decades of uneventful performance by the mains, alongside some pressing needs in other parts of the organisation, justified this policy.

In hindsight, of course, this policy was obviously flawed. The experience of the Leeds burst, in the collective *experience bank*, led to the development of a mains maintenance policy across the authority.

Why had the flooded householders, although satisfied by the prompt response of the insurers, nevertheless felt they could have been better treated?

This was an important issue for the householders whose properties had been flooded. Ian's *experience* at the time of the burst had been one of relief (*emotion*) that this part of the problem was being taken care of promptly by the authority's insurance manager. He was later surprised – *expectations* upset – and dismayed (*emotion*) to learn that householders were somewhat dissatisfied with the way the authority had treated them.

Ian's *own observation* registered the explanation when he heard their views. The financial aspects of the damage were indeed being looked after, but they felt that they had been kept in the dark on the progress of the repair. A second smaller flood had created a belief that the first flood was not a one-off event. They were aware that the repair was taking several days and during that time they felt exposed to further danger from flooding.

To Ian's *reflection/insight* and *credibility checking* processes this made good sense. Viewed from their perspective, they had suffered two floods and could not be sure that more would not follow. The lesson which he incorporated in his *experience bank*, was the *importance of specific communication with everyone affected by an incident*. What had been needed was for an engineer to visit each householder regularly, update them, and answer questions. Any doubts they had about further flooding would have been surfaced and dealt with.

Why had the division employees been so notably supportive, and why had there been so much support from outside the authority?

The *experience*, which was a matter of *own observation* by Ian and his colleagues, was that the reaction by the whole span of staff and operatives in the division had been spontaneously helpful throughout the period of the crisis. Ian's *own experience* would not have automatically assumed this; there had been cases of industrial unrest in Leeds, and following several reorganisations, many staff were in posts which were relatively new to them. His *expectations* would not have been of such a degree of genuine willingness to help, and his *emotions* in the event were of pleasure and a little surprise.

Discussing this response, and hearing his colleague managers' *fellow participants' observations*, together with *informed non-participants' observations*, he concluded (*reflection/insight*) that the motivation was the sudden emergence of an over-riding, single, clear objective – that of maintaining water supplies to the population served by the works. For the week of the crisis, nothing was more important. In the *reflection/insight* and *credibility checking* processes, other *data* supported that view. *Formal knowledge*, from literature and presentations on motivation, stressed the importance of clarity of objectives, and his *own experience*, dating back from early adult life reinforced it. Moreover, another part of his *own experience* was that, for many people in the water industry, an awareness of the vital nature of their work, and a sense of service that went with it, was itself a motivator, which found very practical expression during the crisis.

These reasons did not, automatically, apply outside the authority, however, and yet the *experience* was almost equally supportive. Until the burst could be repaired and the treatment works put water into normal supply, the need was to re-route water from other, unaffected works, and transport water by road to the remaining population. But there was a problem due to lack of transport and bowsers. The division and the authority had some, but they were totally insufficient for serving up to 140,000 people. In the event, bowsers were willingly supplied from other authorities in the north of England, from the Milk Marketing Board, and from the Army.

It was management's *own observation* that the publicity, which reached national level in press, TV and radio, had alerted not only the population affected but many others who were in a position to help. Managers had already approached other water authorities, and had a very positive response; *reflection/insight* suggested that their motivations were similar to the division's own employees. The Milk Marketing Board also recognised the vital need, and management's *own experience* of the generosity of spirit in adversity seemed likely to explain this very welcome gesture. The idea to approach the Army was put forward by a member of staff with services experience, and he followed it up through the night – to very good effect: the Army supplied 195 bowsers.

One of the principal lessons for Ian and his colleagues from this aspect of the burst *experience* was of the importance of clear communications, both internally and externally. Both the GM working through the day, and Ian during the night, were in regular contact with the local media, giving briefings and interviews concerning the implications for the people of Leeds and the progress on the repair. *Reflection/insight* after the event showed how important this had been on many fronts.

Discussion

From this exceptional event Ian was undoubtedly right in believing that the extent of the learning for many people was very great. It is also likely that each individual derived some different lessons as our learning is partly grounded in what we already know. As Arie de Geus (1997) said 'We can only see what we have already experienced' (p. 40).

Of the twelve elements in the model, *opportunity* and *learning orientation* were never mentioned. In some ways they are closely related, because someone with a learning orientation characterised by strong curiosity is likely to make space for opportunities, but this is not automatic as pressure of other events may preclude any possibility of learning. In the burst water main 'exceptional event', the need to avoid a second occurrence, or to handle it more effectively if it should occur, meant that the opportunity to learn from the event was a given. An official inquiry a few weeks later had the effect of formalising, documenting and consolidating the learning.

The significance of opportunity is much clearer in less spectacular events when the need to learn is not as paramount. Following the conclusion of an effective project we can either move on and address the next set of managerial issues, or we can pause to reflect on why the project was successful. A perceptive time-management system would build in some space for reflection using the data gathering sources in the model, as appropriate, rather than leave it to the discretion of the individual manager.

In some ways, Ian's learning orientation was less relevant in a major event than it would be in something more personal. Given his role in the burst, he was obliged to review the event. Driven by external events, his personality was less relevant. His abilities, the combination of intelligences and their development, would have been brought to bear on all the issues raised, although his abilities would have been supplemented by those of his colleagues. Also relevant would have been the number of learned behaviours, such as review techniques learned in earlier experiences.

As with opportunity, the significance of learning orientation is greater in smaller, personal and less public, exceptional events. We would argue that it is the personality traits of openness, alerted by emotion, that start the processes of sense making and learning. Expressed at its simplest, an open personality when roused by a discrepant event would be more likely to work with it, explore it, engage others to help, and come to some learning conclusions than would a more closed personality. A developed intelligence could reinforce this propensity for learning; when faced with a report including an array of figures, someone with a developed logical-mathematical intelligence would be more likely to pursue underlying reasons than someone whose intelligences had developed elsewhere, although the personality characteristics of determination and resilience could influence the extent to which he or she applied that intelligence. And once engaged, a person with well-trained and applied intelligences is likely to reach sounder conclusions than someone whose intelligences remain less developed.

In our discussions with Ian, the nature of his learning orientation was never considered, partly because of the obviously personal nature of the subject but also because of Ian's emphasis on the corporate, almost collegiate, nature of much of the learning. The learning that came from the event was in most respects *group* learning, the product of the exchange of data and ideas amongst the personnel who were most involved. In our experience one of Ian's best developed intelligences is the interpersonal, and real skill in this field facilitated that learning. He established an environment of 'respectful interactions' between all those involved, from the operatives carrying out repairs to the most senior engineers.

An obvious limitation of studying the burst is the fact that it occurred long ago and awareness of the learning processes, insofar as it ever existed, may have diminished. An opportunity to work with a manager in a longitudinal study of an ongoing crisis, with real-time observations, would present fascinating possibilities for further research in this field. Are the twelve elements in the model necessary and sufficient? Are there some track patterns between them which are characteristic of certain types of learning? In an ideal research world, we would have two or more managers going through the crisis, so that the different learning orientations could be explored, as well as interactions between the elements.

Meanwhile, the concept of the learning orientation itself could usefully be studied further. How much of the big five openness cluster of traits is relevant to experiential learning? What other traits, outside openness, as well as determination and resilience, are relevant? From an HRD perspective, what are the learned behaviours, the tools and techniques, which provide personality and ability with cutting edges to learn? There is much to be done by researchers who find cooperative managers, and by reflective managers who are interested in gaining further insights into their own learning.

In closing, we want to express our sincerest thanks to Ian for his very willing help in our studies. With typical thoroughness and integrity he gave us much food for thought, and materially assisted in our learning about learning.

Notes

1 Gardner's (1993) multiple intelligences comprise, in the order in which he presents them in his book: linguistic intelligence; musical intelligence; logical-mathematical intelligence; spatial intelligence; bodily-kinaesthetic intelligence; intrapersonal intelligence; and interpersonal intelligence. Some intelligences may have greater relevance for a given job.

2 'In true dialogue, both of us bring our personal views to the exchange between us and we put these at the disposal of our shared attempt at widening our vision. In dialogue I come forward with my given thoughts and give them new thought, taking my ideas forward. My focus is on the problem, the issue at hand, rather than you or me. If you do the same, then between us the issue receives full attention and neither you nor I stand in the way of clarifying and understanding it, putting it into its right context and place, until obstacles are overcome and contradictions resolved or put back in their right order.' (Deurzen, van E., 1998, pp. 47–52)

References

Bower, G. H. (1994) 'Some relations between emotions and memory' in P. Ekman and R. J. Davidson (Eds) *The Nature of Emotions*, Oxford: Oxford University Press

Boud, D., Keogh, R. and Walker, D. (1985) *Reflection: Turning experience into learning*, London: Kogan Page

Clore, G. C. (1994) 'Why emotions are felt' in P. Ekman and R. J. Davidson (Eds) *The Nature of Emotions*, Oxford: Oxford University Press

Clutterbuck, D. (2001) 'Back to the flaw', *People Management*, 7(21)

Csikszentmihalyi, M. and Sawyer, K. (1995) 'Creative insight: The social dimension of a solitary moment' in R. J. Sternberg and J. E. Davidson (Eds) *The Nature of Insight*, Cambridge: MA Bradford Books, MIT

de Geus, A. (1997) *The Living Company*, London: Brealey

Davis, J.M.L. (2002) 'How experienced managers learn from exceptional events', PhD thesis, Lancaster University

Deurzen van, E. (1998) *Paradox and Passion in Psychotherapy*, John Wiley & Sons

Dewey, J. (1938) *Experience and Education*, Kappa Delta Pi

Festinger, L. (1957) *A Theory of Cognitive Dissonance*, Stanford CA: Stanford UP

Gardner, H. (1993) *Frames of Mind*, London: Fontana

Hampson, S. (1999) 'State of the Art: Personality', *Psychologist*, 12(6)

Honey, P. and Mumford, A. (1992) *The Manual of Learning Styles*, Maidenhead: Peter Honey

Jarvis, P. (1994) 'Learning practical knowledge', *Journal of Higher and Further Education*, 18(1)

Kolb, D .A. (1984) *Experiential Learning*, Englewood Cliffe NJ: Prentice Hall

Louis, M. R. and Sutton, R. I. (1991) 'Switching cognitive gears: From habits of mind to active thinking', *Human Relations*, 44

McCrae, R. R. and Costa, P. T. (1997) 'Conceptions and correlates of openness to experience' in R. R. Hogan, J. Johnson and S. Briggs (Eds) *Handbook of Personality Psychology*, San Diego, CA: Academic Press

Moon, J. A. (1999) *Reflection in Learning and Professional Development*, London: Kogan Page

Schön, D. A. (1983) *The Reflective Practitioner*, London: Maurice Temple Smith Ltd

Storm, C. and Storm, T. (1987) 'A taxonomic study of the vocabulary of emotions', *Journal of Personality and Social Psychology*, 40

Watson, T. J. (2001a) *Organising and Managing Work: Organisational, managerial and strategic behaviour in theory and practice*, Harlow: FT Prentice Hall

Watson, T. J. (2001b) 'The emergent manager and process of management pre-learning', *Management Learning*, 32(2)

Weick, K. E. (1993) 'The collapse of sensemaking in organisations: The Mann Gulch Disaster', *Administrative Science Quarterly*, 38

Part IV

Realities of HR

Aspects of practice

The four chapters in this section each address practice directly, giving examples of ways in which conventional practice needs to be reinterpreted. The section starts with a chapter by Sarah Fraser, who uses the health sector to argue against the imposition of controlling structures designed to overcome feelings of chaos associated with cross boundary working, and offers principles by which such complexity can be better managed. Kiran Trehan and Clare Rigg focus on the educational sector, examining how emotions and complexity intersect with power relations when a critical learning perspective is adopted. The chapter by Christina MacNeil follows. She examines the changing role of the line manager in de-layered, downsized organisations and describes management development designed to equip supervisors with the relevant skills to function as effective facilitators of team learning. The final chapter is by Rosemary Hill, who uses case-study research in small organisations to offer an alternative paradigm to conventional HRD intervention.

Whilst each of the chapters in this volume has practical implications those in this section create a focus for debates that have occurred earlier in the book. In its questioning of boundaries, Sarah Fraser's work resonates with that of Heather Höpfl, David Weir, and Monica Lee. The themes of power and emotion that are central to Kiran Trehan's and Clare Rigg's chapter can be seen in many of the other chapters – particularly those by Tim Hatcher, Jim Stewart, Carole Elliott and Sharon Turnbull, Jamie Callahan and Denis Gračanin, and Lloyd Davies and Paul Kraus. The need to reconceptualise organisational structure, and the implications of this that are apparent in Christina McNeil's work, can also be seen in the two chapters by Paul Iles and Maurice Yolles, and Maurice Yolles and Paul Iles. Finally, by looking at small and medium-sized enterprises, Rosemary Hill is addressing an area that is rarely examined. This highlights the fundamental need that pervades the book to adopt a different approach, and is, perhaps, most explicitly stated by Kim James.

In conclusion, each of the contributors has interpreted the notion of complexity from within their own situation, and in so doing they have provided a wide spread of critique, understanding and context. The theory and practice of working with people needs to develop past the conventional if it is to be able to keep pace with our changing conceptualisation of the world we live in.

13 Leadership principles and reflections for unravelling the stranglehold of organisational boundaries

Challenges for health services

Sarah Fraser

Introduction

The Belgian artist, Magritte, intrigues us with his painting of a pipe that is inscribed '*Ceci n'est pas une pipe*' (This is not a pipe). Naming it *La trahison des images* (The treachery of images) he calls to our attention the importance of not mistaking the image for the real thing.

Do organisational charts stating roles and functions describe the organisation? Do financial rules and procedures define the organisation? Is the painting of the pipe, a pipe? The reality is organisations may have a definable structure as shown through charts, role statements and authority schedules. However, the behaviour of individuals will provide the organisation with its distinctive appearance and level of effectiveness. (Dunderdale, 1994 pp. 23–24). We can easily mistake the work of our organisation for being some *thing* that is tangible and in doing so lose sight of its real nature.

Weick (1979) states that, 'Most "things" in an organisation are actually relationships, variables tied together in a systematic fashion. Events, therefore depend on the strength of these ties, the direction of influence, the time it takes for information in the form of differences to move around the circuit. The word organisation is a noun, and it is also a myth. If you look for an organisation you won't find it. What you will find is that there are events, linked together, that transcribe within concrete walls and these sequences, their pathways, and their timing are the forms we erroneously make a substance when we talk about an organisation'.

Human behaviour is unpredictable, reflecting the different perceptions, feelings and attitudes that people have. The interrelationship between these variables and the social context within which they work, and the way in which they change over time, contributes to the dynamic complexity of our workplace.

Add to this an environment of uncertainty and the notion of 'working it all out' becomes an unrealistic management activity. The public sector in England can be described as turbulent; change is unpredictable, it comes from a mix of technological breakthroughs, government regulation and public demands (Emery and Trist, 1965).

The concept of leadership in this environment is a thorny subject on which many theorists have conflicting and contrasting opinions. What we do know is that the transactional leadership process, where organisations and departments are designed in the back office, roles are defined outside the context in which they are played out, and the business is managed as though it is predictable and controllable, is unlikely to be a successful strategy.

The National Health Service (NHS) in England continues its constant process of renewal and development. The structural changes underway since 2000 have placed new demands on leaders. The endeavour has been to negotiate and discover new management and leadership paradigms that support, rather than diminish, the improvement of health and the delivery of services. As hospital trusts merge with others, primary care groups evolve into primary care trusts, old civil service-led regions dissipate into new forms, and as new mental health trusts are created, we are presented with the opportunity to develop innovative working structures.

Public sector organisations differ from private sector ones in many ways. One of the key differences is the imperative to work together, not only with similar organisations, but also with other allied groups. For example, in order to best provide services for a community, various health organisations (hospitals, primary care, community care, mental health) need to collaborate closely with social care organisations as well as the many voluntary and non-statutory organisations that exist.

Think about it from the perspective of patients who have coronary heart disease. Whilst they may experience an acute intervention in a hospital, the majority of their care will be provided in the community, with support from primary care. They may need to join a supervised exercise session in a local gym, some may choose to join a local voluntary-led support group, some may need special home care from community nurses etc. From the perspective of the patient, the various organisations and their boundaries don't exist (except for when things go wrong); what matters is the connectivity and relationships between all those who provide the appropriate care and support.

The leadership challenge for health and social care is to unravel the stranglehold within which the organisations may be trapped, and to provide the context within which collaboration and partnership working can flourish.

One way is through the appreciation and understanding of the notion of 'boundaries'. By examining the resistance and difficulties we encounter with boundaries we can find principles that provide us with ways to capitalise on change. These principles overlap and combine to provide a leadership focus on the relationships that weave the tapestry of health and healthcare.

Principle 1: create boundaries that are flexible and permeable

We can't work without boundaries; some form of structure is required to give meaning and purpose to our activities. The NHS has statutory obligations and NHS organisations need to demonstrate clinical and financial regularity.

Organisations have been defined (North, 1990) as 'groups of individuals bound by a common purpose who come together to achieve joint objectives'. This suggests organisations can contain a sense of identity created by a common purpose. Those not included are on the outside of the organisation. A boundary is formed. These boundaries can be external to the organisation, or internal. Internal boundaries can exist between various units or departments as well as between the levels of hierarchy in the organisation.

Complexity and opportunity arises when individuals, within one organisation, are perceived as belonging to various groups and networks, all with different purposes and objectives. Most practitioners experience this conflict. How we choose to see boundaries depends very much on the perspective and the context in which we are viewing them. In many cases these co-existing networks with their boundaries are not congruent with the perceived, and conceived, organisational boundary. What is viewed as the legitimate organisation, for example, as displayed by its charted hierarchy of roles and functions and its financial rules and procedures, may bear little resemblance to the healthcare flows and processes within which it participates.

For example, a hospital may have three separate departments called 'medicine', 'surgical' and 'support services'. Where should the radiology department fit? Patients suspected of lung cancer (medicine) need x-rays and CT scans and surgical patients also need x-rays taken. So we may place radiology in support services, as it has a supporting role for other departments, even though many radiology teams carry out interventions of their own. There is probably no right way of organising the various groups as what will matter for the work of the hospital is the relationships between the various professional teams.

The leadership challenge, therefore, is to create team configurations that reflect the dynamic, adaptive and evolving processes that make up healthcare as well as to support those whose roles specifically take them into contact with people in teams and organisations outside their own. Evidence suggests these 'boundary spanning' roles are vulnerable to conflict and can be highly stressful (Margolis and Kroes, 1974).

Reflections for leaders

- How can I go about mapping and increasing my understanding of the various formal and informal networks that operate within my organisation?
- To what extent are teams and individuals working across boundaries and what purpose are they serving?
- Who are the 'boundary workers' and how am I supporting them in their stressful role?
- How am I leveraging existing relationships within and without my organisation to achieve the objectives of our wider health system and local community?
- How can I encourage our 'legitimate' boundaries to be permeable and innovative (e.g. by sharing information with other organisations)?
- What hierarchical boundaries within the organisation are limiting progress and what can I do about them?

Principle 2: regard power as vested in relationships, not roles and functions

I can print a name badge, hand out business cards and use a letterhead that all describe me as the prime minister of Great Britain. However, it's clear I am unable to function and perform the role. The power to accomplish this is directly vested in the relationships and interactions with appropriate individuals and groups.

So, on being promoted to chief executive of Mainstreet Hospital and on receipt of my new business cards – does this mean I am the chief executive? Well, in the formal system I can be defined as such by investigating the signatory and responsibility roles that are laid out in the governance structure. But what does this mean? What power do I actually have?

Power is given meaning as an energy that flows between individuals. The capacity to influence and use power is thus based in the nature and quality of relationships with others. Wheatley (1992) goes so far as to suggest that only relationships and interactions can give meaning to 'things'. An operating theatre has no use without the operating team and the patient. And they are irrelevant and meaningless without interaction. A chief executive who is new to the organisation will need to start by developing appropriate constructive relationships with individuals within and without the formal boundaries of the organisation. Within an organisation, power is relative to the capacity of its individuals to lever such relationships.

Kelly and Allison (1998) remind us of the importance of us examining the nature of power: 'Power hierarchy can become destructive when a leader's position and power becomes fixed and protected from the process of autonomous agents of influence and selection. Protected power permits designated leaders to act for personal rather than system advantage'. The challenge here is for leaders to allow themselves to develop relationships outside the formal hierarchy of their organisation, and to develop the self-awareness necessary to inspect the nature and quality of the power that emanates from such relationships.

So how can the leader, at chief executive or team level, work with power in a way that most constructively supports the organisation's goals and ideals? This is largely a matter of personal reflection and introspection, linked with a sensitivity to environmental conditions.

Reflections for leaders

- How often do I rely on my job title and position to get things done? How often do I rely on others using their roles to get things done?
- If I lost my job tomorrow, how could I continue to influence healthcare in my community? With whom would I network?
- How can I strengthen the influence and performance of other managers and leaders by developing relationships with them? Am I connected to the informal network in my organisation?
- To what extent do our organisational charts reflect the relationships required to deliver both strategic and operational requirements of the organisation?

Principle 3: shape behaviour, not structures or rules

As one chief executive recently commented privately, 'Many practitioners are about to get their fourth employer during my career and there is little evidence that the structures they have worked in have made a significant difference to the way they deliver care. The sad thing is all the energy seems to go into creating the bureaucracies and organisational structures and not in supporting practitioners to improve the quality of healthcare'. He recognises that to lead an improvement in health and care in his local community, he needs to discover and support new ways of behaving.

What the behaviours are and who should demonstrate them should reflect the nature of the local context and priorities. If we consider that the role of leaders in complex systems is to enable workers to evolve so they deliver organisational goals, then it is useful to consider the means by which behaviour can be influenced. This suggests a key role for leaders in dynamic systems is their ability to influence others through inspirational motivation, intellectual stimulation, articulation of goals and by appealing to the individual (Bass and Avolio, 1994).

One of the fundamental principles of any interaction is communication. A simple model (Fraser, 2002) suggests some methods we can use to communicate and their impact on behaviour.

SHARING INFORMATION   SHAPING BEHAVIOUR

General publications	Personal touch	Interactive activities	Public events	Face-to-face
Flyer	Letter	Email	Road shows	One-to-one
Newsletter	Postcard	Telephone	Fairs	Mentoring
Videos	Card	Visits	Conferences	Seconding
Static website		Workshops	Presentations	Shadowing
Manuals		Seminars	Exhibitions	Job swaps
Articles		Training event	Mass meetings	
Guidelines		CD-ROM	Rallies	
Posters		Networks		
Exhibition		Tours		
Reports		Projects		
Benchmarking studies		Audit meetings		
Distance learning				
Briefing				
Bulletins				
Annual report				

Published with permission
Figure 13.1 Accelerating the spread of good practice, Fraser (2002), Kingsham Press.

New groups, networks and organisations arise from common purposes and objectives. These can be created and given meaning through dialogue as conversations provide us with the opportunity to explore differences, perceptions and attitudes. They enable a deeper understanding of issues and if conducted regularly build the foundations for new knowledge, understanding and action. Dialogue is critical for breaking the bonds of boundaries and for creating new and sustainable organisations that reflect current priorities and can adapt to future demands.

For leaders in complex systems, commitment to dialogue is not enough. The ability to tune into weak signals, those seemingly unintelligible and insignificant issues that can trigger large scale change in a system, for better or worse (Underwood, 2002 p. 36). For example, the hospital senior managers who meet informally with their social care counterparts may pick up pieces of information that, although small, may in the future have a considerable impact on their organisation. It could be something like hearing that a nursing home is in financial difficulty. This could mean delayed discharges for some patients and the impact of this on the rest of the operation of the hospital could be very significant.

Reflections for leaders

* What activities do I engage in that would help me discover weak, but potentially significant, signals?
* How much time do I spend talking about structures and roles, in contrast to spending time developing relationships and shaping behaviour? Is this appropriate?
* How often do I engage in meaningful dialogue with leaders across and within the boundaries of my organisation?
* Where do I need to shape behaviour, and why?
* What communication methods can I employ to both share information and shape behaviour?
* What can I do to help other managers and leaders create dialogue and generate new behaviours?

Principle 4: search for a balance between bureaucracy and adhocracy

Who wants to be an NHS manager when the role is perceived and often publicised as the protector and sponsor of bureaucracy? On the one hand there is the requirement to monitor and control and on the other there is a mandate to enter the realm of chaos by breaking down the boundaries and structures perceived as having sustained the delivery of health and healthcare in our communities. Pitched into the turbulence and white water of collaboration and partnership, we tend to cling to the safety of our organisational boundaries. Control is a familiar paradigm and there is comfort in its rules and rituals.

One of the challenges for leaders is supporting individuals through this period of change and allowing this transitory period of ambiguity to be one where creativity and opportunity are foremost. Our human instinct is to simplify and control the messy systems within which we exist. Organisations that institute rules and roles too quickly may live to regret their behaviour.

For example, the formation of a primary care trust (PCT) from a collection of independently run primary care practices is a difficult task. There will be many competing priorities and egos seeking power and comfort in controlling structures. Some new PCTs implemented traditional departmental structures within weeks of being formed. This provided a sense of familiarity for the managers in the new organisation and removed the feeling of 'chaos'. In comparison, some PCT chief executives held back from designing their organisational structures until new members of staff had the time to build relationships within and without their organisation. Many reported they felt this was an uncomfortable time, where they were unsure of their roles and responsibilities and unclear how to meet the demands placed on them. However, with hindsight they reported that the structures which emerged, though not hugely dissimilar to traditional ones, were founded on relationships rather than imposed authority. This also enabled them to continue evolving, they reported their organisational chart seemed to change monthly, and to avoid becoming stuck in a bureaucratic mire where transactional processes rule.

Organisations will always be characterised by a degree of control; the challenge for leaders will be to balance this requirement with the need to create an organisation or set of relationships that meets the challenges facing organisations responding to extensive change within a context of uncertainty.

Networks, relationships and groups that can sense the unexpected (however small the issue), take action quickly and work with a high degree of freedom are most likely to support and sustain healthcare during times of uncertainty and change. Individuals who have supportive connections and alliances with others, as well as a cooperative management team, will be more able to deliver improvements in healthcare. The ability to work with and accept the messiness of an evolving healthcare system can reduce the stress and tension in working across organisational boundaries.

The role of leaders is to support the context in which the above can prosper. This is closely linked with the development of relationships and the shaping of behaviour. Above all, it requires an understanding of the complex clusters of relationships and their relevant boundaries that exist within and across organisations, to appreciate their nature and to seek ways to support those responsible for fostering alliances.

Leadership reflections

- How comfortable am I when not operating in a control mode, and what can I do about it?
- What proportion of my attention and effort is spent perpetuating control, and how does this impact on collaborative activities?
- What is my personal resilience in dealing with uncertainty and ambiguity, and how does this affect my organisation?

- How can I encourage individuals to accept the messy business of change and transition and give them the space so that creativity and innovation can prosper?

Principle 5: seek personal mastery through developing the personal narrative

Leaders influence other people through the stories they tell. These are stories about the self, the group, and values and meaning (van Maurik, 2001 p. 117–118). In an environment of uncertainty leaders need to find ways to develop their own understanding of what is going on and articulate goals and vision in a way that creates meaning for others.

Story-telling is the basic form of transferring knowledge and principles. The traditional poems, rhymes and fairy tales of our forebears were designed to communicate the lessons of life in a time in which email, the printed word and television were unknown and irrelevant.

Leaders who think about and develop their narrative skills develop their self-awareness and force themselves to consider the meaning behind their actions. These stories can be metaphorical or a sharing of real dramas and daily events. For example, the leader who forgets to send a critical document to a counterpart in another organisation, may choose to tell the story of how that action impacted on patient care – from the perspective of the patient who complained about the consequences on their care. If combined with honest reflection and disclosure, this story could have a profound effect on those listening. In a simple story the leader could convey deep values about how care needs to be focused on the patient's perspective, as well as how small things can have a knock-on impact, especially when working across boundaries.

Leadership reflections

- How comfortable am I telling stories about my own feelings and opinions? How often do I do this as a means of helping others see my position on issues?
- How often do I reflect on how my actions may be impacting those with whom I work in other organisations?
- What stories would the leaders in other organisations tell about me and my organisation?
- What stories do I tell about how we can work across boundaries?
- What stories do I hear from those I work with? In what way do these concur with my stories?
- When do I get the chance to listen to stories from patients, carers and other stakeholders in my organisation?

Conclusion

In conclusion, there are no panaceas or prescriptions to ease the pain of working across the myriad of boundaries we encounter. Leaders should avoid the temptation of applying a 'structure' because it fits a personal model or appears to work elsewhere. Instead there is a need to engage with existing local networks of relationships and to find ways to lever these and generate new ones; to create a new culture and structure of working based on mutual support.

These five principles provide the starting point for a personal and organisational learning adventure. We need to break out of our mental model of seeing our organisations as static 'things'. By focusing instead on the clusters of relationships that make up the meaning of how healthcare is delivered, we may discover new and more appropriate working structures. Better still, we can achieve this through the creation of relationships, dialogue and conversation across those boundaries that initially constrained us.

References

Ashkenas, R. Ulrich, D., Jick, T. and Kerr, S. (1995) *The Boundaryless Organization*, San Francisco: Jossey-Bass

Bass, B.M. and Avolio, B.J. (1994) *Improving Organisational Performance through Transformational Leadership*, London: Sage Publications

Dunderdale, P. 'Analysing effective organisations', *Professional Manager*, September 1994, pp. 23–24

Emery, F. E. and Trist, E. L. (1965) 'The causal textures of organisational environments', *Human Relations*, February, 21–32

Fraser, S. W. (2002) *Accelerating the Spread of Good Practice*, Chichester, UK: Kingsham Press

Kelly, S. and Allison, M. (1998) *The Complexity Advantage*, NY: Business Week Books

Margolis, B. L. and Kroes, W. H. (1974) 'Work and the health of man' in J. O'Toole (Ed.), *Work and the Quality of Life*, Cambridge, MA: MIT Press

North, D. (1990) *Institutions, Institutional Change and Economic Performance*, Cambridge: Cambridge University Press

Underwood, J. (2002) *Complexity and Paradox*, Oxford, UK: Capstone Publishing

Van Maurik, J. (2001) *Writers on Leadership*, London: Penguin

Weick, Karl E. (1979) *The Social Psychology of Organizing*, Reading, MA: Addison-Wesley

Wheatley, Margaret J. (1992) *Leadership and the New Science*, San Francisco: Berret-Koehler

14 Propositions for incorporating a pedagogy of complexity, emotion and power in HRD education

Kiran Trehan and Clare Rigg

Introduction

Growing awareness of the influence of power relations in shaping pedagogical agendas has provided considerable impetus for the issue of critical HRD learning. There has been a growing demand in the academic literature of the last few years for HRD educators to engage more critically with their subject than has been the tradition in business schools. The case has been argued for strengthening the critical perspective in contributor disciplines within management (Alvesson and Willmott, 1992) and for a revision of management education generally (French and Grey, 1996). It was probably just a matter of time before well-established critiques of prescriptive approaches to HRD should filter through to the way in which HRD learning is being advanced at a theoretical level. Little attention has been accorded to the issue of complexity, emotion and power in actually operationalising a critical HRD approach with practising managers. It is our belief that much of HRD pedagogy, even that which is intended to support a more critical approach, does not provide a structure or educational processes adequate to the task of working with, and developing an understanding of, emotions and power within HRD. Traditional mainstream HRD practice ignores emotions and power or contributes to their suppression. Alternative HRD pedagogies, while less hierarchical and placing more emphasis on personal and professional experience, reinforce the value of consensus, which either tends to deny power dynamics superficially or attempts to assimilate them. Drawing on the illustrations of students on a part-time Masters course (MA Strategic Human Resourcing), where a critical learning perspective was adopted, this chapter presents an examination of the concrete experiences of advancing such an approach and how emotions and complexity intersect with power relations. The chapter will draw on adult, management education and HRD literature, both mainstream and critical, in providing a review and critique of current practice, and address the following questions.

- What importance is attached to emotions and power in the HRD education domain?
- Are course methods intended to enable an examination of emotions and power, and is the emergent social milieu of the programme influenced by the nature of the power dynamics which students and tutors bring with them?

On the basis of this critique and our own experiences of HRD education programmes, the chapter will draw attention to ways in which course designs and their underpinning values support the examination of power dynamics and emotions, deny its existence or attempt its suppression or assimilation. The intended contribution of this chapter is to identify ways in which emotions and power might be more recognised and valued as a source of learning than we believe to be the case in contemporary HRD education. Moreover, rather than complexity, and emotions and power being overlooked or obscured, the learning milieu of HRD courses should encourage understanding of emotions and power, recognising it as the basis for confrontation and change, both within the programme and, as a consequence, in the workplace.

Our intention is to explore the dynamics involved in operationalising a critical HRD programme. First we review HRD, its rationale and the influence of participative pedagogies more generally. We then describe the postgraduate programme at the University of Central England (UCE) and the way in which critical HRD is undertaken on this programme. From this we present an analysis of students' and tutors' views on the outcomes and impacts of being involved in critical HRD. The next section questions the assumption that such approaches necessarily empower the students taking part and explores the significance of emotions and power relations encountered during the process. The final section examines the implications for critical HRD practice and the role of tutors, particularly in the context of critical HRD education.

We will argue that, by illuminating emotions and the social and power relations embedded within critical HRD teaching, it is possible to present a more contextual and processual account than the idealistic prescriptions that have dominated the study of this practice.

A critical turn in HRD

In the field of management learning critiques of the values, the purpose and approaches to management education and development have become well developed in recent years. At the same time HRD has been another emerging area of academic debate and practitioner focus. Yet whilst there are many potential areas of overlap between HRD and management learning, they have been evolving as parallel discourses, with little attention accorded to exploiting their interconnections.

By HRD we refer to the concern 'with supporting and facilitating the learning of individuals, groups and organizations ...' (McGoldrick, Stewart and Watson, 2002: 396). HRD has tended to be dominated by humanistic approaches and unitary organisation perspectives. For the most part, the critical curriculum in HRD has been disseminated through traditional methods, but increasingly there is interest in the contribution which critical methods could make to a critical pedagogy on HRD (Hughes, 2000). Giroux (1981) has emphasised the value of earlier androgogists because they have 'called into question the political and normative underpinnings of traditional classroom pedagogical styles' (1981: 65). More recently there are a growing number of propositions for pedagogies which apply a critical perspective to method as well as to content. So, for example, the learning community (Reynolds, 1999) is participative in that it offers an opportunity for choice in the direction and content of learning through shared decision-making within the course. Students involved in this approach, as they would be in Willmott's (1997) proposal for 'critical action learning', have an opportunity to base their learning on their professional experience and to select the ideas with which to make sense of it. The 'learning community' and 'critical action learning' therefore, illustrate possibilities for both a methodology and a curriculum which reflect a critical perspective in HRD. Not only is conceptual content and its application based on critical perspectives but methods, procedures and relationships are developed in ways which are consistent with them.

Recent influences from radical education (Giroux, 1992), feminist pedagogy (Weiler, 1991) and from critical theory (French and Grey, 1996) have given fresh impetus to the development of more participative, less hierarchical approaches to teaching and learning – the expression of a critical perspective in both content and methodology. Arguably, in such a context the study of HRD could be enriched through the incorporation of critical perspective. Yet, as we observed at the outset, while there are some examples of a critical pedagogy affecting content and method, corresponding changes in the practice of HRD are harder to find in management education.

Over the last decade there has been an increasing concern for the introduction of a more critical interpretation of practice in adult and higher education (see, for example, Welton 1995 or Barnett, 1997). The same concern is evident in our own field of HRD education, as a response to the considerable influence which managers as a professional group exercise over the lives of employees, the wider community and the environment (Alvesson and Willmott, 1992). In recognition of this, HRD teachers have been urged to 'analyse HRD in terms of its social, moral and political significance and to challenge HRD practice rather than seek to sustain it' (Hughes, 2000). The challenges vary, from critical theory, liberationist (Freirian), feminist and post-structuralist scholarship, to Marxism and labour process analysis. While differences between these schools of thought are too significant to be overlooked, together they comprise a critical perspective which provides a basis for rethinking HRD education.

Whichever critical perspective is applied, its characteristics are likely to include:

- questioning assumptions and taken-for-granteds, asking questions which are not meant to be asked;
- foregrounding processes of power and noting how inequalities of power intersect with social factors such as race, gender or age;
- identifying competing discourses and the sectional interests reflected in them; and ultimately
- developing a workplace and social milieu characterised more by justice than by inequality or exploitation.

The principles of a critical pedagogy in HRD are applied in different ways. Taking HRD education as a case in point, critical perspectives are reflected in the content of the curriculum (Nord and Jermier, 1992), the kinds of material used (incorporating cinema and fictional literature, (for example Thompson and McGivern, 1996), and in drawing on students' work experiences as well as their experience of the course itself (Grey *et al.*, 1996). A critical stance is also reflected in the choice of analytical frameworks introduced to students, whether decon-structionist (Townley, 1994) or applying feminist inquiry and cultural critique (Hughes, 2000).

Approaches such as the learning community (Reynolds, 1999), or more critical interpretations of action learning (Willmott, 1997), apply a critical perspective in both content and method, reflecting longer-standing influences of educators who have 'called into question the political and normative underpinnings of tradi-tional classroom pedagogical styles' (Giroux, 1981: 65) In such approaches, students are able to reflect on their professional experience, to select the ideas with which to make sense of it, and to influence the direction and content of their learning by sharing in decision-making within the structure of the course, which would provide a valuable source of learning for HRD students.

Why be critical?

A key rationale for encouraging human resource developers to be critical lies in the realisation of how powerful managers now are in the world, yet how poorly traditional HRD education has prepared them for considering questions of power and responsibility. Alvesson and Willmott (1992) argue that the practice of man-agement has a dominant effect on the lives of an organisation's employees, its customers and wider society, extending even to the lives of unborn generations through the environmental impact of an organisation's processes. Because of the rise of managers' social importance, French and Grey (1996: 2) reason that '... the management academy has, for better or worse, a crucial role in producing and reproducing the practices of management'.

The traditional view of HRD education has been a technocratic 'development of effective practitioners', as epitomised by the Constable and McCormick (1987) and Handy (1988) reports. Implicit within this tradition has been the presumption of HRD knowledge and practice to be objective, apolitical and value-free. Many writers have challenged this, and argued the need to deconstruct the discourse of practice. Edwards (1997: 155), for example, writing on adult education, argued '... "practice" is already informed by overt or covert discursive understandings and exercises of power'; Watson (1994: 2), writing on management '... managers themselves, however much they tend to scorn the very idea of theory, are inevitably theorists of a sort'. And Schein, writing on shared assumptions about nature, reality and truth:

> A fundamental part of every culture is a set of assumptions about what is real, how one determines or discovers what is real ... how members of a

group determine what is relevant information, how they interpret information, how they determine when they have enough of it to decide whether or not to act, and what action to take.

(Schein, 1987: 97)

In this sense the rationale has been that it is no longer acceptable that HRD educators allow managers to maintain the illusion that their choices and actions are without political consequences.

Hopes and hazards in critical HRD learning

Clearly, given the rationales advanced for critical thinking, the hopes of its proponents have been concerned with transforming society and making it more democratic or emancipatory. Key to this has been the view that through education individuals become conscious of the oppression of, or constraints on, their lives and take action to bring about change for the better. Advocates of critical pedagogy, such as Freire, argue that criticism is the pedagogic route to consientisation, where consientisation is the 'Process in which men (sic, not as recipients, but as knowing subjects), achieve a deepening awareness both of the socio-cultural reality which shapes their lives and of their capacity to transform that reality'. (Freire, 1970, cited in Cavanaugh and Prasad, 1996: 89.) For Fay, critical education provides:

> The means by which people can achieve a much clearer picture of who they are, and of what the real meaning of their social practices is, as a first step of becoming different sorts of people with different sorts of social arrangements.
>
> (Fay, 1987: 89)

Hugh Willmott sets a challenge for critical management learning: 'To envision and advance the development of discourses and practices that can facilitate the development of "management" from a divisive technology of control into a collective means of emancipation' (1997: 175).

Porter *et al.*, in distinguishing between critical thinking and critical management thinking, maintain the latter is to develop 'habits of critical thinking ... that prepare them for responsible citizenship and personally and socially rewarding lives and careers' (Porter et al., 1989: 71).

Other voices challenge this optimism both from theoretical perspectives and as a consequence of empirical experience of critical learning programmes, particularly in adult education. Reynolds (1997) articulates one of the most comprehensive critical reviews, expounding three possible pitfalls or hazards. The first is the potential for management students to resist engagement in critical reflection, because to do so would be to question their profession and challenge their status quo. Reed and Anthony (1992) suggest managers would find the approach 'irrelevant, unreal and impractical' (1992: 607). Jackall (1988) implies managers would find it counter-cultural to the pressures to conform to organisational ideologies. Reynolds (1997) also suggests that, relevant or not, management students might simply find the language of much critical theory impenetrable. The second hazard outlined by Reynolds (1997) is the potential for managers to merely assimilate critical ideas into their existing perspective, without really unpicking the underlying assumptions and ideologies. The third danger relates to the potential adverse psychological and social consequences for individuals of engaging in critical reflection, as Reynolds cautions 'It can prove unsettling, mentally or emotionally and a source of disruption at home or at work. It carries the risk to employment and even – if we include stress related illness – to life itself' (1997: 16).

Brookfield (1994) describes the dissonance produced by critical reflection, as the 'darker side' of such an approach and Reynolds (1997) warns of the production of cultural misfits, facing 're-entry' problems on their return to work, feeling frustrated or powerless with their new awareness. Perhaps most pessimistic are Alvesson and Willmott (1992) in their concern that 'Enhanced ecological consciousness and greater freedom and creativity at work – likely priorities emerging from emancipatory change – may result in bankruptcy and unemployment' (1992: 448).

In the rest of this chapter we examine the aims of critical HRD teaching, in the light of the experiences of students on a postgraduate HRD programme we have run over the past seven years, in order to illustrate the interaction between critical HRD and the complex political and social dynamics of learning groups.

Setting the scene: critical HRD in practice

When applying a critical approach to HRD education, Grey *et al.* argue that a critical pedagogy 'not only offers a challenging view of management as a social, political and economic practice, but does so in a way that stimulates student involvement of a kind that is rare in other forms of management education' (Grey *et al.*, 1996: 109).

Reynolds (1997), drawing from ideas of Giroux (1981), introduces the concept of content radical and method or process radical pedagogies. The latter attempts to address the power asymmetries of the traditional teacher/learner relationship, whilst the content radicals disseminate radical material, but without challenging the contradictions in their power relationships with students. Reynolds outlines characteristics of a perspective which is both content and process radical, that it questions assumptions, analyses power relations and has a collective focus, in the 'sense of acting in concert with others' (Reynolds, 1997: 316).

Students on the UCE Management Development programme encounter critical management learning predominantly in process. The programme takes an experiential learning approach throughout, where, besides a small number of lecture inputs, students spend most of their time working collectively in a specific action learning set (ALS). The ALS fulfils a number of functions; it undertakes group tasks, which are predominantly real organisational problems, and participants are encouraged, through facilitation, to reflect on how they work together and to work through process issues in some depth. Participants are also encouraged to exchange their experiences within the ALS, and of doing their individual course assignments, as well as being involved in the assessment of their own and each other's work. In this sense students' dialogue and social support can be fundamental to the course. The ALS is also often a source of gender, ethnic, age and occupational diversity, where issues mirror some of the patterns in organisations and society. Students are encouraged to reflect on and learn from their feeling and experiences of these power dynamics.

The most content-radical elements occur in the Masters year, through a critical reflection paper and an action research dissertation. In the former, students are asked to reflect critically on their development as a manager, and are introduced to some critical ideas, such as feminism, Foucault's ideas on power, Habermas, Giroux, and critical education. This form of critical self-development is seen as embodying Kemmis's principles of critical reflection, as a form of critical education (Kemmis, 1985). As such it differs from the more instrumental reflection promoted by experiential learning advocates, such as Kolb (1984) or Schon (1983), which does not encourage such a fundamental critique. An action research methodology is deployed for the dissertation and students are encouraged to explore the epistemological basis of action research. Action research has a long history of use for radical community action, and this leads many students to engage with some of the critical theory that it implies. As Carr and Kemmis say, 'in short, action research is a deliberate process for emancipating practitioners from the often unseen constraints of assumption, habit, precedent, coercion and ideology' (1986: 192).

Throughout the programme many features aim to reinforce proactivity. The question of who owns the learning, diagnosis of issues or problems and the solutions to these, is central to the staff roles. Tutors take two basic, mutually supportive roles, those of task consultant, offering information, models, or reading relating to the task, and process consultant, making the participant/group aware of group processes. Tutors take care in their responses to participants' questions not to position participants as dependent and passive. The courses are structured around individual and group tasks, the briefs of which are framed in terms of learning outcomes. However, they have to be interpreted, which provides considerable leeway for participants to determine the curriculum, but this is also a situation of uncertainty, through which they have to direct their own paths, individually and collectively. One participant described this as the 'total refusal, well not so much refusal, more slippery than that, and avoidance of allowing the students to inscribe the tutors as knowledge bearers or themselves as empty vessels to be filled with knowledge' (UCE, 2001). Another said 'the loose style of the Programme acts more rigidly upon the student ... because I had to pace out and set my own boundaries upon my learning ...' (UCE, 2001).

If we are to accept that critical HRD is an important element in the learning process, then questions of power and authority deserve particular attention. What do we really know about participants' experience in which a critical

HRD approach is adopted? Does the student's experience of critical HRD learning reflect in any way their experiences at work? In the next section, and as a way of furthering understanding and development of a more critical approach, we will review such questions in the light of students' experiences of critical HRD practices throughout the programme. The research was phenomenographic, data being collected from discussions within student action learning sets and from reflective papers as well as from our experiences as tutors in the programme described earlier. Marton (1994) explains phenomenography as a research approach for understanding people's way of experiencing the world. He defined it as 'The empirical study of the differing ways in which people experience, perceive, apprehend, understand, or conceptualise various phenomena in, and aspects of, the world around them' (Marton 1994: 424). Phenomenography thus aims to describe qualitatively different ways of experiencing phenomena and was particularly suited to this inquiry, as we intended to examine students' individual experiences of participating in collaborative assessment and to compare this material with the rationale and ideals which had originally informed the course design. The next section is also intended to provide a context to the discussion of the tensions involved in working with critical HRD pedagogy.

Power, authority and the student experience

It might be assumed that questions of power and authority are chiefly confined to traditional HRD methods, and that they are not so problematic in more collaborative approaches; however, the nature of the dynamics of collaborative methods generally would suggest otherwise (Reynolds and Trehan, 2000). Ellsworth (1992) points out, contrary to the rhetoric of critical pedagogy, that concepts of power, empowerment and student voice have become myths that perpetuate relations of domination. If, for example, interpretations of participative HRD education result in an increased emphasis on self-awareness, consciousness-raising or reflexivity in the assessment process, but power, authority and judgement-making are not examined, students have even less control than in more traditional methods. At least within traditional methods the notion of the assessor as an all-knowing, all-powerful entity who has the intellectual authority to make assessment decisions is transparent, with the tutor-student role clearly defined. In critical HRD the individual boundaries are not so clearly defined and this can lead to feelings of disempowerment.

Vince (1996) has suggested that individuals can respond to their anxiety either by entering a cycle that promotes learning, achieving insight through struggle and by being prepared to take risks, or – if the uncertainties are too great – a cycle that discourages learning by way of resistance, denial or defensiveness, ultimately maintaining 'willing ignorance' (1996: 122–133). Not only, therefore, should power and authority be central foci of analysis in the context of a critical pedagogy (Gore, 1993), but such an analysis might be expected to result in visible changes in assessment procedures.

Certainly in practice a participative approach is unlikely to be straightforward (Reynolds and Trehan, 2000). The tutor's intention may be that students will share in the learning and assessment process, even to the extent of collectively managing the entire process. Initially, however, such freedom may cause anxiety and frustration, as the following extracts illustrate:

> I was very uncomfortable with the whole situation and felt almost rejected and unwanted ... my return home that night was even more stressful and emotionally charged.

> I began questioning myself on a number of issues ... I felt as if I had been taken out of myself ... I felt emotionally and psychologically drained.

The above accounts show the dissonance experienced by some participants, in the sense that they felt unsettled and experienced uncertainty and anxiety. However, an experiential course which deploys a critical perspective should, by its very nature, touch participants' emotions.

As Vince (1996) argues, any consideration of learning needs to take account of the emotions experienced by learners in the learning context. A critical course is likely, as a result of the level of social engagement it entails, to touch participants' emotions. Changes to learner-teacher power relations may have similar consequences, as Vince writes; 'Approaches to learning that break free of dependency on the teacher, and place emphasis on the responsibilities of the learner, always create anxiety' (1996: 121).

From our experience, active engagement in critical HRD can be painful and, contrary to its intention, can be disempowering. We should not expect it to be comfortable. Indeed, as has been observed more generally, learning cannot take place without anxiety or critical learning without personal struggle (Hooks, 1993), as the following extract highlights:

> I found myself regularly struggling with the consequences of risk within my group, which tended to involve struggling through other people's reactions, or my emotion at having aired something long suppressed. The result of this cycle of uncertainty, risk and struggle was sometimes a feeling of empowerment involving either a new personal insight or increased authority within the group. There were occasions when the risk seemed too great and my intuition towards defensiveness and resistance won through.

> Anxiety about assessment tended to lead to feelings that set in motion reactions of either fight or flight; there was more than one occasion when I had been tempted not to turn up for group meetings as a result of anxieties about how other group members might react to something I had said or done. As a group during assessment we were also inclined to create a scapegoat in order to avoid and defend decisions.

I can recall incidents when my own uncertainty, that feeling of being on the edge of change, created the conditions for risk and it was in these situations that I think I learned most.

Risks are many and varied in learning groups, the expression of powerful feelings like anger, the risk of speaking or not speaking, the risk of leading, fear and anxiety all have important implications for HRD.

Vince (1996) states that it is the anxiety created from fear that gives rise to the uncertainty which can lead to learning and change, as is illustrated by the above extract. He also observes that learning environments are a powerful and contained arena for viewing negotiations on autonomy and dependence. Within critical HRD therefore, it is important to acknowledge the inequalities of power which can be generated and which in any case can develop between students. Learning groups are permeated with relations of power, which contribute to the construction of individual and group identity.

Similarly, within critical pedagogy, whilst there is an acknowledgement of the socially constructed and legitimated authority that teachers hold over students, there has been a failure to analyse in any depth the institutionalised power imbalances between themselves and their students, giving the illusion of equality while leaving the authoritarian nature of the teacher/student relationship intact. As Ellsworth argues 'empowerment is a key concept … which treats the symptoms but leaves the disease unnamed and untouched' (1992: 98).

The next section explores the complexity of tutor-student relationships in applying a critical HRD perspective.

Understand the complexity of tutor and student roles

When applying a critical perspective to HRD teaching, a critique of the student-tutor relationship needs to be addressed. It seems crucial that tutors are constantly reflexive, so as to question their motives, their style of facilitation, and their awareness of the potential impacts of a critical learning approach to their teaching. In particular, it must be important that tutors are aware of the power they have over resources, structuring the agenda, or controlling assessment. So, for example, within the philosophy of the programme it is hoped that learning will be initiated by the student exchanging ideas freely with the tutor. This exchange echoes the process described by Freire (1972) as 'problem posing, where the traditional assumption of teacher supremacy and student compliance is dismantled'.

Our research suggests, however, that although tutors may support this model of learning from the outset, it can take some time before the student fully adapts to it. One could argue, therefore, that within this problem-posing approach there is a point in time where the student feels there is still a power imbalance, because while the tutor understands the philosophy, the student, initially at least, is to a great extent 'in the dark'. There is an underlying belief that some form of unspoken but expected authority is still present.

In practice, therefore, clarifying the role of the tutor in critical approaches is unlikely to be straightforward, because of the ambiguities that result from the redefinition of the tutor's role. Bilimoria (1995) notes the shift which takes place from a tutor's role based on the 'exercise of control, expertise, and evaluation' to a concept of authority as shared among participants, expressed through collective generation of knowledge and in the 'ownership' of its evaluation (1995: 448). But this is not necessarily how students experience it, as the following extracts illustrate: 'I feel that the tutors create a power base by being vague about the equality between tutors and students, keeping them guessing about whether specifics of an approach are valid or not.' Without recognition of such ambiguities and support in making sense of them, a critical approach to HRD may be experienced as a more subtle technique for disciplining, as this student's reflection on their experience indicates:

> The contribution and involvement of the facilitator felt to me … to use an analogy, like having an arrogant hierarchical senior manager constantly present and expecting great things from you and then disappearing for a round of golf … still expecting everyone to believe his claim [to be] 'part of the team'.

For critical HRD to realise in practice what it promises in principle, it is important to be alert to the tendencies for hierarchical relations to persist in the shape of disciplines which students come to impose on themselves and on each other. This, it could be argued, is a form of govermentality (Foucault, 1979) exercised through the action of 'being one's own policeman', of managing one's own practices. As the following reflection implies: 'At the beginning we were careful not to be too critical of other groups because we feared retaliation … Nothing was stated but it appeared to be an almost unwritten rule.' From this point of view it could be said that critical HRD represents a process of normalisation whereby practices are sanctioned, not by an external authority or an appeal to collective sentiments, but by mundane acts of self authorisation which sustain in the practitioner a compliant identity, a self-policing individual (Usher and Edwards, 1996, p. 56). Applying Foucault's development of the idea of the panopticon as embodying the principle of surveillance, participative assessment could be seen as a shift from darkened cells of the traditional prison to the well-lit panopticon cell, a device which, though seemingly more humane, has the more subtle effect of creating self disciplining subjects.

Orner (1992) argues that discourses of 'liberatory' pedagogy which claim to empower students do not overtly support relations in which students are monitored by others as they discipline themselves. However, we would argue that Foucault's description of the panopticon does raise issues for whether critical HRD can be said to 'empower' students. Within a Foucauldian framework one would need to question the hidden curricula of self-managed groups. As Orner highlights, the 'talking circle', which is a long-cherished form of the democratic classroom, represents an expression of disciplinary power, the regulation of the self through the internalisation of the regulation by others. Similarly, Ball (1990) argues that confessional techniques used in pedagogical practices which encourage students to view the procedures of appraisal as part of the process of self-understanding, self-betterment and professional development is simply a more complex mechanism of monitoring and control.

Conclusion: is critical HRD too risky in practice?

Do these complexities and contradictions mean that critical HRD, however appealing in theory, and however consistent with the principles of a critical pedagogy, is too fraught with difficulties and problematic consequences to contemplate in practice? We embarked on this research project, because of the unanticipated power of our critical HRD programme. The proposal that students should play a significant part in the design, content and assessment of their own and others' learning is clearly a departure from the traditional interpretation of HRD teaching.

However, key to our observations from our own experience of working with critical HRD is that the inevitable presence of power and emotion is an unparalled source of learning about managing and about self-development.

These complexities cannot be reduced to a simplified set of guidelines but it does seem as if there is an argument for tutors being willing and capable of recognising them and openly working with them. From a critical HRD perspective this would entail a reflexive understanding of the processes involved – including the tutor's own part in them, and the skill to support students in working through the implications for the judgements which are being made.

When implementing critical HRD our experience reminds us of the power that tutors can have to influence students' learning, which clearly indicates responsibilities we have for questioning our own intents, motives and practices to be reflexive. Tutors have to be prepared for emotionality and conflict, and be aware of their own needs and biases, and above all to develop an informed understanding of the power situated in their roles and the procedures traditionally associated with them. They need to be constantly developing themselves, in a sense mirroring the task they ask the students to engage in.

References

Alvesson, M. and Willmott, H. (Eds) (1992) *Critical Management Studies*, London: Sage

Ball, S. (1990) *Foucault and Education*, New York: Routledge

Barnett, R. (1997) *Higher Education: A critical business*, Buckingham: The Society for Research into Higher Education and Open University Press

Bilimoria, D. (1995) 'Modernism, postmodernism and contemporary grading practices'; *Journal of Management Education* 19: 440–457

Brookfield, S. (1994) 'Tales from the dark side: a phenomenology of adult critical reflection', *International Journal of Lifelong Education*, 13(3): 205

Carr, W. and Kemmis, S. (1986) *Becoming Critical: Knowing through action research*, Victoria: Deakin University

Cavanagh, J. M. and Prasad, A. (1996) 'Critical theory and management education: Some strategies for the critical classroom', in French, R. and Grey, C. (Eds) *Rethinking Management Education*, London: Sage

Constable, J. and McCormick, R. (1987) *The Making of British Managers*, London: British Institute of Management/Confederation of British Industry

Edwards, R. (1997) *Contested Terrain: The transformation of the workplace in the twentieth century*, London: Heinemann

Ellsworth, E. (1992) 'Why doesn't this feel empowering? Working through the repressive myths of critical pedagogy', in C. Luke and J. Gore (Eds) *Feminisms and Critical Pedagogy*, New York: Routledge

Fay, B. (1987) *Critical Social Science*, Cambridge: Polity Press

Foucault, M. (1979) *Discipline and Punish: The birth of the prison*, Harmondsworth: Penguin

Freire, P. (1970) cited in Cavanaugh and Prasad (1996, p. 89)

French, R. and Grey, C. (1996) (Eds) *Rethinking Management Education*, London: Sage

Giroux, H. A. (1981) *Ideology, Culture, and the Process of Schooling*, Philadelphia, PA: Temple University Press

Gore, J. M. (1993) *The Struggle for Pedagogies*, New York: Routledge

Grey, C., Knights, D. and Willmott, H.C. (1996) 'Is a critical pedagogy of management possible?', in R. French and C. Grey (Eds), *Rethinking Management Education*, London: Sage

Habermas, J. (1972) *Knowledge and Human Interests*, London: Heinemann

Handy, C. (1988) *Making Managers*, London: Pitman

Hooks, B. (1993) 'Bell Hooks speaking about Paulo Freire – the man, his works', in P. McLaren and P. Leonard (Eds) *Paulo Freire: A critical encounter*, New York: Routledge

Hughes, C. (2000) 'Learning to be intellectually insecure: The disempowering effects of reflexive practice', *International Journal of Social Research Methodology*, 1(4): 281–296

Jackall, R. (1988) *The Moral Mazes: The world of corporate managers*, Oxford: Oxford University Press

Kemmis, Stephen (1985) 'Action research and the politics of reflection' in D. Boud, R. Keogh and D. Walker (Eds), *Reflection: Turning experience into learning*, London: Kogan Page

Kolb, David A. (1984) *Experiential Learning*, Englewood Cliffe, NJ: Prentice Hall

Marton, F. (1994) 'Phenomenography' in T. Husen and T. N. Postlethwaite, *The International Encyclopaedia of Education*, (2nd edition) Oxford: Pergamon

McGoldrick, J. Stewart, J. and Watson, S. (2002) *Understanding Human Resource Development*, London: Routledge

Nord, W. R. and Jermier, J. M. (1992) 'Critical social science for managers? Promising and perverse possibilities' in M. Alvesson and H. Willmott (Eds), *Critical Management Studies*, New York: Sage

Orner, M. (1992) 'Interrupting the call for student voice in liberatory education: a feminist post structuralist perspective', in C. Luke and J. Gore (Eds), *Feminism and Critical Pedagogy*, London: Routledge

Porter, L. W., Muller, H. J. and Rehder, R. R. (1989) 'The making of managers: An American perspective', *Journal of General Management*, 14(4): 62–76

Reed, M. and Anthony, P. (1992) 'Professionalizing management and managing professionalization: British managers in the 1980s', *Journal of Management Studies*, 29 (Sept): 591–663

Reynolds, M. (1997) 'Towards a critical management pedagogy', in J. Burgoyne and M. Reynolds (Eds), *Management Learning: Integrating perspectives in theory and practice*, London: Sage

Reynolds, M. (1999) 'Critical reflection and management education: rehabilitating less hierarchical approaches, *Journal of Management Education*, 23: 537–553

Reynolds, M. and Trehan, K. (2000) 'Assessment: a critical perspective', *Studies in Higher Education*, 25(3): 257–278

Schein, E. (1987) *Process Consultation – Vol. 2: Lessons for managers and consultants*, Wokingham: Addison Wesley

Schon, D. (1983) *The Reflective Practitioner: How professionals think in action* New York: Basic Books

Thompson, J. and McGivern, J. (1996) 'Parody, process and practice: Perspectives for management education?', *Management Learning*, 27(1): 21–35

Townley, B. (1994) *Reframing Human Resource Management* London: Sage

UCE 2001, *Postgraduate Management Development Programme Evaluation Survey 1995–2000*, Birmingham: UCE

Usher, R and Edwards, R. (1996) *Postmodernism and Education*, London: Routledge

Vince, R. (1996) 'Experiential management education as the practice of change' in R. French and C. Grey (Eds), *Rethinking Management Education*, London: Sage

Watson, T. (1994) 'Managing, crafting and researching: Words, skill and imagination in shaping management research', *British Journal of Management*, Vol. 5 Special Issue June S77–S87

Weiler, K. (1991) 'Freire and a feminist pedagogy of difference', *Harvard Educational Review*, 61, 449–74

Welton, M. (Ed.) (1995) *In Defense of the Lifeworld*, Albany NY: State University of New York Press

Willmott, H. (1997) 'Critical management learning', in J. Burgoyne and M.Reynolds (Eds), *Management Learning: Integrating perspectives in theory and practice*, London: Sage

15 The line manager as a facilitator of team learning and change

Christina Mary MacNeil

Introduction

The supervisor is defined as the line manager responsible for a section or a team of workers who do not themselves have subordinates. Supervisors represent a link between senior management and the workforce (Evans, 1996). The terms 'supervisor' and 'line manager' are used interchangeably.

Organisations emphasise formalised, planned approaches in their learning and development strategies, suggesting that informal learning, unplanned and often accidental, is an under-utilised learning approach. Thus informal learning in the workplace through facilitating continuous learning in teams could be a powerful means of achieving integration between business strategy and HRD processes (Pedlar and Burgoyne, 1994; Senge, 1990; Walton, 1999).

This chapter proposes that supervisors who are effective facilitators utilise their learning and interpersonal skills to encourage knowledge-sharing in teams. The supervisor as a facilitator of informal learning contributes to a knowledge-sharing environment, where team members create and apply tacit knowledge. In times of continuous change, this collective, knowledge sharing is essential to match competitive challenges.

The first section of this chapter summarises the changing environment, and its impact on the supervisor's role. The second section outlines formal and informal workplace learning processes. A third section explores how the positive learning environment or climate influences knowledge sharing in teams. The fourth section examines how the supervisor as a facilitator could encourage knowledge sharing in their team. The fifth section summarises facilitative skills that enhance informal learning in teams. The final section of the chapter aims to increase understanding of the need for supervisors to be developed as effective facilitators.

The changing, complex environment concerning the supervisor's role

The external business environment generates continuous, and unpredictable change, through globalisation of business and rapid technological development, thus creating highly competitive markets, shorter product-life cycles, and unrelenting demands for service improvement for customers. This hostile environment is exacerbated by pressures for cost reduction in the provision of goods and services to customers (Arkensas *et al.*, 1995; Bartlett and Ghosal, 1989; Leat and Wolley, 1999; Legge, 1995).

The internal environment of organisations must change to respond to the aforementioned competitive forces. Senior management maximise opportunities for cost cutting, communication and innovation through downsizing 'the planned elimination of positions or jobs' (Applebaum, *et al.*, 1999: 14), creating flatter management structures. These complex, business and organisational contexts transfer pressures onto the supervisor to match these changing and challenging demands within their role.

Supervisors operate in an increasingly uncertain and demanding workplace, whilst simultaneously achieving higher levels of performance from diverse teams. The implementation of effective change processes becomes reliant on the capability of the supervisor to support change through learning and development. The supervisor must possess sophisticated adaptation, interpersonal and learning skills to support their team members in continuous learning. A facilitator creates a learning environment and is responsible for providing the resources that enable people to learn. Thus facilitators encourage individuals to 'break through' obstacles to learning, and discover their own potential (Rodgers, 1977).

If change does not occur in organisations in a linear, logical form (Lewin, 1951), but rather as an emergent process incorporating continuous learning and adaptation to circumstances (Mintzberg, 1987), then rational change represents the idealised view or set of intentions of senior management concerning change in organisations. Many senior managers view their contribution to a sophisticated, change management process as explaining the rationale for change to the line management and/or the workforce. The assumption is that intervention from senior management ensures that all employees will accept rather than resist change.

Organisations driving change, focusing only on altering structures, systems and procedures; not allowing people to proceed through different phases of change – 'holding-on, letting-go, moving-on' (Stuart, 1995 p. 469); forcing change without accommodating the need for line management and worker adaptation and learning, will result in outcomes similar to a 'man-made catastrophe' (Stuart, 1995: 467). If the speed employees move through a change process does not match the pace the organisation intends change to occur, then employees will suffer from traumas associated with being 'survivors' of disasters.

Thus rational change conveniently ignores dealing with human feelings concerning change acceptance, which contribute to the totality of a successful change implementation process. Rational change ignores the emotional and political realities, which characterise an individual's employment relationship with their organisation. Thus successful implementation of change involves line management and workforce dealing with their 'intangible' emotions of fear, anger, betrayal and sadness.

If line managers and workers must adjust to continual shifting of cultural values, structures, systems and staffing requirements, then line managers and workers must learn, un-learn and re-learn different knowledge, routines and behaviours. The avoidance of interpersonal and emotional problems inherent in change prevents this learning, because the managers and workers underlying resistance have not been acknowledged (Broussine, *et al.*, 1998).

Attempts to promote learning overlooking the interplay between individual, emotional and organisational political dynamics create 'willing ignorance' (Vince, 2002 p. 79). Individuals experience anxiety due to denial of their emotions, and become involved in a negative learning cycle, whereas risk taking through dealing with the emotions experienced during change, e.g. anxiety, enables individuals to share their new knowledge and insight. Thus for line managers (and the workforce) to achieve an effective change 'journey' through a positive learning cycle, learning must be supported by the organisation.

The supervisor as a change agent

If change in organisations is a continuous process, not a temporary phase to work through before returning to stability and normality, then implementation of change will increasingly be allocated not to a separate, traditional change agent, e.g. a consultant, but the responsibility for change agency will be included in the line managers' expanding remit.

If change processes are acknowledged to be complex and challenging, then the role of the change agent is assumed to be equally complicated and demanding for line managers. Skills and competencies associated with effective change agency are poorly understood and supported by many organisations. It could be assumed that supervisors will lack the relevant expertise to be successful change agents, e.g. emotional resilience, diagnostic, interpersonal and political skills (Stuart, 1995).

It could be assumed further, that the option of learning the change agent role on-the-job could have detrimental consequences for the supervisor and the organisation. For the organisation, there is the importance of getting change right to meet strategic needs, and the costs associated with getting it wrong e.g. loss of business, broken psychological contract, loss of organisational memory and competence (McHugh *et al.*, 1999). For the supervisor, lack of expertise could have detrimental consequences for their self-esteem: individuals may be unable to reconcile the emotional and ethical dilemmas experienced when implementing change, dealing with peers and colleagues e.g. 'not being one of us anymore' (Doyle, 2002: 466).

The supervisor transition from 'novice' to 'expert' change agent requires different, developmental pathways (Doyle, 2002: 466). Thus skills for change agent expertise are derived not from formal management development approaches, e.g. training programmes, but from experiential, informal learning approaches, e.g. coaching, mentoring and project leadership (Buchanan and Boddy, 1992). Thus learning and change are inevitably, inextricably linked (Kofman and Senge, 1993).

Formal and informal workplace learning

Differences between formal and informal learning processes in organisations are not necessarily clear. It is important to summarise differences that distinguish formal and informal learning from the perspective of both the organisation and the individual. Most obvious ones are in the areas of control, physical location and prediction of learning outcomes. The degree of control that workplace learners have over the learning process is determined by the extent of autonomy they have in expressing their choice of learning approach. The physical location – in the workplace or away from the workplace – determines where workplace learners are actively engaged in the learning process. The third difference concerns the extent to which the learning process is designed to achieve predetermined outcomes, and the extent to which learning outcomes can be reliably predicted by the organisation.

If informal learning cannot be specifically designed, then learning outcomes cannot be predicted with accuracy, because the range of variables influencing the learning process prevents outcomes being fully determined in advance. However, some take the opposite view, namely that informal learning can be planned – for instance see Marsick and Watkins (1990). In formal learning situations, the goal of personal development is paramount, and some individual change may occur at a later stage, whereas in the informal, work-based learning situations, the work task is of paramount importance for the team member, and the process of learning in a team is secondary.

Yet, to be effective in an informal learning situation, workplace learners need to gain highly developed skills in critical reflectivity, including the ability to question their own tacit assumptions and beliefs. The development of these important skills for maximising informal learning from team members requires support from both the supervisor and the organisation.

A work team is defined as a number of people with relevant skills, who work together to achieve their task objectives. A work team has a range of roles, and rules for the members' interaction, with an agreed system of decision-making (Heron, 1999). Team learning is a process where the team creates knowledge for both its own members, and for others within the organisation.

The learning generated by work teams is particularly valuable in organisations where it is difficult to create standardised processes to deal with unique problems or non-routine tasks. Wherever standardised processes cannot be identified in advance, enabling the workforce to deal with the frequency or type of problems, the benefit of structuring the workforce into teams is to bring delegation of decision-making that allows problem solving at the local level, thus utilising shared team knowledge (Cohen *et al.*, 1996; Molleman, 2000).

A fragmented individual learning process is characterised by learning separately without any inclination to share knowledge. An effective knowledge-sharing process will enable the team to make the transfer from individualised, fragmented knowledge into team-based communication and knowledge sharing. The team's learning becomes a habitual process, which can develop into a shared knowledge base to assist organisational learning (Kasl *et al.*, 1996).

The positive learning climate supporting shared learning in the team

A positive learning climate, is 'a constructive organisational environment encouraging individuals to have positive attitudes towards learning and recognise the need to develop learning, to overcome their own resistance to change, understand their own short comings as learners and to be more open to experiences and ready to learn from them' (Antonacopoulou, 1999: 220).

To encourage a climate of continuous learning in work teams, there must be regular interplay between individual and organisational learning (Kim, 1993; Kolb, 1984; Pedlar *et al.*, 1991). To maximise the transference between individual and organisational learning, there needs to be some mechanism for communicating mental models throughout the organisation. The creation of a positive learning climate encourages critical enquiry amongst participants, and willingness to subject individual thinking processes to public enquiry. This will not occur in atmospheres of defensiveness and control (Argyris and Schön, 1978). A positive learning climate incorporates double-loop learning, where employees question reasons for existing problems, and find solutions preventing those problems in future (Argyris, 1985; 1986).

The manner in which the organisation rewards or punishes the behaviour of individuals, has a powerful influence on reinforcing or impeding individual learning and transfer into shared learning (Ellinger and Bostrom, 1999). Political forces expressed in the norms and values of the learning climate influence an individual's receptivity or resistance to learning. An important difference between adaptive and generative learning environments is found in organisation's learning norms and values, which influence the supervisor's response to staff making mistakes. In generative learning environments, mistakes are opportunities for learning and change, not occasions for allocating blame (McGill *et al.*, 1992). In a generative learning environment, supervisors encourage admission of mistakes, so that team members share knowledge through this informal learning process without fearing negative consequences.

Supervisors who have transferred from firms that operate in an adaptive learning environment to firms that operate in a generative learning environment will demonstrate a defensive reaction to learning. These supervisors are reluctant to be seen by peer supervisors or team members to make mistakes because of the negative consequences, which they or others experienced, causing negative outcomes for status or promotion prospects.

To convince the supervisors of the genuine existence of the positive learning environment, there must be firm evidence from senior management that supervisors and their team members can admit to mistakes. It is not sufficient for the organisation to espouse positive, generative learning values, when negative, adaptive values are built into the organisation's culture and HRD systems, e.g. reward processes, criteria for promotion (Antonacopoulou, 1999; MacNeil, 2001).

Supervisors' facilitative skills and informal learning

Supervisors can enhance the process of informal learning through knowledge sharing in teams – if they are encouraged to contribute their facilitation skills. Thus supervisors working as facilitators of teams can encourage knowledge sharing, supporting learning through mistakes, and creating a form of team learning that is continuous – not individual and fragmented. Organisations cannot capture tacit learning nor benefit from its existence, if this learning remains fragmented and embedded in the individual (Nonaka and Takeuchi, 1995).

Thus it is the supervisor as facilitator who provides linkage of both individual and organisational learning. The facilitation skills of the supervisor enable the organisation to use the shared knowledge of the team members.

The organisation's knowledge of its environment is enhanced by two-way communication. Lack of interactive communication between the senior and lower levels of management inhibits the organisation's capability to focus on its environment, learn and manage change (Smith, 1995). This is important where competitive pressures have encouraged de-layering, team working and empowerment, so the remaining workforce must maximise the available opportunities for increasing creativity, motivation, and work output (Proehl, 1996). Thus involvement of team members is important to encourage creativity and innovation through sharing individual knowledge during teamwork (Manz and Sims, 1987; Parry *et al.*, 1998), and translating individual learning into team learning which becomes a powerful focal point for organisational learning (Wilson, 1996).

The supervisor working as a facilitator

This chapter refers to a facilitator approach, but it is not intended to imply that there is only one way for a facilitator to operate in all learning contexts. The accomplished facilitator has a range of highly developed learning and interpersonal skills: an instructor, coach or conflict handler according to the learning situation (MacNeil, 2001). The facilitator must vary the approaches used according to his/her assessment of the learning needs of individuals or teams at any particular time (Sheenan and Kearns, 1996). The continuum of approaches and skills used will incorporate different levels of direction, knowledge input, process input, process intervention and coaching to achieve the learning objectives (Van Maurick, 1994).

Facilitation is 'empowering people to take control and responsibility for their own efforts' (Bentley, 1994: 1) and in this process the facilitator has responsibility for creating the appropriate learning environment. The facilitator creates the learning environment through the provision of opportunities and resources, whilst not actually trying to control the learner's process. Thus facilitators enable the learning process; but the ultimate act of learning is embedded in the individual or team (Prokopenko, 1998).

It is assumed that in formal learning situations responsibility for learning will be controlled by the trainer rather than the learner, although it is recognised that learners have to be motivated and cannot be made to learn. In informal learning situations, responsibility for learning belongs to the self-directed learner, and only secondarily with the facilitator. The facilitator concentrates not on teaching, but developing the learning process (Heron, 1999). The facilitator approach should not be a directive process; however, there may be some occasions when the facilitator has a directive input. This is acceptable if the intervention meets the learning objectives, which have been jointly determined between the facilitator and the team.

Problems preventing effective facilitation in practice

The use of facilitation skills by supervisors could be inhibited in practice by some problems. There is concern regarding the actual effectiveness of supervisors as facilitators, and thus their ability to develop their team members. This can occur in organisations where the inadequacy of past training and development of managers is repeated, due to historical lack of overall strategic integration between individual and organisational needs in management development. It can also happen in organisations that choose to adopt a policy of cost cutting in the provision of training and development policies and processes (Harrison, 1997; Kolb *et al.*, 1994; Mabey and Salaman, 1999; Mumford, 1997). Although supervisors have traditionally been 'gatekeepers' controlling the access of their team members to development opportunities and career progression (Walton, 1999), ironically this role has not included achieving access to their own development opportunities in the organisation.

Operational constraints prevent supervisors from concentrating on facilitating their teams, competing pressures include heavy workload, short-term problem solving, underdeveloped coaching skills, conflict between the coaching and directional styles of management. Further constraints can arise through confusion in the communication from senior management concerning expectations of the supervisor's role (Mink *et al.*, 1993), and in particular, through lack of support from senior management to long-term investment in people via HRD policies and processes (de Jong and Versloot, 1999; de Jong *et al.*, 1999).

The shifting power relationship between the supervisor role and team

Team working alters the demands on the role of supervisors, because of an implied change in the power relationship with their team. The traditional command and control style of management (Drucker, 1955) is less effective when management accountability is devolved to a team instead of the individual supervisor. This power shift is evident in the supervisor's behaviour in the team, demonstrated by the requirement that he/she adopts a different leadership approach as a facilitator (Horner, 1997). Otherwise, there is a contradiction between empowering team members to think autonomously, whilst simultaneously expecting them to be instructed by their supervisor. This approach to leadership involves the supervisor facilitating the team towards shared goals through joint agreement (Gardner, 1990; Stewart and Manz, 1995). To meet the changing and challenging demands of leading teams supervisors must facilitate, not impose direction on teams through command and control (Zucchi and Edwards, 2000).

However, some supervisors will resist the change to using a facilitation approach. These supervisors perceive the facilitator approach as removing the hierarchical boundary between themselves and workers, and that losing the command and control approach to the facilitative approach undermines their job and/or is a threat to their claim (albeit at a low status level) to be managers (Arkensas *et al.*, 1995; Balkema and Molleman, 2000; Stewart and Manz, 1995). Kirk and Broussine (2000) and Morgan (1986) suggest that some supervisors find it difficult to be neutral in dealings with the work team. The supervisor is part of the organisations political, power structure as a member of management. These supervisors have a tendency to over-direct their work teams' learning process, dominating, implementing their own individual, personal goals, at the expense of the teams' learning goals (Darling, 1996; Messemer, 1990).

Empowerment: implications and contradictions for the supervisor role

If supervisors' power is traditionally based on one-sided instruction and communication of tasks to workers, then this expertise is based on experience and knowledge of former work processes. This technical knowledge is less important in a rapidly changing environment, where the generation of new and shared knowledge is vital to enable the work team to respond to rapidly changing situations (MacNeil, 2001). 'The idea that workers should have control over work processes has once again resurfaced, as change in technology for many industries has made traditional managerial control mechanisms redundant' (Morrell and Wilkinson, 2002: 120).

The thorny issue of management control over employees continues despite the delegation of authority assumed to take place during empowerment. Trends for empowerment and team working are based on the organisation's need to maximise human capital, mirroring 'soft and hard' HRM approaches (Storey, 1991). Where the organisation adopts the soft HRM approach, utilising creativity and problem solving, then soft empowerment could meet the employees' needs for two-way communication with management. However, the hard HRM approach to empowerment increases personal accountability of employees' behaviour through measurement of tasks, combined with senior management's expectation of continuous improvement in employee performance. Often hard empowerment can be linked to planned reduction of jobs, thus creating instability in the employee relationship through rationalising the need for contingent, flexible employment patterns in organisations, e.g. peripheral, temporary workforces. Any training opportunities offered to employees actually represent not learning opportunities, but the employees' obligation to ensure their survival by increasing their

employability in the internal and external job market. The hard HRM employment relationship is characterised by the workforce operating as a disposable
commodity for organisational profit, and as willing conspirators for their own
expendability (Claydon and Doyle, 1996; Legge, 1995).

Developing supervisors as effective facilitators

The changing role of the supervisor can be summarised as managing business
issues, coping with continuous change, and leading downsized teams to achieve
on-going continuous improvement. Still, supervisors gain their position largely
due to technical skills; the technical expertise may not match the extent to which
their supervisory jobs are evolving in size and complexity.

Many organisations traditionally undervalue the supervisor's role; this is
reflected in inadequate or non-existent training and development provision for
supervisors. Yet supervisory training has the potential to bring about improved
competence in problem solving, team management, project management, leading
to cost savings and ultimately increased profits for the organisation (Bunning,
1996).

A major determinant of the effectiveness of supervisory training is the supervisors' capability to transfer and apply their learning to different workplace
contexts. Thus supervisors will be resistant to learning and development, which
they perceive as relating to theoretical, abstract situations, not applicable to everyday problems (Garavan and Sweeney, 1994). It is important that management
development is targeted at supervisory staff, enabling them to learn the relevant
interpersonal and learning skills for the facilitator role. Supervisors can find it
uncomfortable, to switch between their supervisor role and the facilitator
approach (Ellinger *et al.*, 1999). To ensure supervisors can manage the different
relationship with their teams, supervisors need to learn different expertise and
skills. The facilitator approach requires practice and training; this will include
supervisors learning both soft process skills, e.g. communication, and hard, task-
based skills (Beech and Crane, 1999).

Kolb, (1984) has identified the value of using personal experience to reflect on
learning processes. Professional practice (including management) is based not
only on technical approaches, but also on the use of tacit knowledge. A crucial
competence for supervisors is to learn reflective competence (Schön, 1983; 1987),
allowing individuals to analyse, modify and build their existing competencies,
achieving further development.

The effective facilitator should be highly competent in promoting reflective
processes, generating 'discursive validity checking' to create shared, team understanding. The critical facilitator is an active rather than a neutral participant,
confronting reflections belonging to themselves and others. The facilitator subjects their own reflection to powerful challenges from team members, creating
critical discourse (Gregory and Romm, 2001). Thus development for supervisors
should emphasise informal learning processes, and building reflective skills
through the exchange and sharing of information (Kessels, 1999). Development

for supervisors as facilitators cannot be designed using the individualised, systematic training processes, because the systematic training processes cannot deal with the levels of complexity and uncertainty facing individuals and organisations during change.

To ensure that both learning and change happen simultaneously, organisations must eliminate internal learning boundaries and barriers to instigate an open culture, creating a positive learning climate where individuals are confident to challenge their own thinking (Senge, 1991).

Conclusion

The purpose of this chapter was to explore the complex, changing role of the line manager at supervisory level in organisations. If organisations are to meet their strategic objectives, there needs to be alignment between HRM and HRD policies and processes. The line manager role as a driver of policies and practices to facilitate strategic change is strongly emphasised in HRM. Historically supervisors have been reluctant gatekeepers of HRD processes for their teams, and organisations have tended to emphasise formal as distinct from informal learning in their HRD strategies. Thus the contribution of the supervisor as a facilitator of both learning and change in teams is an important often overlooked resource.

Complexity of change increases the demands facing the supervisor's role. If change in organisations can be described as a continuous, uncertain process, rather than a temporary phase, then supervisors need sophisticated skills for promoting learning through knowledge sharing in their teams. The supervisor and their teams are required regularly to learn, un-learn and re-learn new organisational meanings through sharing tacit knowledge. The supervisor's approach to learning, through communication of learning norms, can powerfully influence a positive learning climate encouraging team members to share their tacit knowledge.

The facilitator approach represents a change from the command and control approach, a change which some supervisors find difficult, fearing loss of status or role. Thus supervisors must be developed to perform this different, facilitator approach for a demanding, continuum of learning situations. The reluctance of organisations to invest in supervisory training and development is shortsighted, given supervisors' potential contribution to learning and change. There should be further research, for a fuller understanding of supervisors as facilitators.

References

Antonacopoulou, E. (1999) 'Developing learning managers within learning organisations', in M. Easterby-Smith, J. Burgoyne, and L. Araujo (Eds), *Organisational Learning and the Learning Organisation: Developments in theory and in practice*, Sage, London

Appelbaum, S. H., Lavigne-Schmidt, S., Peytchev, M. and Shapiro, B. (1999) 'Downsizing: Measuring the costs of failure', *Journal of Management Development*, 18(5): 436–463

Arkensas, R., Ulrich, D., Jick, T. and Kerr, S. (1995) *The Boundaryless Organisation*, San Francisco: Jossey-Bass

Argyris, C. (1985), *Strategy, Change and Defensive Routines*, Boston: Putman

Argyris, C. (1986) 'Reinforcing organisational defensive routines: On unintended human resource activity', *Human Resource Management Journal*, 25(4): 541–555

Argyris, C. and Schön, D. (1978) *Organisational Learning: A theory of action perspective*, San Francisco: Jossey- Bass

Balkema, A. and Molleman, E. (1999), 'Barriers to the development of self-organising teams', *Journal of Managerial Psychology*, 14(2): 134–149

Bartlett, C. A and Ghosal, S. (1989) *Managing across Borders: A transnational solution*, Cambridge, MA: Harvard Business School Press,

Beech, N. and Crane, O. (1999) 'High performance teams and a climate of community', *Team Performance Management*, 5(3): 87–102

Bentley, T. (1994), 'Facilitation providing opportunities for learning', *Journal of European Industrial Training*, 18(5): 1–14

Broussine, M., Gray, M., Kirk, P., Paumier, K., Tichelar, T. and Young, S. (1998) 'The best and worst time for management development', *Journal of Management Development*, 17(1): 56–67

Bunning, R. (1996) 'Supervisory training that has turned a profit', *Journal of European Industrial Training*, 20(9): 9–13

Claydon, T. and Doyle, M. (1996) 'Trusting me, trusting you?: The ethics of empowerment', *Personnel Review*, 25(6): 13–25

Cohen, S. G., Ledford, G.E. and Spreitzer, G. M. (1996) 'A predictive model of self-managing work team effectiveness' *Human Relations*, 49: 643–676

Darling, M. (1996), 'Empowerment: Myth or reality', *Executive Speeches*, 10(6): 23–28

de Jong, J. A., Leenders, F. J. and Thijssen, J. G .L. (1999) 'HRD tasks of first level managers', *Journal of Workplace Learning: Employee Counselling Today*, 11(5): 176–183

de Jong, J. A. and Versloot, B. (1999), 'Job instruction: its premises and its alternatives', *Human Resource Development International*, 2(4): 391–404

Doyle, M. (2002) 'From change novice to change expert: Issues of learning, development and support', *Personnel Review*, 31(4): 465–481

Drucker, P. (1955) *The Practice of Management*, London: Heinemann

Ellinger, A. D. and Bostrom, R.P. (1999) 'Managerial coaching behaviours in learning organisations', *The Journal of Management Development*, 18(9): 752–771

Ellinger, A. D., Watkins, K. E. and Barnas, C. M. (1999), 'Responding to new roles: A qualitative study of managers as instructors', *Management Learning*, 30(4): 387–412

Evans, D. (1996) *Supervisory Management: Principles and practice*, London: Cassell

Garavan, T. N. and Sweeney, P. (1994) 'Supervisory training and development', *Journal of European Industrial Training*, 18(2): 17–26

Gardner, J. W. (1990) *On Leadership*, New York: Free Press

Gregory, W. J. and Romm, N. R. A. (2001) 'Critical facilitation: Learning through intervention in group processes', *Management Learning*, 32(4): 453–467

Harrison, R. (1997) *Employee Development*, The Charted Institute of Personnel and Development, London

Heron, J. (1999) *The Facilitator's Handbook*, London: Kogan Page

Horner, M. (1997) 'Leadership theory past, present and future', *Team Performance Management*, 3(4): 1–12

Kasl, E., Marsick, V. J. and Dechant, K. (1996) 'Teams as learners – a research based model of team learning', *Journal of Applied Behavioural Science*, 33(2): 227–246

Kessels, J. (1999), 'Successful programme implementation in corporate education', chapter presented at the CIPD Professional Standards Conference at Warwick University on 13 July

Kim, D. H. (1993) 'The link between individual and group learning', *Sloan Management Review*, Fall, 35(1): 37–57

Kirk, P. and Broussine, M. (2000) 'The politics of facilitation', *Journal of Workplace Learning: Employee Counselling Today*, 12(1): 13–22

Kofman, F. and Senge, P. M. (1993) 'Communities of commitment: The heart of learning organisations', *Organisational Dynamics*, 22(2): 5–23

Kolb, D. A. (1984) *Experiential Learning*, Englewood Cliffe, NJ: Prentice Hall

Kolb, D., Lublin, S., Sproth, J. and Baker, R. (1994) 'Strategic management development using experiential learning theory to assess and develop managerial competences', in Mabey, C. and Isles, P. (Eds), *Managing Learning*, London: Open University Press

Leat, M. and Wolley, J. (1999) 'Multi-nationals and employee relations', in Hollinshead, G., Nicholls, P. and Tailby, S., *Employee Relations*, London: Financial Times Management

Legge, K. (1995) *Human Resource Management: Rhetoric and realities*, London: Macmillan Press

Lewin, K. (1951) *Field Theory in Social Science*, New York: Harper & Row

Mabey, C. and Salaman, G. (1999) *Strategic Human Resource Management*, Blackwell, London

Manz, C. C. and Sims, H. P. (1987) 'Leading workers to lead themselves: The external leadership of self-managed work teams', *Administrative Science Quarterly*, 32: 106–128

Marsick, V. J. and Watkins, K. E. (1990) *Informal and Incidental Learning in the Workplace*, London: Routledge

MacNeil, C. (2001) 'The supervisor as a facilitator of informal learning in work teams', *Journal of Workplace Learning*, 13(6): 246–253

McGill, M. E., Slocum, J. W. (Jr) and Lei, D. (1992) 'Management practices in learning organisations: Adaptive and generative styles of organisational learning' *Organizational Dynamics*, summer, 35(1): 37–57

McHugh, M., O'Brien, G. and Ramondt, J. (1999) 'Organisational metamorphosis lead by front line staff', *Employee Relations*, 21(6): 556–576

Messemer, M. (1990) 'How to put empowerment into practice', *The Woman*, CPA.: 25

Miller, D. (1996) 'A preliminary typology of organisational learning: Synthesising the literature', *Journal of Management*, Fall, 22(3): 1–86

Mink, O., Owen, K. Q. and Mink, B. (1993) *Developing High Performance People: The art of coaching*, Reading, MA: Addison-Wesley

Mintzberg, H. (1987) 'Crafting strategy', *Harvard Business Review*, 65(5): 66–75

Molleman, E. (2000) 'Modalities of self-managing teams: The "must", "may", "can" and "will" of local decision-making', *International Journal of Operations and Production Management*, 20(8): 889–910

Morgan, G. (1986) *Images of Organisations*, London: Sage

Morrell, K. and Wilkinson, A. (2002) 'Empowerment: Through the smoke and past the mirrors?' *Human Resource Development International*, 5(10): 119–130

Mumford, A. (1997) *Management Development Strategies for Action*, London: CIPD

Nonaka, I. and Takeuchi, H. (1995) *The Knowledge-creating Company*, New York: Oxford University Press

Parry, I. J., Transheld, D., Smith, S., Foster, M. and Wilson, S. (1998) 'Reconfirming your organisation: A team work approach', *Team Performance Management*, 4(4): 1–8

Pedlar, M. and Burgoyne, J. (1994) 'Applying self-development in organisations', in Mabey, C. and Isles, P. (Eds) *Managing Learning*, London: Open University Press

Pedlar, M., Burgoyne, J. and Boydell, T. (1991) *The Learning Company*, London: McGraw Hill

Proehl, R. A. (1996) 'Cross-functional teams – A panacea or just another headache?' *Supervision*, 57(7): 6–23

Prokopenko, J. (1998) 'The next century: A focus on human resource development', *Human Resource Development International*, October, 1(3): 268–272

Rodgers, C. (1977) *Freedom to Learn*, London: Kogan Page

Schön, D. (1983) *The Reflective Practitioner: How professionals think in action*, London: Maraca Temple Smith

Schön, D. (1987) *Educating the Reflective Practioner*, San Francisco, CA: Jossey-Bass

Senge, P. (1990) *The Fifth Discipline: The art and practice of the learning organization*, London: Century Books

Sheenan, M. and Kearns, D. (1996) 'Using Kolb, implementation, and evaluation of facilitation skills', *Industrial and Commercial Training*, 27(6): 8–14

Smith, D. (1995) 'The learning organisation: Change proofing and strategy', *Journal of Management Development*, 14(9): 17–20

Stewart, G .L. and Manz, C. C. (1995) 'Leadership for self-managing work teams: A typology and integrative model', *Human Relations*, 48(17): 747–770

Storey, J. (1991) 'Introduction: From personnel management to human resource management', in Storey, J. (Ed.) *New Perspectives on Human Resource Management*, London: Routledge

Stuart, R. (1995) 'Experiencing organisational change: Triggers, processes and outcomes of change journeys', *Personnel Review*, 24(2): 1–39, (pp. 467 and 469)

Van Maurick, J. (1994) 'Facilitating excellence: Styles and processes of facilitation', *Leadership and Organisational Development Journal*, 15(8): 30–34

Walton, J. (1999) *Strategic Human Resource Development*, London: Prentice Hall

Wilson, D. A. (1996) *Managing Knowledge*, Oxford: Butterworth Heinmann

Vince, R. (2002) 'The impact of emotion on organisational learning', *Human Resource Development International*, 5(1): 73–85

Zucchi, F. and Edwards, J. S. (2000) 'How similar are human resource management practices in re-engineered organisations?', *Business Process Management Journal*, 6(3): 214–223

16 A practitioner's reflections on HRD research

A case of internalized complexity?

Rosemary Hill

Introduction

The chapter originates in my doctoral research (Hill, 2001) into human resource development (HRD) in small and medium-sized enterprises (SMEs). The central research problem concerned the poor take-up of UK national HRD programmes – such as the Investors in People standard (IIP UK, 1996) – by small organizations. Fundamental to understanding that problem was an examination of SME HRD in general, and it is from this second strand of the research that the arguments and ideas advanced in the chapter have emerged. Whilst the research design and outcomes are discussed more fully further on, a little more background is offered here.

Preliminary literature searches and investigations indicated that the whole area of SME HRD was characterized by conditions of absence and deficiency. Simply put, it appeared that small organizations neither train nor develop their workforce. But how sensible or practical would it have been to explore SME HRD with a negative logic – that is, looking for what was apparently not there? With this in mind, the research assumed a positive logic by focusing on an exploration of 'how' and 'why' small organizations adopt the HRD approaches they *do* employ, rather than seeking evidence of HRD policy and practice in any conventional form or sense. So, a priori, SME HRD was conceptualized as an organic component embedded in a small organization's infrastructure and normal routines. It was also noted that this conceptualization was typified by an absence of formality, structure and substance; was founded in the natural development and deployment of tacit knowledge and skills; and was individually shaped through a combination of '*naturally-occurring interventions*' such as SME owner/manager perspectives, organizational/industry cultures and norms, everyday operational pressures and sudden catalytic crises. If, as implied here, HRD is embedded in the mechanics of 'business as usual', then HRD and work become one and the same, united as inseparable processors of learning – hence the notion of a 'naturally-occurring intervention' as mooted above. Empirical case-study work both confirmed and added new dimensions to the foregoing arguments.

This brings us to the main point of discussions in the context of this chapter. The notion of SME HRD being shaped by 'naturally-occurring interventions' seems a rather complex and difficult concept. In literal terms, it is a seemingly impossible oxymoron. As such, I suggested in my thesis that researchers might like to revisit the whole area of HRD as a (deliberate?) intervention – not just in small organizations but across organizations in general. For instance, does HRD, and by implication learning, require formal intervention at all? And, how ethical is it to intervene in human agency that is fundamentally driven by a natural instinct towards self preservation, fulfilment and growth? Stewart (1998), for example, is but one commentator who points the HRD profession towards circumspection in this regard. The invitation to rethink the notion of 'HRD as intervention' holds great significance for me personally. For, as a reflective HRD practitioner-scholar/researcher, the practitioner part of me makes a living through 'deliberate intervention', whilst the scholar/researcher in me feels a need for further enquiry that clearly challenges the basis of how I make that living.

The main aim of this chapter is, therefore, to explore the ideas introduced above, in an attempt to resolve the dialectic that my hybrid professional identity – the HRD practitioner-scholar/researcher – seems to have spawned. In this sense, an exploration of the validity and value of 'HRD as intervention' becomes a means to an end in a search for personal meaning. To accomplish this dual agenda, the chapter next builds upon arguments already presented to further develop a conceptual- and a research-based case as to why researchers might like to revisit the notion of 'HRD as intervention'. It then proceeds to discuss potential implications for both self and other HRD professionals and suggests an alternate way of thinking about the nature of 'intervention' in relation to HRD, from both a philosophical and terminological perspective. The chapter concludes with a résumé of key learning points and, in accordance with a further chapter aim, reviews what it has contributed to the continuing debate about the diverse, complex and mutable nature of HRD as a whole.

A conceptual base for revisiting 'HRD as intervention'

Much of the academic and practitioner literature about HRD and organization development (OD) seems to position HRD theory, design and delivery – either explicitly or implicitly – within a framework of intervention (see, for example: Becker *et al.*, 2001; Cacciope, 1998; Garavan and Deegan, 1995; French and Bell, 1990; Harrison, 1997; Klasen and Clutterbuck, 2002; McGoldrick *et al.*, 2002; Russ-Eft, 2001; Stewart, 1996 and 1998; Stewart and McGoldrick, 1996; Versloot *et al.*, 2001; Weinberger, 1998). The Concise Oxford Dictionary defines intervention as 'interference' or 'mediation' and suggests that to intervene is to 'come between so as to prevent or modify the result or course of events'. Associating the fundamental nature of HRD as advanced in the literature and practised in organizations with notions of interference and prevention would seem to seriously undermine both the quintessence of HRD and the human condition itself.

But what is the quintessence of HRD? Garavan *et al.* (2000) examine in some depth a major philosophical debate about whether HRD, as an organizational activity, should promote 'performance' or 'learning', and suggest that this debate is '... generally posited in (such) a dichotomous way' (ibid: 65). They go on to comment on how the performance focus is generally advanced by HRD practitioners and the learning focus more often by academics and researchers. Clearly, such arguments further underline the sense of personal confusion about my standing as an HRD professional explored in the previous section. But perhaps the performance-practitioner/learning-academic perspective is not so dichotomous after all. For example, Stewart (1992) believes that learning is the focus of HRD. As a professor of HRD, he may be considered an academic. Academics Iles and Yolles (this volume), however, seem to present a performance orientation of HRD in their viable systems model of OD. As they explore OD from an academic perspective, their arguments would appear to cross the putative performance-practitioner/learning-academic divide to shape a *performance-academic* paradigm. On the other hand, if OD methodologies such as process consultation, action research and group survey feedback (French and Bell, 1990) are also seen as 'tools' of the HRD practitioner – and OD is about enabling and enhancing individual and organizational learning – then this particular marriage transverses that divide also to forge a *learning-practitioner* paradigm.

Many HRD interventions engage a facilitative rather than direct teaching or training approach. Facilitation, for example, is a common feature of process consultation and teambuilding activities. Shaw (2002) invites us to consider what 'facilitation' has come to mean. Acknowledging a derivation in the French word *facile* (easy), she argues that although seeing facilitation as something that is '... intended in a positive sense to help complicated, difficult, conflictual situations of human engagement flow more easily and productively' (ibid: 2), she cannot help but gravitate uneasily towards the connotation of 'facile' in the English sense – something she defines as potentially reductive, insensitive and crass. In this context, it would appear that facilitation aligns with intervention in its negative gist.

Conceptually then, 'HRD as intervention' is complex, contextual and charged with the emotion of human agency and involvement. Furthermore, intervention may be emotionally indistinguishable from the supposed self-generative and supportive practice of facilitation. As Callahan and Gračanin (this volume) argue '... emotions may be seen as an important element in understanding complex systems'. It is, perhaps, emotional dissonance that has prompted me to reflect critically upon the complexity of my professional being and to advance a case for re-conceptualizing the interventionist disposition of HRD. The next section presents empirical support for this case.

A research base for revisiting 'HRD as intervention'
Overview of the research design

As the central research issue in my doctoral project was concerned with the poor take-up of UK national HRD programmes by SMEs and as part of this problem was perceived to reside in the 'why' and the 'how' of SME HRD approaches, the study aimed to explore and compare HRD in SMEs with the characteristics of UK national HRD in order to understand this problem. Fieldwork was carried out in a range of small organizations in the north west of England over the period 1996 to

2000; the bulk of empirical data was collected by means of three case studies, accessed by a large survey. As discussions at the beginning of the chapter signal, the starting point for empirical investigations was the proposition that HRD approaches developed by SMEs may be a natural barrier to their engaging in national HRD programmes. Figure 16.1, both illustrates this proposition and reiterates the general a priori 'shape' of SME HRD already described. The two portrayals of HRD in the figure were developed and positioned in the research design as Key Variables 1 and 2 – SME HRD and UK National HRD, respectively.

Whilst it is interesting to compare the obvious distinctions and differences between the two HRD typologies displayed in the figure, our main concern here is with the SME HRD key variable. The table indicates that, due to a lack of formal structure and substance, SME HRD may perhaps best be described as a set of fuzzy, individualistic perspectives, organically generated and shaped by owner/manager ideologies, organizational cultures, external pressures and operating environments. It seems that, unlike national HRD, HRD approaches in small organizations are not enforced through the implementation of scientific models but grounded in the spontaneous deployment of tacit knowledge and skills (Baumard, 1996; Nanda, 1996; Nonaka, 1996; Spender, 1996a and b). Arguably, planned intervention has no place in this arrangement, whereby – like the knowledge and skills being acquired – 'intervention' is fundamentally instinctive, intangible and unexplainable. Although commonly thought more prevalent in smaller organizations (Harrison, 1997), tacit knowledge and skills are by no means the sole preserve of the SME sector. Tacit knowledge and skill have an important cognitive dimension in any organization, as they are vital components of regeneration, particularly in the context of innovation and creative capability (Nonaka, 1996). By implication, this means that the concept of a 'naturally-occurring intervention' could apply to an organization of any size.

Key Variable 1 HRD in SMEs (informal perspectives)	• Notable absence of formality, structure and substance • Individually shaped through a combination of naturally-occurring 'interventions' such as owner/manager perspectives, organizational/industry cultures and norms, external pressures and operational needs: internally generated through need and necessity • Founded in the natural development and deployment of tacit knowledge and skills
Key Variable 2 UK National HRD (formal model)	• Notable presence of formality, structure and substance • Generically designed and implemented through a model derived in the ethos and delivery of UK National HRD (N/HRD), and large-firm logic: externally imposed through planned intervention • Founded in the 'enforced' development and deployment of explicit (scientific) knowledge and skills

Figure 16.1 Summary of *a priori* differences noted between HRD in SMEs and UK National HRD (N/HRD).
Source: Hill (2001)

From Figure 16.1, above, it can be seen that a 'naturally-occurring intervention' was proposed as an indigenous *influence* arising out of everyday activities, circumstances and pressures, both internal and external to the organization. Research questions were, therefore, developed to explore the nature and impact of these influences in the context of the research problem. The following are examples of questions applied in the case-study work in order to unpack the 'how' and 'why' of the three cases' HRD approaches.

- What are owner/manager perspectives about HRD?
- What are owner/manager views about organizational formality?
- What are the key needs and features of each organization?
- What are key internal/external imperatives and influences on each organization?
- How does each organization learn?
- How is all this shaping each organization's culture?
- How is all this shaping each organization's HRD approach?

The research questions were used to inform a variety of interview topic guides and questionnaires. Managed in this way, interviews and questionnaires encouraged case-study respondents – usually the owner/manager, director or managing director – to talk about things within the realms of their own experiences and descriptive powers rather than to regurgitate stereotyped (and perhaps externally indoctrinated) views of why they (SMEs) were doing things the way they were. This reinforced the positive logic of the research design by looking for signs of existing processes and activities that could be construed, even loosely, as 'developmental', rather than expecting to see examples of conventional HRD models and practices.

Findings and conclusions

Empirical data gathered in the research substantiated the proposition about SME HRD contained in Figure 16.1, above. That is HRD approaches emerged, not as a result of deliberate planned intervention, but through the *interaction* of daily routines or in response to acute crisis – thus uniting work and HRD as both inseparable processes and inseparable processors of learning. A corollary to all of this – or more likely because of it – is that HRD was aimed at the development of the organization above, or to the detriment of, the training and development of individuals. To draw upon an example from one of the cases studied, a sudden and unexpected loss of a major customer had a profound effect upon the development and shape of HRD in this organization. This incident served as an important catalyst for change, causing the managing director to negotiate a new market position and to seek a welter of information from employees, via a rudimentary staff appraisal scheme, about how they perceived the performance of the organization, themselves and their fellow workers. It can be argued that in this organization 'HRD' emerged '... from disorder through processes of spontaneous self-organization in the absence of any blueprint'. (Stacey *et al.*, 2000: 1). Without any such blueprint or plan, it can also be argued that this organization was moving towards an unknowable future and that the rudimentary HRD process emerging out of the catalytic incident described above was part of the organization's own perpetual construction of its unknowable future (Stacey *et al.*, 2000).

A building block in that organizational construction process was HRD 'getting done' without the benefit of any planned, or unnatural, intervention. The research revealed several similar illustrations of 'naturally-occurring interventions', that facilitated developmental outcomes to the organization – or more typically the disorganization – they emerged from. Figure 16.2, below, summarizes the HRD approach noted in each case-study organization.

Embedded in the descriptions of the cases in the figure is a sprinkling of what have been interpreted as 'naturally-occurring interventions'. For instance, according to the technical manager in Case 1, everything happened 'against the background of the product', an organizational philosophy that focused routine activities and priorities on building capability in design innovation and computerized engineering technology. This meant that the senior management team continually geared itself to maintain a continual flow of discussion and dialogue about design and process improvement strategies and techniques. Case 1's senior management team unwittingly practised the principles of action research and action learning (French and Bell, 1990; Revans, 1983) as an organization development method. The causative 'intervention' in this instance was a requirement for the organization to do everything 'against the background of the product' – in essence a 'naturally-occurring intervention'.

Reviewing other data in Figure 16.2, it is not difficult to identify other parallel examples springing from the mechanics of 'business as usual' that can be located in some formal HRD model or practice. The circumstances of Case 2's major contract loss has already been discussed above; Case 3 was, too, a turbulent organization in dire need of a sustained period of tranquil operating conditions and quiet reflection. On becoming a provider of services to the UK government's new flagship welfare-to-work programme, the New Deal, Case 3 was obliged to develop a more formal organizational structure and set of operating procedures, primarily for purposes of satisfying external audit obligations. This change agenda incorporated a requirement for more formality and transparency in both generalist HR and specific HRD processes. Whilst this may constitute an example of compulsion rather than 'natural intervention', arguably the intervention was not an 'HRD intervention' in its customary guise.

Four main conclusions were advanced from the study as a whole, but only those elements most relevant to this chapter are presented here. Overall, there was no evidence to suggest that SME HRD was anything other than its depiction in Figure 16.1, above. The HRD approaches found were individualistic and informal reflections of industry norms and expectations, and owner/manager perspectives and influences, that in turn had been shaped by life and industry experiences and capabilities. The study also showed that the context for SME

Case-study organization	Approx. no. of employees	Approach to HRD ('How and why do SMEs develop the HRD approaches they do?')
Case 1: Design and build engineering Trading as a limited company	20	Shaped by traditional engineering values and needs located in rather entrenched owner/manager perspectives. 'Development' revolved around day-to-day product/process design activities, especially those focused on the construction of computer aided design and management systems. Case 1's stated HRD needs were more aspirational than operational. No internal HRD expertise to enable development of alternative HRD perspectives and approaches.
		Case 1's HRD approach was contained within the limits of the knowledge and capabilities of individuals in the organization. Complete organizational focus on a need for everything to be done 'against the background of the product' – a phrase frequently used by a member of the senior management team.
Case 2: Providers of security systems, telecommuni- cations and CCTV Initially a limited company then trading as a PLC following an organizational restructure and refocus	70, reducing to around 50 by time of research disengagement	Case 2's HRD approach reflects the MD's view of HRD/T and D as lost time and a work disruption, balanced against a need to retain customer confidence and limit legislative liability. HRD focus is on engineers as both MD and sales and technical directors are former engineers; no other HRD initiatives to cater for staff T and D in general. MD also seen as an obstruction to this happening. Loss of major contract was a catalyst for change that led to a period of deep reflection about the way forward for the organization as a whole and the introduction of a rudimentary staff appraisal system. No internal HRD to capitalize on what was being learned and to develop the appraisal system beyond its original intent as an organizational intelligence gathering exercise. Redundancies were made following an organizational restructure.
Case 3: Voluntary organization – youth & community projects Trading as a charity and run by a management committee	6, rising to *circa* 20 by time of research disengagement	Case 3's HRD approach reflects the industry it serves – i.e. 'people focused' with a concern for the pastoral care and development of individuals and the local community. Although restricted by funding, this approach evolved over time under the influences of three different leaders, all of whom have some sort of HRD experience and acumen. An organizational need for Case 3 to become involved in the New Deal – the UK government's flagship 'welfare to work' programme – served as a catalyst for Case 3 to develop more formal operational and HR processes in general. Then experienced a period of rapid and turbulent growth.

Figure 16.2 Summary of HRD approaches in the three cases.

HRD is important, both in terms of researching it and understanding it. This relates to the organic nature of HRD in small organizations and its inception through what has been termed as 'naturally-occurring intervention'.

In making a bridge from this section (the empirical) into the next (the post-empirical/creative-conceptual), I enlist the support of another co-writer in this volume. In his chapter 'The urge to destroy is a creative urge', James suggests that 'Creative thinking is dependent upon a paradigm that is creative'. He also suggests that a creative mind-set can only be achieved through the destruction of existing structures and cognition. My research concluded that HRD approaches in the three cases emerged, not as a result of planned *intervention*, but through the spontaneous *interaction* of daily routines and problem solving. It would seem that a key difference between *intervention* and *interaction* in this context is that the former is externally shaped and applied from the outside, whilst the latter arises naturally from within the complexity of the organism itself to find its own unique shape. To create a new paradigm, I propose not to destroy but to re-arrange the old one by turning it inside-out, and suggest that HRD be conceptualized as aesthetically (see the definition of 'aesthetics' advanced by James, this volume) *interactionist* rather than systematically interventionist.

'Interaction' as an alternative to 'intervention'?

Figure 16.3, compares and contrasts the interactionist and interventionist nature of HRD. Understanding the first set of variables is key to unpacking the rest. A comparison of *becoming* and *being* highlights the difference between an organism that exists in a state of perpetual journeying (becoming) and one that exists in a 'finished' state, or feels compelled to seek one (being). In keeping with a basic principle of complexity theory (Stacey *et al.*, 2000), 'becoming' is *complex*, whilst 'being' is *complicated*. According to Lee (this volume) 'A complicated system or a problem might be very complicated indeed, but with time and effort all its parts, and its whole can be measured and understood. In contrast, a complex system might be quite simple, yet its parameters cannot be measured or quantified (in the normal sense) and the whole is more than the sum of the parts'. An example of a complicated system would be a jigsaw puzzle – complicated indeed, yet all parts will eventually come together within a pre-ordained structure, the whole never more than the sum of the parts. An example of a complex system might be the development of a garden – simple in concept and on paper at the design stage perhaps, but once the garden has been planted the 'whole' is continually evolving towards an unpredictable and unknown end-point through an iterative cycle of growth, death and replenishment. The cycle itself is continually subjected to a sphere of unknown and unpredictable influences both internal and external to the organism (the garden), such as weather and climate changes, the presence or otherwise of a knowledgeable and caring gardener, pests and disease, the influences (good and bad) of wild and domestic creatures, and perhaps most crucially, the interaction of individual plants with each other and with the system as a whole, both above and beneath the soil.

HRD as interaction may be perceived as a *complex* system – internally generated, emergent from disorganization, having to find its own order due to a (mostly) unknown or unpredictable end-point – with an overall consequence of not being thought of, talked about or recognizable as 'HRD' in any conventional sense. The research findings and conclusions set out in the previous section illustrate this. On the other hand, HRD as intervention *is* complicated, as any manager or HR practitioner will attest. But when applied systematically within predefined parameters to deliver predetermined outcomes, the result of HRD intervention is, by and large, measurable, understandable and wholly recognizable as 'HRD'.

The traits in Figure 16.3 are clearly identifiable too in the 'Four types of development' model (Lee, this volume). The interactionist paradigm (Figure 16.3) fits well with Lee's processual/phenomenological view of management, whilst the interventionist position leans more towards the classic/scientific management orientation. Through her own research, Lee suggests that these four approaches to management link quite closely to four ways in which the word 'development' is used. She attributes the processual/phenomenological domain with notions of emergent development through internal discovery and interaction with others leading to an unpredictable world and unknown end-point; and the classic/scientific domain with a development ideology that encompasses inevitable stages, planned steps and a structured and known end-point.

The end-point of the chapter follows in a summary of key points and a critique of main contributions.

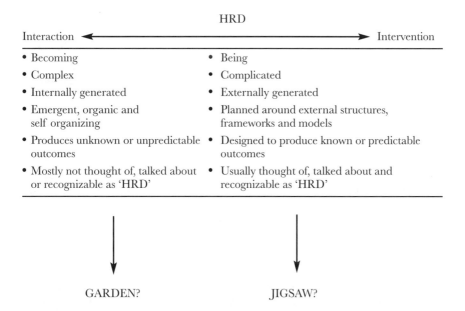

HRD

Interaction ⟵———————————————————⟶ Intervention

• Becoming	• Being
• Complex	• Complicated
• Internally generated	• Externally generated
• Emergent, organic and self organizing	• Planned around external structures, frameworks and models
• Produces unknown or unpredictable outcomes	• Designed to produce known or predictable outcomes
• Mostly not thought of, talked about or recognizable as 'HRD'	• Usually thought of, talked about and recognizable as 'HRD'

GARDEN?   JIGSAW?

Figure 16.3 A comparison of HRD interaction and intervention.

Conclusion and contributions

The chapter began by explaining the origins of the notion that HRD may be thought of as a naturally-occurring intervention, and ends with the development of two HRD typologies. One typology focuses on 'HRD as intervention' in its conventional sense, whereas the other introduces 'HRD as interaction' as both an alternative to 'intervention' and a rationalization of the term 'naturally-occurring intervention'. The chapter content between these start and end-points has advanced a conceptual- and a research-based case as to why researchers might like to revisit the interventionist nature of HRD. The typologies and their comparison at Figure 16.3, above, potentially offer a framework for that research agenda.

In thinking more broadly about what the chapter has contributed, it challenges the idea that HRD needs to shape and modify human behaviour and capability via external intervention. As well as offering this challenge, the chapter also commits to the public domain an alternative HRD paradigm that is fundamentally self-determining and self-organizing through processes of internal interaction. As far as the HRD practitioner is concerned, this paradigm shift may mean that he or she will be required to interact with and *become* a player *in* HRD, rather than intervene in and *be* a shaper *of* HRD. The chapter also adds to the general debate about the complex and often subjective nature of HRD – a debate that for me at least increasingly indicates that there should be no attempt to frame and engage a universal definition of HRD.

On a personal level, has writing the chapter has helped me to resolve the personal dialectic discussed in the introductory section? Probably not. Do I need to resolve it? Probably not. Perhaps my professional identity is best left in a state of 'becoming' to find its own way out from the inside. A further question remains. Should I opt to operate exclusively in either a practitioner or an academic world where aims and priorities might have more clarification and where emotions might be less impugned? Again probably not, as that would undoubtedly deny the richness and the copious learning opportunities inherent in the complexity of 'becoming' in a variety of operational models. Running with and nurturing the tension will, I hope, continue to foster a rounded sense of perspective, purpose and receptiveness. In short, I choose to work assiduously and predominantly in the glory of my garden – maybe taking the occasional solace in the construction of a jigsaw puzzle.

So, there is a sense of personal resolution of sorts after all. At the outset of developing the chapter, there was no absolute clarity on what the outcome would be. The complex act of writing has served as a personally-defining and interactionist learning experience in itself.

References

Baumard Philippe (1996), 'Organizations in the fog: An investigation into the dynamics of knowledge', in Bertrand Moingeon and Amy Edmondson (Eds), *Organizational Learning and Competitive Advantage*, London: Sage Publications, 74–9

Becker, Brian E., Huselid Mark A., and Ulrich, Dave (2001), *The HR Scorecard: Linking people, strategy, and performance*, Boston, Massachusetts: Harvard Business School Press

Cacciope, Roy (1998), 'An integrated model and approach for the design of effective leadership development programmes', in *Leadership and Organizational Development*, 19(1): 44–53

French, Wendell L. and Bell, Cecil H. Jr (1990), *Organization Development: Behavioural science interventions for organization improvement*, 4th edn, New Jersey: Prentice Hall

Garavan, Thomas N. and Deegan, Joe (1995), 'Discontinuous change in organizations. Using training and development interventions to develop creativity', in *Industrial and Commercial Training*, 27(11): 18–25

Garavan, Thomas N., Gunnigle, Patrick and Morley, Michael (2000), 'Contemporary HRD research: A triarchy of theoretical perspectives and their prescriptions for HRD', in *Journal of European Industrial Training*, 24(2/3/4): 65–93

Harrison, Rosemary (1997), *Employee Development*, London: Institute of Personnel and Development

Hill, Rosemary (2001), *Human Resource Development in Small and Medium-sized Enterprises: Barriers to national HRD*, unpublished PhD thesis, Nottingham Trent University

IIP UK (1996), *Investors in People the Revised Indicators: Advice and guidance for practitioners*, London: IIP UK

Klasen, Nadine and Clutterbuck, David (2002), *Implementing Mentoring Schemes*, Oxford: Butterworth-Heinemann

McGoldrick, Jim, Stewart, Jim and Watson, Sandra (Eds) (2002), *Understanding Human Resource Development: A research-based approach*, London: Routledge

Nanda, Ashish (1996), 'Resources, capabilities and competencies', in Bertrand Moingeon and Amy Edmondson (Eds), *Organizational Learning and Competitive Advantage*, London: Sage Publications, 93–120

Nonaka, I. (1996), 'The knowledge creating company', in Starkey, Ken (Ed.), *How Organizations Learn*, London: International Thomson Business Press, 18–31

Revans, R. (1983), *The ABC of Action Learning*, Bromley: Chartwell-Brant

Russ-Eft, D. (2001), 'Improving learning and performance: Theory and methods', in Jan N. Streumer (Ed.), *Perspectives on Learning at the Workplace: Theoretical positions, organizational factors, learning processes and effects, proceedings second conference on HRD research and practice across Europe 2001*, University of Twente, Enshcede, The Netherlands, 13–32

Shaw, Patricia (2002), *Changing Conversations in Organizations: A complexity approach to change*, Routledge: London

Spender, J. C. (1996a), 'Organizational knowledge, learning and memory: Three concepts in search of a theory', in *Journal of Organizational Change Management*, 9(1): 63–78

Spender, J. C. (1996b), 'Competitive Advantage from Tacit Knowledge', in Bertrand Moingeon and Amy Edmondson (Eds), *Organizational Learning and Competitive Advantage*, London: Sage Publications, 56–73

Stacey, Ralph D., Griffin, Douglas and Shaw, Patricia (2000), *Complexity and management: Fad or radical challenge to systems thinking?*, London: Routledge

Stewart, J. (1992), 'Towards a Model of HRD', in *Training and Development*, October 1992, 26–29

Stewart Jim (1996), *Managing Change Through Training and Development*, second edition, London: Kogan Page Limited

Stewart, Jim (1998), 'Intervention and assessment: The ethics of HRD', in *Human Resource Development International*, 1(1): 9–12

Stewart, Jim and McGoldrick, Jim (Eds) (1996), *Human Resource Development: Perspectives, strategies and practice*, London: Pitman Publishing

Versloot, Bert M., de Jong, Jan A. and Thijssen, Jo G. L. (2001) 'Organizational context of structured on-the-job training', in *International Journal of Training and Development*, 5(1): 2–22

Weinberger, Lisa A. (1998), 'Commonly-held theories of human resource development', in *Human Resource Development International*, 1(1): 75–93

Index

Notes: cited authors are referenced only
where they receive frequent or detailed
mention, or extended quotation; b =
boxed section; f/d = figure/diagram; n
= endnote; t = table

advertising, corporate 44
aesthetic(s): defined 122; role in human
behaviour/organisation 123–4, 158,
178
agriculture 169–70
al-Wazan, Hasan (Leo Africanus) 72
alchemy 59
ALS (action learning set) 209–10
Ang, Soon 107
'Anglo-American' management style 71;
domination of HRD theory/procedure
69, 78, 100
Arab world/culture: business methods 69,
71, 75–8; economics 73–4, 75;
education 75; HRD's compatibility
with 69, 78, 79–81; influence on
Western culture 71–2; internal
divergences/similarities 74; religious
identity 72–3
archetypes, in human developmental
systems 13–14, 21
Aristotle 157, 171
autocatalysis 52
autonomy; see community; self
autopoiesis; see self-regulation

Bateson, Patrick 87–8, 93, 95–6, 97
Bauman, Zygmunt 103, 104–5, 109
Beckmann, Max 172
behaviour, human, theories of 86–8,
157–8
Benedetti, Carlo De 59b
Bernard, St 126

bounded vs. unbounded worldviews 48–52
Bowie, Norman E. 91, 93
BPR (business process re-engineering) 9
British Airways 177–8
Brown, Andrew 91–3, 93
Bukharin, Nikolai 117
bureaucracy, in health services 199, 200–1
Burke, W. Warner 79
Butterfield, Herbert 70–1

CAS (complex adaptive systems) 52
catastrophe theory 119–20
Catholic dogma 63
cave paintings 172–3, 174
Ceausescu, Nicolai 118
change, processes of: global (politico-
economic) 117–18; organisational 16,
26, 60b, 150–2, 218–20, 227;
paradigmatic 119–21, 124–7, 148–9;
resistance to 118, 121, 150–1;
technological 167–8
chaos theory 119–20, 131
Chinese philosophy 171
'classical' management style 8
cognition: and HRD 33f, 33t, 34; and
purpose 157–8; role in learning 14,
155–7; and VST 154
Coleridge, Samuel Taylor 122
communication: role in organisational
structure 199t, 199–200; technology
167–8
'community': autonomy,
conflict/reconciliation with 101–2,
108–10, 113nn; HRD in relation to
105–6, 110–12; role in modern society
104–5, 106, 107
complexity (theory): definitions 7–8, 51–2,
131; and GTA 133–4; relation to social
sciences/HRD 1–2, 21, 25–7, 42–3,

52; scientific development of 119–21; see also systems, complex
congruence (in organisational functioning) 148
Conley, J. 107–8
consultation, role in decision-making 80
creativity: components of 122–4; role in modern business/thought 117, 124–7, 238
critical approach (in education): practical application 204, 209–11; theoretical basis 205, 206–9; tutor-student relationships 213–15
Cushman, Philip 103–4

Daly, Herman 46
Darwin, Charles 87, 93
data gathering, role in learning 183–5
debt, as basis of economy 103–4
decision-making processes 80
deep ecology 50–1
Descartes, René 171
determinism 49; in Islamic thought 75–6
Deurzen, E. van 191n
development: forms of 9–10, 10d; individual 9, 175–6; see also HRD; OD
Donaldson, Thomas 84
Douglas, Danielle 85
Du Gay, Paul 104, 108–9, 110, 111
Durkheim, Emile 109, 113n
Duska, Ronald F. 91, 92

Eagleton, Terry 63, 65
Eco, Umberto 92–3
ecology: deep 50–1; importance to HRD/social sciences 53; see also environment
economics: in Arab world 75–6, 77; limitations of 49–50, 53; neoclassical 45–6; as personal motivation 8–9, 112–13n; shifts in 103–4; and socal responsibility 43–4, 45, 46–7, 49–50
education 204–15; in Arab world 75; critical approaches see separate main heading; Western (new) methods 126, 205–7
Einstein, Albert 122
Eliot, T.S. 131
Emirates Airlines 80
emotion: means of analysis 136–7, 140–4ff; role in HRD 131, 132–3; role in learning 133, 182–3; theoretical bases 133–6, 166

Engels, Friedrich 118
environment: corporate exploitation of 44, 45–7, 53; impact on organisational development 16; and systems theory 50–1
EOC (edge of chaos) 52
error, learning from 171–2, 174, 222; practical investigations 186–90
ethics: business 84–5; general theories of 91–3, 158; HRD's relationship with 83, 93–7, 94d, 98b; see also economics; social responsibility
'European' management style 69, 71, 78
evolution, and human behaviour 86–7
expectation, role in responses 182
experience: domains of 94–5; role in learning 15–16, 179–80, 181f, 182–5
Exxon Valdez disaster 45–6

family relationships: role in Arab culture 74–5; role in psychological development 13
feedback: role in complex systems 26; role in organisational structure 30, 110–11
feminine, the: definitions/identifications 57–8, 63–4; denial in organisational structures 62–3, 64–5; mythical symbolism 58, 59; psychological theories of 60–2; religious symbolism 59–61, 63, 65–6
Foot, Philippa 94
Foucault, Michel 103, 210, 214
Freud, Sigmund 113n

Gaia hypothesis 50, 51
Gama, Vasco da 72
Gardner, H. 191n
Gestalt theory 47
Ghazali (Arab scholar) 73
Gibson, James 120, 122, 123–4, 176
Giroux, Henry A. 205–6, 207, 209, 210
globalisation, processes of 73–4, 218–19
Gnosticism 59
goals: importance in modern society 169; role in organisational development 33–4; role in personal development 19, 76
Gorringe, Timothy 92, 93, 94, 96, 97
Grail myths 58–62; feminine symbolism 58, 65; later reinterpretations 60–2
graphic art: role in childhood devlopment 175–6; role in human (pre-)history 172–3, 174–5; role in modern society 121–2, 124, 167, 173–4, 176–8

Greek philosophy 170–1
GTA (general theory of action) 133–4, 135*d*, 136

Habermas, Jürgen 155–6, 160, 163, 210
Harrison, Michael 29–34
Hatcher, Tim G. 98*b*
Hayel Saeed Anam group 80
health services, organisation of; see NHS
Heraclitus 170
hero worship, need for 105, 109
Hesse, Hermann 65*b*
Hicks, Sir John 46
Hochschild, Arlie Russell 133, 135, 136
Hoghelande, Theobald de 60
holism: in ecological systems 50–1; in employment structures 110; in learning processes 15–16
HRD (human resource development): adaptation to complex systems 35–9*ff/tt*, 51–2; in Arab world 78, 79–81; definitions 69, 89*f*, 89–90, 91; as discipline 42, 51, 53, 69–71, 132, 232; education in 204–5, 206–9, 215 (see also UCE); history 70–1; influences on 43, 45, 69; nature of 131, 232–3, 240; and organisational structures 102, 103, 104, 150–2, 218, 222, 224, 231–2; research into 20, 45, 70, 78, 84, 231–40; in small/medium organisations 231, 233–8, 234*f*, 237*f*; strategies of 25; theories of 25–6, 32–5*tt*, 42–3, 48–52, 85–6
HRM (human resource management): in Arab world 79; 'hard/soft' 225–6; high-commitment 57*b*; history/development 70, 81; HRD's integration with 25, 227
Hume, David 96
hunter-gatherer societies 168–9, 172–3

Ibn Khaldun (Arab scholar) 71
image (public), importance to corporations 44
images; see graphic art
imagination, role in creativity 122
industrial revolution 118–9
information: defined 175; technology 167–8
infrastructure, personal, role in learning 133, 182–3
inquiry, methodologies of 35–9*dd/tt*
intelligence, types of 191*n*
intervention, role in HRD 97*b*, 97–8,

231–3; practical investigations 233–8, 234*f*, 237*f*; vs. interaction 238–9, 239*f*, 240

James, William 132
'Japanese' management style 69, 71, 78
Jung, Carl Gustav 11, 61–2, 166
Jung, Emma 59

Kaptchuk, Ted J. 171
Klee, Paul 125, 166, 176–7
Kristeva, Julia 63

Laborit, Henri 123
leaders/leadership: desirable attributes 195–6, 199–203; requisite thought processes 197, 198, 200, 201–2
learning: approaches to 11, 12*d*, 14–16, 15*d*, 90–1; facilitation of 218, 223–5, 226–7, 233; orientation 183, 190–1; practical investigations into 180–1, 186–90; role in life 166, 172; workplace 179–85, 221–2, 226–7; see also education
Lee, Monica 69–70
Lewin, Kurt 47
Lewis, Bernard 70
line managers; see supervisors
logical positivism 49–50

Mabey, Christopher 29–34
Magritte, René 195
Mahfouz, Naguib 74
management: learning processes 179–80; research 180–1, 186–90; rights/duties 71; types, defined by approach 8–9, 9*f*, 10*f*; types, defined by nationality 69, 71, 78–9 (see also Arab world); see also leadership; supervisors
Mandela, Nelson 118
Martin, Paul 87–8, 93, 95–6, 97
Marx, Karl 97
matrix/ces: creative 61; organisational 64–5
Maturana, Humberto 172
McGoldrick, Jim, Prof. 86
Midgley, Mary 85, 93, 95, 96–7
Morris, William 119
Muna, Farid 75
Myers Briggs Type Indicator (MBTI) 11

Nadler, David A. 149–52
narrative, role in leadership 202
newness, as criterion of excellence 117

Newtonian science 118–19, 131;
     supercession by new models 52,
     119–21, 126
NHS (National Health Service) 196;
     administration 199, 200–1; changes in
     196; subsidiary organisations 201
Nissani, Mati 121

OD (organisational development) 27–8,
     233; history 72, 147; newer
     developments in 30–3*ff*, 148–52,
     158–63; traditional procedures 28–30*tt*,
     147–8
Olivetti (corporation) 59*b*
Organ, Dennis W. 106
organisational citizenship behaviour
     (OCB) 106–7, 113*n*
organisation(s): business ethics 44, 45–6;
     internal conflicts 18, 101–2;
     operational models 149–52*tt*;
     patterning 158–63*tt*; processes of
     change 16, 26, 60*b* (see also OD);
     relationship with environment 53;
     relationship with individual(s) 20, 60–1,
     76–7, 100–2, 104, 195, 222;
     small/medium, HRD in 231, 233–8,
     234*f*, 237*f*; social interaction within
     137–8, 140–3; and spiritual values
     107–9, 113*n*; structuring 52, 57, 62–3,
     64–5, 77, 195, 196–7

paradigm shift; see change
Pareto, Vilfredo 171
Parker, M. 107
Parsons, Talcott 133–4, 136
PCTs (primary care trusts) 201
penicillin, discovery of 174
personality: development of 13, 175–6;
     and management qualities 8–9, 183–4,
     190
Peters, Tom 110, 111, 117
Petri nets 137–40*ff*, 142–3; examples
     140–2
'phenomenological' management style 9
philosophy, history of 170–1
postmodernism 7
power: distribution in work teams 224–5;
     educational approaches to 204, 207–8;
     nature of 198
'processual' management style 8–9
professions, requirements of 42
psychology: limitations 47, 53; theories of
     11, 13, 47, 48, 183–4; vs. social
     responsibility 47–8, 86–7

public vs. private sector organisations 196
purpose, behavioural/universal 157–8,
     171

reductionism 49
reflection, role in learning 179, 185
Reynolds, Michael 105, 208–9
Rose, Nikolas 103

Sadler, Philip 125–7
Schein, Edgar H. 207–8
Schon, Donald 179
Schumacher, E.F. 46
'scientific' management style 8
self, sense/expression of 102–4
self-organization, tendency towards 52
self-regulation (autopoiesis) 50, 52, 172
Shakespeare, William 102
social responsibility, and HRD 43–5; see
     also economics
society: evolution of 13; organisation of
     126–7; units of 14; see also social
     responsibility
Socrates 171
Sorrell, Tom 84–5
Soviet Union, collapse of 117–18
'stakeholder,' concept of 9, 34
supervisors: as agents of change 218, 220;
     as educators 218, 223–5; obstacles
     facing 224, 225–6; position in
     organisation 218, 219, 222, 225
SWOT analysis 30
systems, complex: adaptation of HRD to
     35–9*ff*/*tt*; HRD as 239; leaders' role in
     200
systems theory 26–7; and HRD 32–5*tt*;
     and OD 28–30*tt*; and self-regulation
     50; see also systems, complex

Taylorism 70
time, Arab/Western perceptions of 76
training: in Arab world 77, 80; role in
     managerial development 8, 48, 69;
     theoretical basis 78
Trinity, Holy, doctrine of 61
Trotter, Wilfred 121
trust, role in organisational structure
     110–11
Turnbull, Sharon 109
Turner, Ralph 102–3
typologies, schematised 16–20, 17*d*

Union activity 71
University of Central England (UCE), MA

in Strategic Human Resourcing 205,
209–11; course content 210; student
comments on 212–13, 214; tutor-
student relationships 213–15
uterus, symbolic depiction of 60

Van Dyne, Linn 107
Vaz (vase), as symbol of self/femininity 60,
65
visualisation methods 137; see also Petri
nets
VSM (viable systems model) 149, 152–4,
153*f*
VST (viable systems theory) 148–9;
compatibility with HRD 149, 151–2,
160, 161–3; domains 154, 155f, 156*t*

Wager-Marsh, F. 107–8
wasta (influence), role in Arab business 76,
77
Wataniya Telecom 80
water main, accident to 186b, 186–90;
causes 187–8; lessons learnt 187, 188,
189, 190
Watson, Sandra 86
Weick, Karl E. 195
Weinberg, Steven 123
women, employment opportunities 77–8,
87; see also feminine
Woodall, Jean, Prof. 85
World Trade Center, attacks on 71, 117,
118
World Wide Web, visualisation of
structure 137, 143–4